PENGUIN

THE WAY OF THE SUFI

I... ...han was born in 1924 into a family that traces itself through the Prophet Mohammed and the Sassanian Emperors of Persia and, beyond that, back to the year 122 B.C. – perhaps the oldest recorded lineage on earth. Shah is the author of many books published throughout the world. Their subject matter ranges over travel, bibliography, literature, humour, philosophy and history, but their author is most prominent for his writings on Sufi thought as it applies to the cultures of both East and West. Despite the extraordinary success of these books, Shah refuses newspaper interviews and declines to play the role of a 'guru', preferring hard and silent work in his chosen *milieu* of thinkers and artists. He holds the Dictionary of International Biography's Certificate of Merit for Distinguished Service to Human Thought. His books, *Thinkers of the East* and *Learning How to Learn*, are also published in Penguin.

IDRIES SHAH

THE WAY OF
THE SUFI

PENGUIN BOOKS

Penguin Books Ltd, 27 Wrights Lane, London w8 5tz (Publishing and Editorial)
and Harmondsworth, Middlesex, England (Distribution and Warehouse)
Viking Penguin Inc., 40 West 23rd Street, New York, New York 10010, USA
Penguin Books Australia Ltd, Ringwood, Victoria, Australia
Penguin Books Canada Ltd, 2801 John Street, Markham, Ontario, Canada l3r 1b4
Penguin Books (NZ) Ltd, 182–190 Wairau Road, Auckland 10, New Zealand

First published by Jonathan Cape 1968
Published in Penguin Books 1974
Reprinted 1975, 1977, 1979, 1982, 1986, 1987

Made and printed in Great Britain by
Richard Clay Ltd, Bungay, Suffolk

To be a Sufi is to detach from fixed ideas
and from preconceptions; and not to try
to avoid what is your lot.

ABU-SAID, SON OF ABI-KHAIR

Do not look at my outward shape,
But take what is in my hand.

JALALUDIN RUMI

CONTENTS

Contents

INTRODUCTION

> The Sufi is one who does what others do – when it is
> necessary. He is also one who does what others cannot
> do – when it is indicated.   Nuri Mojudi

So many people profess themselves bewildered by Sufi lore that
one is forced to the conclusion that they want to be bewildered.
Others, for more obvious reasons, simplify things to such an
extent that their 'Sufism' is just a cult of love, or of meditations, or of something equally selective.

But a person with a portion of uncommitted interests who
looks at the variety of Sufi action can see the common characteristic staring him in the face.

The Sufi sages, schools, writers, teachings, humour, mysticism, formulations are all concerned with the social and psychological relevance of certain human ideas.

Being a man of 'timelessness' and 'placelessness', the Sufi
brings his experience into operation within the culture, the
country, the climate in which he is living.

The study of Sufic activity in distant cultures alone is of
value only to those working in the narrow field of scholasticism. Considering Sufi activities as merely religious, literary or
philosophical phenomena will produce only garbled renditions
of the Sufi way. To try to extract theory or system and to attempt the study of it in isolation is just as comparatively profit-
less.

This book is designed to present Sufi ideas, actions and report: not for the microscope or as museum-pieces, but in their
relevance to a current community – what we call the contemporary world.

London, 1968   IDRIES SHAH

Part One

THE STUDY OF SUFISM
IN THE WEST

THE STUDY OF SUFISM IN THE WEST

Theories about Sufism

LET us presume no background of Sufi ideas on the part of an imaginary student who has recently heard of Sufism. He has three possible choices of source-material. The first would be reference books and works written by people who have made this subject their special province. The second might be organizations purporting to teach or practise Sufism, or using its terminology. The third could be individuals and perhaps groups of people, not always in Middle Eastern countries, who are reputedly Sufis. He may not yet have been induced to believe that Sufism is to be labelled 'Mohammedan mysticism' or 'the cult of the dervishes'.

What does this man learn, and what are his problems?

One of the first things that he could discover is that the very word 'Sufism' is a new one, a German coinage of 1821.[1]

No Sufi ignorant of Western languages would be likely to recognize it on sight. Instead of Sufism, our student would have to deal with terms such as 'the Qadris', named after the founder of a certain rule who died in 1166. Or he might come across references to 'the People of Truth', 'the Masters', or perhaps 'the Near Ones'. Another possibility is the Arabic phrase *Mutassawif*: 'he who strives to be a Sufi'. There are organizations called 'the Builders', 'the Blameworthy', which in constitution and sometimes even minor symbolism closely resemble Western cults and societies like Freemasonry.[2]

These names can ring oddly, and not always felicitously, in the contemporary Western ear. This fact alone is a real psychological problem, though a concealed one.

As there is no standard appellation for Sufism, the inquirer may turn to the word *Sufi* itself, and discover that it suddenly became current about a thousand years ago,[3] both in the Near

East and in Western Europe;[4] and it is still in general use to describe particularly the best product of certain ideas and practices, by no means confined to what people would conventionally call 'religious'. He will find plenty of definitions for the word, but his problem is now reversed: instead of coming up against a mere label of no great age, he gets so many descriptions of *Sufi* that he might as well have none at all.

According to some authors, and they are in the majority, *Sufi* is traceable to the Arabic word, pronounced *soof,* which litrally means 'wool', referring to the material from which the simple robes of the early Muslim mystics were made.[5] These, it is further claimed, were made of wool in imitation of the dress of Christian anchorites who abounded in the Syrian and Egyptian deserts and elsewhere in the Near and Middle East.

But this definition, plausible though it may appear, will not solve our problem as to name, let alone ideas, in Sufism. Equally important lexicographers, however, stress that 'wool is the garb of animals'[6] and emphasize that the Sufi objective is towards the perfectioning or completing of the human mind, not the emulation of a herd; and that the Sufis, always highly conscious of symbolism, would never adopt such a name. Furthermore, there is the awkward fact that the Companions of the Bench[7] – the *Ashab as-Safa* – are traditionally supposed to have been the Sufis of the time of Mohammed (who died in A.D. 632). It is said that they formed themselves into an esoteric group in the year 623, and that their name is a derivation from the phrase *Ashab as-Safa*. Although some grammarians have pointed out that the 'wool' origin is etymologically more likely – and more probable than, say, the derivation from *safwa* ('piety'), or even *saff* (contracted from the phrase 'First Rank of the Worthy') – others have contested such opinions on the ground that nicknames do not have to abide by the rules of orthography.

Now the name is important as an introduction to the ideas, as we shall see in a moment. Meanwhile let us look at its associations. The Sufis claim that a certain kind of mental and other activity can produce, under special conditions and with particular efforts, what is termed a higher working of the mind, leading to special perceptions whose apparatus is latent in the ordinary man. Sufism is therefore the transcending of ordinary limitations.[8] Not surprisingly, in consequence, the word *Sufi* has been linked by some with the Greek word for divine wisdom (*sophia*) and also with the Hebrew cabbalistic term *Ain Sof* ('the absolutely infinite'). It would not reduce the problems of the student at this stage to learn that it is said, with all the authority of the *Jewish Encyclopaedia*, that Hebrew experts regard the Cabbala and the Hasidim, the Jewish mystics, as originating with Sufism or a tradition identical with it.[9] Neither would it encourage him to hear that, although the Sufis themselves claim that their knowledge has existed for thousands of years, they deny that it is *derivative*, affirming that it is an equivalence of the Hermetic, Pythagorean and Platonic streams.[10]

Our still uninitiated student may by now be thoroughly confused; but he has had a glimpse of the problems of studying Sufi ideas, even if only because he can witness for himself the unproductive struggle of scholastics.

A possible refuge would be found if our man could accept the affirmation of a specialist – such as Professor R. A. Nicholson – or if he asked a Sufi.

Now Nicholson says: 'Some European scholars identified it with Sophos in the sense of "theosophist".[11] But Nöldeke ... showed conclusively that the name was derived from *suf* (wool) and was originally applied to those Muslim ascetics who, in imitation of Christian hermits, clad themselves in coarse woollen garb as a sign of penitence and renunciation of worldly vanities.'[12]

This characteristic, if not venturesome, opinion was published in 1914. Four years earlier, Nicholson himself had offered his translation of the eleventh-century *Revelation*, the earliest available Persian treatment of Sufism, and one of the most authoritative Sufi texts. In its pages the author, the venerable Hujwiri, specifically states – and this is doggedly translated but ignored by the Professor – that *Sufi* has no etymology.[13]

Nicholson shows no curiosity about this claim, but thinking

about it could have led him to an important idea in Sufism. For him, quite clearly, a word *must* have an etymology. Unconsciously assuming that 'no etymology' must be absurd, he looks no further in that direction but, all undismayed, continues to seek an etymological derivation. Like Nöldeke and many others, such a mind will prefer the word 'wool' to the seeming paradox of 'no etymology'.

This is surely the reason why, in his recent book on Sufism, the learned Dominican Father Cyprian Rice (an admirer and pupil of Nicholson) says, half a century after the publication of the English translation of Hujwiri's text (a version which he praises): '... from their habit of wearing coarse garments of wool (*suf*) [they] became known as Sufis.'[14]

But acquaintanceship with Sufis, let alone almost any degree of access to their practices and oral traditions, could easily have resolved any seeming contradiction between the existence of a word and its having no ready etymological derivation. The answer is that the Sufis regard the *sounds* of the letters S, U, F (in Arabic, the signs for *Soad, Wao, Fa*) as significant, in this same order of use, in their effect upon human mentation.

The Sufis are therefore, 'the people of SSSUUUFFF'.

Having disposed of that conundrum (incidentally illustrating the difficulties of getting to grips with Sufi ideas when one thinks only along certain lines) we immediately see a fresh and characteristic problem arising to replace it. The contemporary thinker is likely to be interested in this explanation – this idea that sound influences the brain – only within the limitations imposed by himself. He may accept it as a theoretical possibility in so far as it is expressed to him in terms which are regarded as admissible at the time of communication.[15]

If we say: 'Sounds have an effect upon man, making it possible, other things being equal, for him to have experiences beyond the normal,' he may persuasively insist that 'This is mere occultism, primitive nonsense of the order of Om–Mani–Padme–Hum, Abracadabra and the rest.' But (taking into account not objectivity but simply the current phase of accepted thought) we can say to him instead: 'The human brain, as you are doubtless aware, may be likened to an electronic computer. It responds to impacts or vibrations of sight, sound, touch and so on, in certain predetermined or "programmed" ways. It is held by some that the sounds roughly represented by the signs S, U, F are among those for reaction to which the brain is, or may be, programmed.' He may very well be able to assimilate this wretched simplification into his existing pattern of thinking.

This condition existing in our *vis-à-vis*, the special problem in the study of Sufi ideas here, is that many of those who are anxious to study them are in fact unwilling, because of a systematic psychological commitment, to allow certain contentions about Sufism, held by Sufis, to be retained in the mind. This situation, whose existence is demonstrated by much personal experience, is far more widespread than this single example might suggest.

The problem for both parties is not made any easier by the common tendency of the individual addressed to attempt to deal with Sufi ideas by outright rejection. A common answer goes something like this: 'To think in the terms suggested by you would wreck my established ways of thought.' This individual is quite mistaken in believing this; to the Sufi he is really a man undervaluing his own capacities. Another reaction is to try to rationalize or reinterpret the ideas being offered him in the terms of some system (anthropological, sociological, sophistical, psychological) which he himself finds more to his taste. In our example this subjective condition would perhaps be expressed in the statement: 'Ah, yes, this theory of the influence of sound has obviously been produced in order to give a more esoteric twist to the rather mundane derivation from wool.'

But this kind of thinking will not ultimately succeed on a wide scale because, far from being found only among primitive tribes or buried in books in dead languages, the Sufi ideas are in varying degrees contained in the background and studies of over fifty million people alive today: those connected in some way with Sufism.

Limitations of Contemporary Approaches to Sufism

A large part of this problem is the powerful tendency nowadays to place all people, things, ideas, into specialist categories. Categories may be all very well – who could do without them? – but when any matter is being studied and there is only a limited choice of label offered, the experience can seem like being told by Henry Ford that 'You can have any colour automobile, providing that it is black.' This problem which the inquirer is possibly even unaware of – his preoccupation with a few categories – is matched by that of the Sufi in attempting to convey his own ideas under other than ideal conditions.

Here is an illustrative example, chosen from recent experience. I give it because it will incidentally, and not in a forced 'system', tell us something about Sufi ideas.

In a recent book[16] I mentioned, among much else, that Sufi ideas and even literal texts were borrowed by or lay behind theories, organization and teachings of such diverse aspect as those of Chivalry, of St John of the Cross,[17] St Teresa of Avila,[18] Roger Bacon,[19] Geber, the father of Western alchemy[20] – surnamed the Sufi – Raymond Lully the Majorcan,[21] Guru Nanak, the founder of Sikhism,[22] the *Gesta Romanorum*,[23] as well as Hindu Vedantist teachings.[24] Certain deteriorated psychological procedures, too, have passed into the western literature of magic and occultism,[25] as well as legitimate psychological ideas and processes, sometimes thought of as recent discoveries.[26]

This book created, among reviewers and others, a quite remarkable and manifold reaction.[27] Some were enthralled, not always for good reasons; but it is the others of whom I am speaking. What I had actually done was to collect the results of whole lifetimes of other people's academic research, often buried in monographs and seldom-read books, always by highly respected orientalists and specialists of one kind or another. I also contributed 'live' material from Sufic sources. But although the quoted material was by no means a complete selection of the material available, it was too rich a mixture for some readers. And yet many of them should have been far more familiar than I was with work already done in their own fields. One celebrated expert had uncomplimentary things to say about me, to say nothing of those who attacked what they only *thought* they found in my work!

Shortly after this phase, in conversation with a certain 'specialist', I mentioned that not only had I been relying in my thesis upon such authorities as Professors Asín, Landau, Ribera, Tara Chand, Guillaume, and others of equally unimpeachable integrity, but that I had in my own text freely quoted their names and works; and that in other cases I had quoted the books by such ancients as Lully, Bacon, Geber, and others who all mentioned the Sufis by name, Sufi books, or Sufism specifically. His reaction was not to agree that the experts should have known their job better, but to repeat the name of my main critic. Settling back in his armchair and chuckling, he said: 'You've got him, my boy. Make your choice: do you just want to discredit him, or do you want his job?'

My 'error', as far as treatment of the subject was concerned, had simply been that instead of quoting authority and building up, step by step, an unassailable 'case', I had assumed that the book would be read thoroughly and that the facts would speak for themselves.

My friend automatically assumed that I was engaged in a game of displacement of someone in authority. The original critic had propelled himself into the attack on an equally false assumption: that I lacked good material because I had not hammered it home triumphantly enough.

What is perhaps more astonishing, when we look at problems in the study of Sufi ideas, is the treatment given to them by people who, if not experts in the field itself, might have familiarized themselves with the academic resources available. Hence, to take an instance of a not uncommon trend in the West, we find a professor writing a book on philosophers of the East,[28] in which, out of nearly one hundred thousand words, only about three hundred (one page out of over three hundred) are concerned with the Sufis. And this in spite of the fact that the same author had published a work on the philosophers of the West,[29] both types of thinker having been influenced by Sufi sources. This influence is never mentioned. The redoubtable English philosopher Bertrand Russell too, is found to have written a huge book, *Wisdom of the West*,[30] in which Western thinkers whose connection with Sufi thought is clear are named, but where no mention of Sufis or Sufism may be found.

It may be said that both of these books are popularizations intended for the general reader; but they do, after all, carry the names of scholars, and they do lack information.

General readers, or members of the non-orientalist disciplines, consulting these books, would have little means of knowing what had been left out.

Verification of the Literary Materials by Direct Contact with Sufism

Quite revealing among the problems facing anyone who wants to study Sufi ideas is the constant repetition of unproved theories, represented as facts, by 'specialists' and others who themselves have little objectivity.

Since Sufic study is carried out mainly by direct methods (and it has been known to be conveyed entirely by gesture, symbol and demonstration), when we lose this element in our study, relying upon books, we must be at the mercy of those who advance all kinds of subjective theories.[31]

There are those who say that Sufism is developed from historical Islam; and they include some Sufi apologists writing in this vein for good reasons. Some say that it is the reverse: a reaction against Islamic attitudes. There are those who would believe that its ideas stem from Christianity as they know it; or that they are partially or wholly attributable to the effect of Persian dualism; or that it is from China, or India; or again, that it is non-Indian. There are champions of the Neoplatonic theory, of Shamanism and we could extend this list. The picture starts to look like one of people debating whether iron comes from Sweden or Japan.

We may call Sufi ideas 'a psychology', not because this term adequately describes Sufism, but because nowadays 'wisdom' is not a popular word. It is to be noted, however, that because the dictionary-makers do not understand us, the possibility of Sufi ideas being understood at all is not thereby excluded.

In the problem of permissible categories of study we see that Sufism straddles many of them. We can find materials bodily taken from Sufism, ideas which are characteristic of it, methods, tales, legends and even poetry of the Sufis in the phenomenon of the Troubadours,[32] in the William Tell legend of Switzerland,[33] in the Near Eastern cult of the 'Peacock Angel',[34] in Gurdjieff and Ouspensky,[35] in Maurice Nicoll, in the Swede Dag Hammerskjöld,[36] in Shakespeare,[37] in the psychology of Kenneth Walker,[38] in the tales of the Dane Hans Christian Andersen,[39] in the works of Sir Richard Burton (himself a Qadiri dervish),[40] in a recently issued series of textbooks on learning English from the Oxford University Press,[41] in contemporary children's books,[42] in the religion of the 'witches',[43] in the symbolology of the Rosicrucians,[44] and of the Illuminati,[45] in many medieval scholastics of the West,[46] in the Bhakti cult of the Hindus[47] – though this is much popularized in the West as a traditional Hindu system – in the secret books of the Ismailis,[48] in the organization, name and techniques of some of the so-called Assassins,[49] in tales and techniques of supposedly Japanese Zen origin,[50] or reputedly connected with Yoga,[51] in material relating to the Knights Templar,[52] in psychotherapeutic literature, in Chaucer[53] and Dante Alighieri[54] – and I am only enumerating the sources almost at random.

Misunderstandings of Sufi Ideas and Formulations

What is a Sufi idea, how is it expressed, where do we look for it?

Many ideas we can easily identify as being derived from the Sufis because of their context or actual attribution in the text. But the special problem beyond this is the fact that there is no record of any other body or ideas or system which has penetrated so widely and so far into so many departments of life and thought, in the East and the West. No mind has been trained to expect such a thing, except that of the Sufi, who does not need the material. As a consequence we get this questioning: is Sufism a series of shamanistic cults, a philosophy, a religion, a secret society, an occult training system, the mainspring of whole ranges of literature and poetry, or a military system, a chivalric, or perhaps a commercial, cult?

Serious problems in locating genuine and relevant Sufi ideas and practices exist, too, for any student who has already met a watered-down, generalized or partial variety of Sufism, whether in the East or the West. There are many hundreds of people in Europe and America who practise 'dervish dance, whirling or turning' in spite of the fact that it is specifically on record in easily accessible dervish literature[55] that this practice was especially 'prescribed', for local reasons, by Rumi for the people of Asia Minor in the region of Iconium.[56] In a similar way, when those influenced by the Western 'work' or 'system' which attempts to follow Gurdjieff and Ouspensky – and there are many thousands of them – are forthrightly told that their exercises and methods are well known and applied in certain Sufi schools, but that they are to be used in a different way and a more intelligible manner corresponding to the community involved, they are – more often than not – incapable of assimilating this statement. The Sufi gains in such cases are beginning to be overwhelmed by the losses due to misunderstanding or misapplication.

Another, and until recently a rapidly growing, phenomenon, making use of some Sufi ideas and practices, is known to thousands in the West as 'Subud'. Its procedure is mainly based upon Naqshbandi–Qadiri[57] methods, but in its current presentation these have been turned upside down. In the Subud meeting called the *Latihan*,[60] the member waits for certain experiences, believed to be the working of God within him. Some are slightly affected, some profoundly, some not at all. The interesting thing here is that the Subud attitude values the experience, and many people who are not affected or who cease to perceive it drift away. The remainder are the stalwarts of the movement.

But, according to Sufi ideas and practice, it is precisely those who do not feel subjective states, or who have at one time been affected by them and no longer feel them, who may be real candidates for the next stage.[59] To the Sufi, one who does not know this may appear like a man, trying to exercise his muscles, who thinks the exercises are no good because he no longer feels stiffness in his limbs. The gains of Subud are offset, at least in part, by the losses.

This is the real problem in the attempted study of the original Sufi ideas through such popularizations. As this inversion has invoked Sufi terminology, the student may very well not be able to shed the Subud associations when he approaches Sufism.

Yet another problem, strongly characteristic of Sufism, awakens a great deal of opposition. This may be stated by saying that Sufi literature contains material which is ahead of its time. Certain Sufi books, some translated into Western languages and therefore a matter of verifiable record, contain material which seems to become comprehensible only when 'new' psychological and even scientific technical discoveries are made and become well known. A verification of claims which once seemed bizarre or impossible then becomes possible. Western orientalists and others have noted, for instance, that the Afghan Jalaludin Rumi (died 1273),[60] Hakim Sanai of Khorasan (fourteenth century),[61] El-Ghazali of Persia (died 1111),[62] and Ibn El-Arabi of Spain (died 1240)[63] speak of psychological states, theories of psychology and psychotherapeutic procedures which would have been incomprehensible to readers without the contemporary 'infrastructure' which we have lately acquired in the West. These ideas are called 'Freudian' and 'Jungian' and so on, in consequence.

Sufi claims that 'man rose from the sea', and that he is in a state of evolution, covering an enormous period of time, appeared to be fanciful nonsense until the nineteenth-century Darwinists seized upon this material with delight.[64]

References said to be to the forces contained in the atom,[65] to a 'fourth dimension',[66] to relativity,[67] to space travel,[68] telepathy, telekinesis, are frequent; sometimes these are treated as facts, sometimes as due to techniques, sometimes as man's present or future capacities. Accounts of precognitive awareness and other phenomena of this kind are to be judged only in the light of comparatively recent knowledge, or still await verification by conventional scientists. Over seven hundred years ago, Ibn el-Arabi stated that thinking man was forty thousand years old, while orthodox Jewish, Christian and Moslem belief was still committed to scriptural 'datings' of the Creation at only four to six thousand years before. Some recent research, however, now dates 'modern' man as about thirty-five thousand years old.[69]

Some of the strongest ridicule, still maintained in some circles, to which Sufis have been subjected, is due to their having stressed in their classics the dangers of obsessions being implanted in people, and to their having pointed out the undesirable nature of indoctrination and emotion being confused with spiritual gifts, to the horror of religious enthusiasts. Only in the past few decades have other people come to know better than the clerics.[70]

The especial secondary problem here, too, is that although scientists will, rightly, await verification of this material, or try to investigate it, gullible occultists will crowd around the Sufi who speaks of these things as deriving from Sufism, urgently demanding, as of right, magical knowledge, self-mastery, higher consciousness, hidden secrets and the rest.

For the Sufi, these trustful and sometimes unbalanced people can be more of a problem than the sceptics. The believers create a further problem because, baulked of easy magical knowledge, they may quite quickly turn to those organizations (well-meaning and otherwise) which seem to them able to satisfy this thirst for the unknown or the unusual; or to offer 'short cuts'. It is not to be denied that we use this phrase – but always with qualifications: 'Adepts have, however, devised short cuts to an attainment of a knowledge of God. There are as many ways to God as there are souls (selves) of men.'[71] Several such bodies exist in Britain and America. If you write for the literature of one of them, for example, you will receive a publication in which it is claimed that Sufis prefer a vegetarian diet and that students must be 'free of caste, colour and creed' before developing 'occult powers'.

Other movements, using the name Sufi, idealize their founders, giving members a sort of inter-religious ceremony. More than one practises musical recitals supposed to throw the seeker into an advantageous ecstasy – in spite of the fact that Sufi teaching is widely on record that music can be harmful[72] and that it is what is taught, not the teacher, which is the point of Sufism. The gains in Sufi information are once more offset by losses due to faulty practice and selectively biased reading.

Asiatic immigration – Arab (mainly from Aden and Somaliland), Indian and Pakistani – into Britain has introduced another form of 'Sufism'. This centres around groups of Muslim religious zealots who gather for communal prayer-exercises which stimulate them emotionally and sometimes have a cathartic effect. Using Sufi terminology and similitudes of Sufi organization, these have branches in many industrial and seaport cities of Britain.

The problem here is not only that many of the participants will not now be able to study Sufi ideas (since they believe that they already know them) but that just anyone – sociologist, anthropologist or ordinary members of the public – cannot always know that this does not represent Sufism, any more than snake-handling represents Christianity, or the game of 'Bingo' mathematics. The gains, once more, are on a low level; the losses are not slight.

Like their indoctrinated confrères throughout the Muslim world from Morocco to Java, those coteries are often in reality groups of fanatics using the Sufi form. Some are plainly hysterics. Others have never heard of any other form of Sufism.[73] To them such claims as that of Ibn El-Arabi – 'Angels are the powers hidden in the faculties and organs of man' – would seem utter blasphemy – and yet they revere Ibn El-Arabi![74]

It is not impossible that these entities (through sheer enthusiasm, efficient deployment of money and recourse to modern mass-publicity methods) will become generally considered by observers to be real Sufis or representative of Sufi ideas. It is probably true to say that religion is too important a matter to leave to speculative non-expert intellectuals or clerics. The latter tend to 'scramble' devout activity. This is an ancient error. Ghazali was once believed in the West to be a Catholic theologian of the Middle Ages. 'St Jehosaphat' has been shown to be Buddha, and 'St Charalambos' of the Greeks has been revealed as none other than the dervish master Haji Bektash Wali, who founded the Bektashis.[75] The fifteenth-century Christian saint Therapion is the dervish poet Turabi.[76]

Such developments can already be seen in countries of the East where enthusiasts, often pleasant enough characters, outshout the Sufis, maintaining that their own antics are the true Sufism. This, in turn, has posed a sore and largely unrecognized problem for many Westerners interested in the Sufi heritage. Faced with acceptance or rejection, convinced that this must be Sufism because so many people locally consider it to be so, numbers of these students have reacted either by revulsion or by total, uncritical acceptance. In Britain, to say nothing of other Western countries, there are examples of the 'Sufi conversion syndrome' – sometimes in the case of not inconsequential persons, ready to leap into print to 'prove' that this cult, as they have seen it among ecstatics, is something to be adopted in the West.[77]

It can give one an almost uncanny sensation to compare this state of affairs with a hypothetical situation in an underdeveloped area where advanced ideas have penetrated but – through lack of accurate and appropriately systematized information – have been adopted by the local inhabitants in a superficial or untoward manner. One is tempted to think in terms of the 'cargo cults'[78] among less advanced communities, whose members built tin-can replicas of aircraft, believing that they could thus magically reproduce the wonders of supply of good things from the skies.[79]

And yet there is no real lack of basic information on Sufi ideas. There is information, but much of it is not studied and

assimilated by those who could do so. There is another characteristic problem here: the problem caused by the places where
the material appears.

Much material on Sufism and the Sufis, some of it the product of excellent observation, inquiry and field-work in Asia,
Africa and Europe, appears from time to time in the general-
circulation press. But because the work is not always by 'recognized specialists', or because it sees the light of day in media
which are not regarded as authoritative in 'the field', it can be
missed.

Here are a few recent examples:

In two brilliant articles in *Blackwood's Magazine*[80] in 1961
and 1962, O. M. Burke described the ideas and practices of
Sufis in Pakistan, Tunisia, Morocco and elsewhere. He outlined
theories and exercises well known in Sufi practice but not always literally represented in its overt literature. In 1961, a
Delhi newspaper[81] carried a good report of Sufi beliefs and de-
liberations in Paris. In a specialized scientific journal in 1962[82]
there was an important contribution by an Egyptian physician
in which ideas and psychotherapeutic procedures of a Central
Asian dervish community with international ramifications were
delineated. None of this material will ordinarily be quoted in
orientalist, or even occultist, literature.

No citation seems yet to have been made from an important
article by another worker dealing with the living, oral tradition of 'secret teaching' in the Middle and Far East, which was
published in 1960 in the *Contemporary Review*.[83] The desire
to diffuse Sufi ideas and practices and the special manner in
which this is done, and also symbolic demonstrations of Sufi
ideas carried out in a large Hindu-Kush community which has
branches in Europe, provide another first-class document. Because, no doubt, it was published in the *Lady*,[84] a women's
weekly magazine, this could be considered lost as research
material.[85]

A resolute correspondent of *The Times*,[86] writing in 1964,
imparted an account of ideas and practices in Afghanistan and
their ramifications in the Arab world. It seems unlikely that

this valuable report will ever form a part of the formal literature on Sufism. An article in *She* in 1963, and another in 1965,[87] contained at least some material of interest and some previously unrecorded facts.

Forms of Sufi Activity

What else do the Sufis teach, how do they do so, and what special problems does this study pose for those who would wish to learn of the ideas from a reputable source?

The Sufis state that there is a form of knowledge which can be attained by man, which is of such an order that it is to scholastic learning as adulthood is to infancy. Compare, for instance, El-Ghazali, 'A child has no real knowledge of the attainments of an adult. An ordinary adult cannot understand the attainment of a learned man. In the same way a learned man cannot understand the experiences of enlightened saints or Sufis.'[88] This, for a start, is not a concept which would instantly recommend itself to the scholar. This is no new problem. In the eleventh century, Mohamed El-Ghazali (Algazel), who saved the Muslim theologians by interpreting Islamic material in such a way as to defeat the attack of Greek philosophy, informed scholastics that their mode of knowledge was inferior to that gained through Sufi practice. They made him into their hero, and their successors still teach his interpretations as orthodox Islam, in spite of his stating that the academic method is insufficient and inferior to real knowledge.

Then there was Rumi, the great mystic and poet, who told his audiences that like a good host he gave them poetry because they demanded it; providing what was asked for. But, he continued, poetry was tripe compared with a certain high development of the individual. Nearly seven hundred years later he could still sting people with this kind of remark. Not long ago a reviewer in a reputable British newspaper was so affronted by this passage (which he found in a translation), that he said, in effect, 'Rumi may think that poetry is tripe. *I* think that *his* poetry is tripe in this translation.'

But Sufi ideas, in being put in this manner, are never intended to challenge the man, only to provide him with a higher aim, to maintain his conception that there may be some function of the mind which produced, for instance, the Sufi giants. Inevitably the contentious collide with this idea. It is because of the prevalence of this reaction that Sufis say that people do not in fact *want* the knowledge that Sufism claims to be able to impart: they really seek only their own satisfaction within their own system of thinking.[89] But the Sufi insists: 'A short time in the presence of the Friends (the Sufis) is better than a hundred years' sincere, obedient dedication.' (Rumi.)

Sufism also states that man may *become* objective, and that objectivity enables the individual to grasp 'higher' facts. Man is therefore invited to try to push his evolution ahead towards what is sometimes called in Sufism 'real intellect'.[90]

Sufis contend that, far from this lore being available in books, a great part of it must be personally communicated by means of an interaction between the teacher and the learner. Too much attention to the written page, they insist, can even be harmful. Here is a further problem; for it appears to oppose the scholar no less than the member of the vast modern literate community who feels, if at times only subconsciously, that all knowledge must surely be available in books.

Yet Sufis have worked long and hard to adapt the written word to convey certain parts of what they teach. This has led to the use of manipulated and enciphered material – not designed especially or always to conceal a real meaning, but intended to show, when decoded, that what on its outward face seemed like a complete poem, myth, treatise and so on, is susceptible of another interpretation: a sort of demonstration analogous to a kaleidoscopic effect. And when Sufis draw diagrams for such purposes as these, imitators merely tend to copy them, and use them at their own levels of understanding.[91]

Another Sufi technique provides a further problem. Many Sufic passages, even whole books or series of assertions, are designed to stimulate thought, even sometimes by the method of arousing healthy criticism. These documents are only too often taken by their literalist students as faithful renderings of beliefs held by their authors.[92]

In the West in general we have plenty of translations. Mostly they are literal renderings of only one facet of multi-dimensional texts. Western students actually know that the internal dimensions exist, but they have not yet applied them to any extent in their work. To be fair, it must be said that some have admitted that they cannot do this.[93]

Another Sufi idea, producing a problem which many have found impossible to integrate in their minds, is the Sufi insistence that Sufism can be taught in many guises. Sufis, in a word, do not stick to any one convention.[94] Some quite happily use a religious format, others romantic poetry, some deal in jokes, tales and legends, yet others rely on art-forms and the products of artisanship. Now, a Sufi can tell from his experience that all these presentations are legitimate. But the literalist outsider, however sincere he may be, will often testily demand to be told whether these Sufis (or this or that group of Sufis) are alchemists, members of guilds, religious maniacs, jokers,[95] scientists – or what. This problem, while it may be special to Sufism, is by no means new. Sufis have been judicially murdered,[96] hounded out of their homes or had their books burned, for using non-religious or locally unacceptable formulations. Some of the greatest Sufi classical authors have been accused of heresy, apostasy, even political crimes. Even today they come under fire from all kinds of committed circles, not just religious ones.[97]

Even a cursory examination of reputed origins of Sufism will reveal that, although Sufis claim that Sufism is an esoteric teaching within Islam (with which it is therefore regarded as entirely compatible), it also stands behind formulations which many people consider to be quite different from one another. Hence, while the 'chain of transmission' of named teachers extends back to the Prophet Mohammed in this or that line of attribution used by a school or teacher, it may also be referred to – by the same authorities – as stemming from such as Uwais el-Qarni (died in the seventh century) who never met Mohammed in his life.[98] The authoratitive Suhrawardi, in common with (though much before) the Rosicrucians and others, specifically states that this was a form of wisdom known to and practised by a succession of sages including the mysterious ancient Hermes of Egypt.[99] Another individual of no less repute – Ibn el-Farid (1181–1235) – stresses that Sufism lies behind and before systematization; that 'our wine existed before what you call *the grape and the vine*' (the school and the system):

> We drank to the mention of the Friend,
> Intoxicating ourselves, even before the creation of the vine.[100]

There is no doubt that dervishes, would-be Sufis, have traditionally collected together to study whatever remnants of this teaching they could find, awaiting the possible moment when an exponent might appear among them and make effective the principles and practices whose active meaning was for them lost. This theory is to be found in the West, of course, in Freemasonry (with its concept of the 'lost secret'). The practice is duly confirmed, for instance, in the textbook *Awarif-ul-Maarif* and it has been regarded by those interested in such things as an indication of the occurrence of a messianic-expectation characteristic in Sufism. However that may be (and it belongs only to a 'preparatory phase', not to Sufism proper), there is evidence that people in Europe and the Middle East, whatever their psychological commitment or faith, have from time to time been located and inspired in the Sufi doctrines by teachers, sometimes of mysterious origins, who came among them. These people have for centuries been referred to as Universal, or Completed, Men (*Insan-i-Kamil*). Such was the case with Rumi and Shams of Tabriz; of Bahaudin Naqshband* (fourteenth century) of Bokhara; of Ibn El-Arabi, who taught in terms of religion, figures of antiquity and love poetry; and of many others less well known in Western literature.

The problem for the student here may be not whether this 'irrational' form of action or refreshment of a tradition took place or not; but rather the psychological difficulty of accepting such people as really having any special function to 'reunite

---

* Incorrectly but frequently rendered as 'Naqshiband.

the beads of mercury' or to 'reactivate, awaken, the inner current in man'.

But we have not even started to enumerate the fields in which Sufis and entities known to have been devised by them (these latter being a minority of the real number, because Sufism is action, not institution) have carried out social, philosophical and other forms of action, in the past thousand years. Characters as seemingly diverse as the forthright Rumi, the saintly Chishti, the 'God-intoxicated' Hallaj,[101] the statesmen of the Mujaddids, have worked for centuries to further the actual reunification of communities seemingly irrevocably parted.

For their pains, and again assessed by the inadequate and often inaccurate standards of their commentators, these people have been accused of being secret Christians, Jews, Hindus, apostates and sun-worshippers. When the Bektashis used the number twelve, and gave, like Arabi and Rumi, Christian myths a high place in their teachings, it was (and still is) assumed that they were capitalizing on the local abundance of Christians without an effective leadership. The validity of this charge awaits the verification of the Sufi answer that Christian, as well as numerous other, formulations, contain a valuable measure of insights which can, under suitable circumstances, be applied to man.

The followers of Haji Bektash (died 1337) were and still are in some places regarded as immoral simply because of their practice of admitting women to their meetings. Nobody could, or would, understand them when they said that it was necessary to redress the social balance of a society based upon male supremacy. 'Social reinstatement of women' simply sounded, until it recently became a 'respectable' objective, like a cloak for orgies.

Nobody of consequence, even in the nineteenth and early twentieth centuries, bothered himself to look at the claim, made by such men as the distinguished Turkish Sufi and savant Zia Gökalp,[102] that Sufi writers centuries ago had outlined and employed theories later identified with the names of Berkeley, Kant, Foullée, Gruyeau, Nietzsche and William James.

This brings us to another important Sufi projection, one which causes bafflement – and even rage – in certain types of person, but which should nevertheless be faced. It is the assertion that when Sufic activity becomes concentrated at one point or in one community in a very active and 'real' (not imitation) form, it does so only for a limited time and for distinct purposes. It is the type of person who says 'I want it here and now or not at all' who dislikes this statement. Put in another way, the idea is that no society is ever complete, neither are its needs exactly the same as those of other societies. No Sufi sets up an institution intended to endure. The outer form in which he imparts his ideas is a transient vehicle, designed for local operation. That which is perpetual, he says, is in another range.

Difficulties in Understanding Sufi Materials

In this age of creeping institutionalization it is at least as difficult as it has ever been to make this point effectively. Yet a thousand years ago the dervish wanderer Niffari in Egypt, in his still influential classic, the *Muwaqif* ('Stops'), energetically stressed the danger of mistaking the vehicle for the objective.

Coming hard on the heels of this problem is the one of guidance or teachership. The Sufi teacher is a conductor, and an instructor – not a god. Personality-worship is forbidden in Sufism.[103] Hence Rumi: 'Look not at my exterior form, but take what is in my hand'; and Gurgani: 'My humility which you mention is not there for you to be impressed by it. It is there for its own reason.'[104] Yet such is the attraction of personality to the ordinary man that the successors of Sufi teachers have tended to produce, rather than a living application of the principles taught, hagiographies and bizarre and deficient systems. The theme of the temporary nature of the 'cocoon' is conveniently forgotten. Hence the constant need for a new exemplar.

A further problem for the student who is not aware of the above situation is the existence of what have been called 'illustrative biographies'. These contain material designed for study, to cause certain effects, much in the way in which myths can contain dramatized fact. With the passage of time they outlive their usefulness, and are then taken as lies or records of literal truth. Where is the historian who will willingly relinquish such source-material? Hence, for example, because in a biography of Maulana Jalaludin Rumi[105] he is stated to have spent long periods in his Turkish bath, seekers of higher consciousness and would-be illuminates have actually been known to endow this report with such significance as to build and frequent their own steam-baths. They, in turn, have their own imitators . . .

Those who remember their nursery rhymes may be able to grasp one aspect of Sufic study by thinking about the unfortunate Humpty-Dumpty. Like Humpty, Sufi ideas have had a great fall – when they have been adopted at their lowest level. They have, in consequence, fallen in all sorts of strange places. Looking at the pieces of Humpty, we can call the emotionalists and conventional scholars the 'king's horses' and the 'king's men' of the rhyme. Like them, there is an inevitability about their helplessness to deal with the problem. A man and a horse – or any number of them – belonging to a king or otherwise, are suitable for just so many tasks, no more. Something is missing, as in the nursery rhyme: and, unless they are Sufis or use Sufic methods, they cannot 'put Humpty together again'. They have the horses, and they have the men; but they have not got the vehicle, the knowledge.

If Sufi ideas, as expressed in books and among preparatory or 'orphaned' communities, and given shape by the teachings and existence of a human exemplar, are in fact designed to produce a form of mentation more valuable than mechanical thought, the student might argue that he is entitled to know about the product. He may expect to find Sufis taking an invariably significant or even decisive part in human affairs. While the Sufi would not accept that public acclaim is what he seeks (most of them flee it), and that he is not anxious to become a sort of Albert Schweitzer-cum-Napoleon-cum-Einstein, there is nevertheless massive evidence of the powerful Sufi heritage.

More surprising than that, for those who seek to label and limit Sufism as simply this or that cult, is the extent and variety of the Sufi impact, setting aside the Sufi claim that their greatest figures are almost always anonymous.

During the periods of mainly monarchical rule over the past millennium, Sufis in the East have been kings or stood behind them as advisers. At the same time, under other conditions Sufis have worked against the very institution of kingship, or to mitigate its abuse. The names of many of these men and women are well known. The Mogul Dara Shikoh of India sought to form an esoteric bridge between his Hindu, Muslim and other subjects.[106] Sufi patriots have fought against foreign tyrants, just as Sufi soldiers have fought for the preservation of existing states – sometimes on a grand scale, as with the Sufi-inspired Janissaries of Turkey, the resistance leader Shamyl of the Caucasus, the Senussi of Libya, or the dervishes of the Sudan. Almost all the literature of Persia in the classical period is Sufic, and so are innumerable scientific, psychological and historical works.

The citations just made are a matter of historical record, and could be greatly increased in range and number.

Whereas the fragmentary researches of committed scholars upon which I have often drawn in this discourse have their inestimable value in the preservation of fact, it remains for a new spirit of learning to assemble and collate the extent and value of Sufi activity in human society. In this way we may preserve the gains and reduce the losses.

Such students – and here is another problem – in addition to being less prone to indoctrination than their predecessors, would have to take into account the contention of the Sufis themselves when they say: 'Sufism must be studied with a certain attitude, under certain conditions, in a certain manner.'[107]

Many people, unthinkingly in too many cases, have rebelled against this dictum. But is it, after all, so very different from saying: 'Economics must be studied with a certain attitude (the desire to understand) under certain conditions (the discipline of scholasticism and the right books) in a certain manner

(following a curriculum devised by those who know the subject properly)'?

The study of Sufism cannot be approached, for instance,
from the single standpoint that it is a mystical system designed
to produce ecstasy and based on theological concepts. As a Sufi
poem by Omar Khayyam[108] states:

> In cell and cloister, in monastery and synagogue,
> Here one fears hell, another dreams of paradise.
> But he who knows the true secrets of his God
> Has planted no such seeds within his heart.

It seems unlikely that much progress towards the widespread
understanding of Sufi ideas will be made until more scholars
avail themselves of Sufi interpretative methods. If they do not,
they will continue to waste effort on secondary phenomena.
This, in turn, poses a special problem for the Sufi himself. As
Ibn El-Arabi has said: 'The Sufi must act and speak in a manner which takes into consideration the understanding, limitations and dominant concealed prejudices of his audience.'[109]

The correct study of Sufi ideas depends upon the supply and
right use of the literature and also the contact with the Sufi
instructor.

As to supply of literature, time may put that right in the
ordinary course of events, although two recent experiences indicate that the losses, again, may be serious.

One of my books was criticized by an eminent scholastic
and expert on Sufism in the middle East on the ground that
Mulla Nasrudin the joker was no Sufi instruction-figure. He
did not know at the time, and perhaps still does not know,
that at that moment a European student was actually living in a
dervish community in Pakistan which was using Mulla Nasrudin, and nothing else, as instruction-material. An account of
these studies was recently published in a British journal of
religion.[110]

But merely adding to the information on Sufism is not
enough. Not long ago, when I was innocently inquiring about
holiday prospects from a Western intellectual whom I button-

holed on a Greek island, he rounded on me with a fair amount of abuse. Brandishing a copy of one of my books, he said: 'You are wasting your time thinking about a holiday, and trying to waste the time of a man who is reading this book: something more important than all your holidays!'

We must not confuse those who think that they are interested in Sufism, or those who think that they are Sufis, with those who really can study Sufism and benefit from it. Sufism has always been something which cannot be judged from a study of those who claim to be its friends.

The effective study of Sufism today, above all in the West where interest in it is so remarkably widespread, requires the following of the would-be student:

1. Understanding that the bulk of translations available are unsuitable. This is mainly because the originals were intended for specific communities and local audiences and cultures which do not now exist in the same form.

2. Seeking authoritative written and oral materials and activities designed by Sufis to operate in the student's own culture, time and other circumstances.

3. Recognizing that all organizations except genuinely Sufic ones are always conditioning instruments, whether consciously so or otherwise.

4. Being prepared to abandon preconceptions about what 'study' constitutes. Readiness to study matters and materials which may not appear to be 'esoteric'.

5. Deciding whether his search is or is not a disguised form of a search for social integration, a manifestation of sheer curiosity, a desire for emotional stimulus or satisfaction.

6. Crediting, even as a working hypothesis, the possibility that there is a conscious, efficient and deliberate source of legitimate Sufic teaching actually in operation in the West.

This book is intended to illustrate for the general reader something of the richness and range of Sufi ideas.

Its materials have also been chosen and are presented as applicable to the people of the contemporary culture, offering an introductory course of study.

NOTES AND BIBLIOGRAPHY

WHERE possible, citations have been made of European, American and other comparatively available works.

All dates are expressed in Christian Era term.

1. Thöluck, F. A. G., *Ssufismus sive Theosophia Persarum panthe-isitica* (Berlin, 1821) (in Latin).

2. Masonic rituals, words, terms, etc., can often be 'decoded' by using Sufi systems. For instances and references see my *The Sufis* (New York, 1964; London, 1966), pp. xix, 50, 178, 179, 182, 183, 184, 186, 188. According to traditions (see J. P. Brown, *The Darvishes* (London, 1927), p. 229) the Sufi Masons have a warrant from the Grand Lodge of Tiberias, whose members fled there from the destruction of Jerusalem. They became widely known in the Near East through Zounoun (Dhun-Nun) (died 860).

3. According to the fifteenth-century poet and Sufi master, Jami (in his *Nahfat el-Uns*). Sheikh Suhrawardi dates the word from the ninth century, and the word is not sufficiently established to be found in dictionaries of such a comparatively early date. Imam Qushairi in his *Rasail* places the appearance of the word at about A.D. 822. Earlier Sufis used many names, including 'The Kindred', 'The Recluses', 'The Virtuous', 'The Near Ones'.

4. E.g., in Ibn Masarra of Córdoba (Spain) (833–931). For Sufic influence in Europe see, e.g., Garcin de Tassy, introduction to *Mantic-Uttair* ('Parliament of the Birds') (Paris, 1864).

5. *Suf = wool*. Externalists in the East and West have often adopted this etymology, which therefore often appears in reference books as the derivation.

6. 'Wool is the garb of animals' 'As-Suf libas al-Inam': Arabic quotation from Hujwiri's *The Revelation of the Veiled*. See Sirdar Ikbal Ali Shah, *Islamic Sufism* (London, 1933), p. 17.

7. This and other derivations have been used by Sufis themselves, explaining that 'bench' is not the original word, but the nearest equivalent which the Companions could find to their own word for themselves.

8. Higher functions of the mind: e.g., cf. the Persian couplet, 'Ba Murshid beshudi Insan / Be Murshid mandi Haiwan' ('With a Guide you may become a real man, without one you will remain an animal'); and Rumi: 'From realm to realm man went, reaching his present reasoning, knowledgeable, robust state – forgetting earlier forms of intelligence. So, too, shall he pass beyond the current forms of perception ... There are a thousand other forms of Mind...' and 'The degree of necessity determines the development of organs in man ... therefore increase your necessity.' (*Mathnavi-i-Maanavi*: Couplets of Inner Meaning).

9. *Jewish Encyclopaedia,* vol. XI, pp. 579, 580, 581 *et passim.* Jewish sages regarded by Western scholars as following the Spanish Sufi schools include: Juda Halevi of Toledo, in his *Cuzari*; Moses ben Ezra of Granada; Josef ben Zadiq of Córdobo, in his *Microcosmus*; Samuel ben Tibbón; Simtob ben Falaquera.

10. Identity of Sufi ideas with ancient Egyptian, Pythagorean and Platonic schools noted, e.g. by M. A. Ubicini, *Letters on Turkey* (London, 1856).

11. See Thöluck, op. cit. This book appeared ten years before Mme Blavatsky was born, and nine years before the birth of Col. Olcott, co-founder of the Theosophical Society.

12. R. A. Nicholson, *The Mystics of Islam* (London, 1914), pp. 3–4. Professor Nicholson was in his time believed to be a great authority on Sufism and published several useful books and translations. 'Nicholson was the greatest authority on Islamic mysticism this country has produced, and in his own considerable field was the supreme authority in the world.' (*The Times*, 27 August 1945.)

13 R.A. Nicholson, (translator), *The Kashf al-Mahjub* ('Revelation of the Veiled') (London, 1911), p. 34.

14. Fr. Cyprian Rice, *The Persian Sufis* (London, 1964), p. 9. Increasing Roman Catholic interest in Sufism, already shown to have had a significant effect upon Catholic mystics and academicians, is recently evidenced by the fact that this book was given *Nihil Obstat* and the *Imprimatur* of the Dominican and Diocesan authorities of

Rome. Its author believes that the future purpose of Sufism will be 'to make possible a welding of religious thought between East and West, a vital oecumenical commingling and understanding, which will prove ultimately to be, in the truest sense, on both sides, a return to origins, to the original unity' (ibid, p. 10).

15. Summed up by the Sufi ancient Abdul-Aziz Mekki (died 652) as: 'Offer a donkey a salad, and he will ask you what kind of a thistle it is.'

16. *The Sufis* (New York, 1964; London, 1969).

17. Prof. Miguel Asín y Palacios, 'Un precurso hispanomusulman de San Juan de la Cruz', *Andalus*, I (1933), pp. 7 ff. See also P. Nwyia, 'Ibn Abbad de Ronda et Jean de la Croix, *Andalus*, XXII (1957), pp. 113 ff.

18. Asín, 'El Simíl de los Castillos y moradas del alma en la mística islámica y en Santa Teresa', *Andalus*, II (1946), pp. 263 ff.

19. Shah, *The Sufis*, p. 239; and Baron Carra de Vaux in *Journal Asiatique*, XIX, p. 63. The Franciscan, Roger Bacon (died 1294), wearing Arab dress, discoursed at Oxford, quoting the *Hikmat el-Ishraq* ('Wisdom of Illumination') identified with the Sufi school of Sheikh Shahabudin Yahya Suhrawardi, who had been executed for apostasy and carrying on 'the ancient philosophy' in 1191. For Franciscan connection with Sufism, see *The Sufis*.

20. Shah, *The Sufis*, pp. xvi, 155, 191, 194, 196, 199, 202–4, 243, 370.

21. Asín, *Abenmasarra*; and Shah, *The Sufis*, pp. xvii, xix, 42, 140, 203–5, 243, 244, 246, 247, 261, 370, 388, 389. See also J. Ribera, *Origines de la filosofia de Raimundo Lulio*.

22. C. F. Loehlin, 'Sufism and Sikhism', *Moslem World*, XXIX (1939), pp. 351 ff; and see Shah, *The Sufis*, pp. 358 f.

23. C. Swan, *Gesta Romanorum* London, 1829), etc. The first known Western manuscript of this collection dates from 1324. Its stories are the source of Shakespeare's *King Lear, The Merchant of Venice, Pericles, The Rape of Lucrece*. Chaucer, Lydgate and Boccaccio all included material from this source.

24. A. Barth, *Religions of India*; Dr Tara Chand, *The Cultural History of India* (Hyderabad, 1958), p. 153; and Shah, *The Sufis*, pp. 356 ff.

25. See Shah, *The Secret Lore of Magic* (London, 1957). For the Sufi attitude to magic, see *The Sufis*, pp. 326 ff; and Shah, *Destination Mecca* (London, 1957), pp. 169 ff. For supernormal faculties exercised by Sufis, see J. P. Brown, *The Darvishes* (London, 1867; repub. 1927); L. M. J. Garnett, *Mysticism and Magic in Turkey* (London, 1912); S. A. Salik, *The Saint of Gilan* (Lahore, 1953); J. A. Subhan, *Sufism, its Saints and Shrines* (Lucknow, 1939).

26. Freud's psychological method of interpreting symbols is used in the Sufi El-Ghazali's *Niche,* nine hundred years before Freud. See (s.v. Symbolism) Gairdner's translation of *The Niche* (Royal Asiatic Society, London, 1924). The 'Jungian Archetypal theory' was known to Sufis in ancient times: see R. Landau, *The Philosophy of Ibn Arabi* (New York, 1959), pp. 4 f. Freud's debt to Cabbalism and Jewish mysticism, which Jewish authorities regard as derived from Sufism or identical with it, is treated in Professor David Bakan, *Sigmund Freud and the Jewish Mystical Tradition* (New York, 1958).

27. Certain reviewers and others, ignorant of the fact that Sufi books seldom have indices (so that the reader shall read the book in its entirety), have deplored the lack of an index to *The Sufis*. The Coombe Springs Press issued an independent index to *The Sufis* in 1965.

28. E. W. F. Tomlin, F.R.A.S., *Great Philosophers of the East* (London, 1959), p. 295.

29. E. W. F. Tomlin, *Great Philosophers of the West* (London, 1959).

30. Published London 1959 and 1960.

31. Some experts' opinions about the 'origins' of Sufism: 'The influence of Christian mysticism is paramount' (Tomlin, *Great Philosophers of the East,* p. 295); 'A reaction from the burdens of a dry monotheism, of a rigid law and a stiffened ritual' (Rev. Dr Sell, *Sufism* (Madras, 1910), p. 11); '... having its origins in the religious conceptions of India and Greece' (J. P. Brown, op. cit., p. v); 'appear to be a kind of Gnostics' (J. W. Redhouse, *The Mesnevi* (London, 1881), p. xiv); '... the emotional character of Sufism, so different from the cold and bloodless theories of the Indian philosophies, is apparent' (E. G. Browne, *A Literary History of Persia* (London, 1909), p. 442); 'a little Persian sect' (F. Hadland Davis, *The Persian Mystics: Jalaludin Rumi* (London, 1907), p. 1); 'great perversion of Mohammed's teaching' (Miss G. L. Bell, *Poems from the Divan of*

Hafiz (London, 1928), p. 51); 'derived in part from Plato, "the Attic Moses", but mainly from Christianity' (E. H. Whinfield, *Masnavi I ma'navi: the Spiritual Couplets* (London, 1887), p. xv); 'Orientalists ... have indeed attributed the origins of Sufism to Persian, Hindu, Neoplatonic or Christian sources. But these diverse attributions have ended by cancelling one another' (T. Burckhardt, *An Introduction to Sufi Doctrine* (Lahore, 1959), p. 5).

32. R. A. Nicholson, Selections from the *Diwan-i-Shams-i-Tabriz* (Cambridge, 1898; rev. 1952), pp. xxxvi ff. Professor Edward Palmer has recorded for Western students the fact that *mutrib,* the Arabic equivalent of troubadour, also stands for 'Sufi teacher' (*Oriental Mysticism*, p. 80). Professor Hitti is even more explicit:

In southern France the first Provençal poets appear full-fledged towards the end of the eleventh century with palpitating love expressed in a wealth of fantastic imagery. The troubadours (*tarab*: music, song) who flourished in the twelfth century imitated their southern contemporaries, the *zajal* singers. Following the Arabic precedent the cult of the dame suddenly arises in south-west Europe. The *Chanson de Roland*, the noblest monument of early European literature, whose appearance prior to 1080 marks the beginning of a new civilization – that of Western Europe – just as the Homeric poems mark the beginning of historic Greece, owes its existence to a military contact with Moslem Spain. (P. K. Hitti, *History of the Arabs* (1951 edition), p. 562.)

33. See Robert Graves's Introduction to Shah, *The Sufis*, p. xvii. The most accessible English rendering of Attar's *Parliament of the Birds* is the 1954 version, translated by C. S. Nott from a French copy, reissued in London in 1961. The Rev. Baring-Gould had shown in Victorian times the Tell legend lacked historical backing. Haydn's *Dictionary of Dates* says (s.v. 'Tell'): 'The popular stories respecting him were demonstrated to be mythical by Professor Kopf of Lucerne, 1872.'

34. Peacock Angel cult: Founded by the Sufi master Sheikh Adi ben Musafir (died 1162). A chapter on this society is to be found in Chapter 15 of Arkon Daraul, *Secret Societies* (London, 1961), published in New York in 1961 as *A History of Secret Societies*. The symbology of the cult can be unlocked by applying the 'Abjad-notation' enciphering system used by the Sufis, described in Shah,

The Sufis; this was extensively used by poets and Sufis. See also note 93.

35. G. I. Gurdjieff left abundant clues to the Sufic origins of virtually every point in his 'system'; though it obviously belongs more specifically to the Khagjagan (Naqshbandi) form of the dervish teaching. In addition to the practices of 'the work', such books as Gurdjieff's *Beelzebub* (otherwise known as *All and Everything*) (New York, 1950) and *Meetings with Remarkable Men* (2nd impression, 1963) abound with references, often semi-covert ones, to the Sufi system. He also cites by name the Naqshbandis, Kubravis and other Sufis, in his 1923 (Paris) 'prospectus' of a public presentation (*The Echo of the Champs-Élysées*, I, 37, part 2 (Paris: 13–25 Dec. 1923), quoting as sources, *inter alia*, the Naqshbandi, Qadiri, Qalandar, Kubravi and Mevlevi Dervish practices, Maurice Nicoll, *Psychological Commentaries* (London, 1952) and *The New Man* (London, 1950) abound with examples of Sufic methods used to interpret religious and other documents. These works depart from Sufi usage in dealing with subjects in a random fashion, and in being aimed at an 'accidental' rather than a chosen community of students.

With regard to P. D. Ouspensky: largely through his contact with Gurdjieff this Russian philosopher names the Sufis as a source of ancient psychology, e.g. in *The Psychology of Man's Possible Evolution* (London, 1951), p. 7. Ouspensky, however, had no direct contact with dervishes and was unable to effect the necessary transposition of Sufic ideas from their literary sources in Eastern and other literature into the terminology used in his 'system'. Had he been able to do so, he would have realized that his 'system' had ignored the Sufi requirement of 'time, place and certain people'. He attempts to systematize the material of Gurdjieff in *In Search of the Miraculous* (London, 1950), in which he records conversations with Gurdjieff. Both the Naqshbandi Sufis and the Gurdjieff-Ouspenskians call their studies 'The Fourth Way'. See Ouspensky, *The Fourth Way* (London, 1957).

36. *Hammarskjöld and Sufis*: Jalaludin Rumi is quoted literally by him (Hammarskjöld, *Markings* (London, 1964), p. 95 *et passim*); see also – in *Reader's Digest*, quoting *Dagens Nyheter* (Stockholm 1962) – his copy of the Sufi poem translated by Sir William Jones (1746–94):

On parent knees, a naked new-born child,
Weeping thou sat'st while all around thee smiled.
So live, that sinking in thy last long sleep,
Calm thou may'st smile while all around thee weep.

37. Shakespeare's plays contain not only many stories of Persian, Arabian and other Eastern origins, but also what might seem to be almost literal quotations from Sufi literature. Professor Nicholson has noted one or two equivalents from the *Diwan-i-Shams-i-Tabriz* in his translation of that book (see note 32 above) pp. 290 and 291 *et passim*. See also Garcin de Tassy, *Philosophical and Religious Poetry of the Persians* (Paris, 1864).

38. Professor Kenneth Walker, in *Diagnosis of Man* (London, 1962), quotes the Sanai-Rumi Sufi school usage of the legend of the 'Elephant in the Dark', to show how modern man may fumble with parts of a problem, instead of going to the heart of it. Walker follows Gurdjieff; see his *Study of Gurdjieff's Teaching* (London, 1957).

39. As 'The Tale of the Ugly Duckling'; see Shah, *The Sufis*.

40. F. Hitchman, *Burton*, I, p. 286.

41. By L. A. Hill.

42. E.g. J. G. Saxe, *The Blind Men and the Elephant* (London, 1964); and C. Downing (trans.), *Tales of the Hodja* (London, 1964).

43. Shah, *The Sufis,* pp. 208 ff., 243. For Eastern origins of 'witches', see J. L. Bracelin, *Gerald Gardner – Witch* (London, 1960), p. 75; and A. Daraul, *Witches and Sorcerers* (New York, 1966), pp. 20, 23–4, 73, 204 f., *et passim*.

44. See Shah, *The Sufis,* pp.187, 191, 223, 389 f.; and A. Daraul, *Secret Societies* (London, 1961). Rosicrucians claim that their founder brought his knowledge from Arabia, Fez and Egypt. The origins have been traced by Daraul (ibid., p. 195), to the Qadiri Sufi Order.

45. Daraul, *Secret Societies,* Chap, 22; E. J. Jurji, *The Illuministic Sufis*, JAOS 57, pp. 90 ff., 1937; and Brown, *Darvishes*.

46. See Shah, *The Sufis, passim,* for references of the influences of El-Ghazali and others on Western Europe. Most books on medieval scholasticism and the history of its thought carry references to this source. Cf. Hitti, *History of the Arabs*; and G. Leff, *Mediaeval Thought* (London, 1958).

47. Leff, ibid.; and O. B. Kapor, 'Research Thesis on the Mystic Philosophy of Kabir' (Allahabad University Studies, 10, 1933), p. 166.

48. W. Ivanow, *The Truth Worshippers of Kurdistan* (Leiden, 1953), pp. 57–68 *et passim.*

49. The people who became known as the Assassins were a Sufi organization originally called *Asasin* ('People of the Foundation, the Fundamentals'), a branch of which was taken over in the tenth Christian century by Hasan, son of Sabah, known as the Great Assassin or Old Man of the Mountains. This name is a mistranslation of his usurped title, *Sheikh El-Jabal* (Master of the Mountains), erroneously rendered by Westerners in the alternative meaning (Sheikh) of 'Senex del Monte', which Crusaders called him. The 'Aga Khans' are reputed to be descended from this Hasan. Another, rival leader of the cult is located in Bombay. The original 'order' however, continues independently. See Sirdar Ikbal Ali Shah, 'The General Principles of Sufism' (*Hibbert Journal,* vol. 20 (1921–2), pp. 523–35). Great confusion has been created in the West by the literal translation of the meaning of Arabic names. Hence, for instance, while 'Algazel' may be seen to be Al-Ghazali, not everyone recognizes 'Doctor Maximus' ('The Greatest Teacher') as El-Sheikh El-Akbar (Ibn El-Arabi); or 'Basil Valentine' ('The Triumphant King') as El-Malik El-Fatih, the alchemist; or, for that matter, the anti-witch tract *Errores Gaziorum* as 'Ghulat aljazair' ('Sects of Algeria').

50. Shah, *The Sufis,* pp. 309, 362–4.

51. ibid., p. 309. Yoga and Zen material nowadays tend to ignore the special requirements of choice of disciple and type of teacher.

52. ibid., pp. xiv, xix, 225–7, 399.

53. ibid., pp. xxii, 50, 104, 106, 115, 163, 166, 223, 393.

54. Professor M. Asín Palacios: *Islam and the Divine Comedy* (Ibn el-Arabi, 1165–1240), tr. H. Sunderland (London, 1926). (*La Escatologia Musulmana en la Divina Comedia,* Madrid, 1961.)

55. See, e.g., Shamsudin Ahmad El-Aflaki, *Munaqib El-Arifin:* trans. Redhouse as *The Acts of Adepts* (London, 1881); reprinted in facsimile ed. Kingston as *Legends of the Sufis* (London, 1965). See also El-Ghazali, *Alchemy of Happiness.*

56. Rumi (1207–73) was born in Balkh, Afghanistan and died at Konia (Iconium), Turkey, where 'dervish dancing' in public is now proscribed except as a tourist spectacle.

57. Abdul-Qadir of Gilan ('Sultan of the Friends') (1077–1166); Hadrat Bahaudin Naqshband (El-Shah) (1318–89).

58. 'Subud' was founded by an Indonesian, Mohammed Subuh, in 1934. Indiscriminate indulgence in the *Latihan* exercise has been known to give rise to a condition now referred to in medical literature as 'Subud psychosis'.

59. 'Truth comes after "states" and ecstasy, and takes its place' (Kalabadhi, *Kitab El-Taaruf*, quoting Junaid of Baghdad (d. 910)). In A. J. Arberry's version, *The Doctrine of the Sufis* (Cambridge, 1935), p. 106: 'But when Truth cometh, ecstasy itself is dispossessed.'

60. In *Fihi Ma Fihi* (translated by A. J. Arberry as 'Discourses of Rumi' (London, 1961)); *The Mathnavi* (trans. R. A. Nicholson, London, 1926; J. W. Redhouse, London, 1881; E. H. Whinfield, London, 1887; C. E. Wilson, London, 1910, etc.).

61. First Book of the *Hadiqa* (trans. J. Stephenson as 'Walled Garden of Truth', Calcutta, 1910); *Karnama* ('Book of the Work'); and *Diwan*.

62. *Mishkat El-Anwar* (trans. W. H. T. Gairdner as *Niche for Lamps*, Royal Asiatic Society, London, 1924; Lahore, 1952). *Ihya El Ulum El-Din* ('Revival of Religious Sciences').

63. *Futuhat Al-Makkia* ('Openings in Mecca'); *Fusus El-Hikam* ('Bezels of the Wisdoms'); *Kimia-i-Sadat* ('Alchemy of Happiness'); *Tarjuman El-Ashwaq* ('Interpreter of Desires', trans. Nicholson).

64. See Dietrici, *Der Darwinismus im 10. und 19. Jahrhundert* (Leipzig, 1878); and Rumi, *Mathnavi*.

65. Shabistari, *Garden of Mysteries/Secret Garden* (thirteenth-fourteenth centuries); Sayad Ahmad Hatif Isfahani, *Tarjiband*; and others.

66. E.g. 'The Hidden World has clouds and rain, of a different kind ... made apparent only to the refined, those not deceived by the seeming completeness of the ordinary world' (Rumi, *Mathnavi*):

Ghaib ra abri wa abi digar ast
Asman wa aftab-i-digar ast.
Nayad an illa ki bar pakan padid
Barqiyan fi labs min khalkin jadid.

67. E.g. in Hujwiri's (eleventh century) *The Revelation of the Veiled*, s.v. 'Recapitulation of their Miracles'.

68. See, for example, No. IX in Nicholson's *Diwan-i-Shams-i-Tabriz*, p. 32 (thirteenth-century Persian text).

69. Professor Mohammed Ali Aini, trans. A. Rechid, *La Quintessence de la philosophie de Ibn-i-Arabi* (Paris, 1926), pp. 66–7.

70. Junaid of Baghdad (d. 910) answered conditioned minds thus: 'None reaches the rank of Truth until a thousand honest people testify that he is a heretic.'

71. In Arabic: 'Al-turuqu illahi ka nufusi bani Adama' (see Sirdar Ali Shah, *İslamic Sufism*, p. 211).

72. See, e.g. Saadi (1184–1263), *Gulistan* ('Rose Garden'), 'On the Manners of Dervishes', Agha Omar Ali-Shah's translation, *Gulistan* (Sheikh Muslihuddin Saadi Shirazi, *Le Jardin de Roses*), Paris, 1966. Cf. Ibn Hamdan, cited in Hujwiri's *Kashf*: 'Be sure that you do not train yourself to music, in case this holds you back from even higher perceptions.' Contemporary dervishes of the Chishti 'order' have strayed far from the instructions of their founder in this matter, settling for a dissociated or ecstatic state induced by listening to or playing music. Muinudin Chishti himself wrote against this practice: 'They know that we listen to music and that we perceive certain "secrets" as a result. So they play music and cast themselves into "states". Know that every learning must have all its requirements fulfilled, not just music, thought, concentration. Remember: what is the good of a wonderful milk yield from a cow which kicks the pail over?' (Risalat, *Epistles to Disciples*).

73. Although all pay lip-service to the teachings of Ibn El-Arabi, for instance, they have not absorbed such words as these, where he refers to Sufism:

She has confused all the learned of Islam,
All who have studied the Psalms,
Every Jewish Rabbi,
Every Christian Priest.

Or the famous words of Abu-Said ibn Abi-Khair (1040):

> Until college and minaret have crumbled
> This holy work of ours will not be done.
> Until faith becomes rejection, and rejection becomes belief
> There will be no true Muslim.

On the limitations of religious 'vehicle': 'What can I do, O Muslims? I do not know myself. I am no Christian, no Jew, no Magian, no Musulman. Not of the East, nor of the West', *Divan-i-Shams-i-Tabriz*, xxxii, p. 124 (Persian version).

74. Ibn el-Arabi, *Fusus el-Hikam* ('Bezels or Segments of the Wisdoms'), s.v. El-Fas El-Adamia ('Segment of Adam'): paraphrased in S. A. Q. Husaini, *Ibn Al Arabi* (Lahore, 1931); French version: Burckhardt, T., *La Sagesse des Prophètes* (Paris, 1955), pp. 22 f.

75. J. K. Birge, *The Bektashi Order of Dervishes* (London, 1937), p. 39, n. 3.

76. Brown *The Darvishes*, p. 475.

77. These cults are sometimes deteriorations of such communities as I describe in *Destination Mecca*, pp. 169 ff.

78. A penetrating perception of the fact that many Sufi ideas have filtered into primitive communities was written by the well-known poet Ted Hughes two years ago: 'One would almost be inclined to say that Shamanism might well be a barbarized, stray descendant of Sufism.' (The *Listener*, 29 October 1964, p. 678.)

79. P. Lawrence, *Road Belong Cargo* (London, 1964), contains a description of this cult and has an excellent bibliography.

80. Vol. 290, no. 1754, pp. 481–595; and vol. 291, no. 1756, pp. 123–35.

81. *Siraat* (English language), Delhi, vol. 1, no. 5, 1 January 1961, p. 5, cols. 1–3, 'Sufism in a changing World', by Selim Brook-White ('Murid').

82. *International Journal of Clinical and Experimental Hypnosis*, vol. 10, no. 4 (October), pp. 271–4: J. Hallaj, 'Hypnotherapeutic Techniques in a Central Asian Community'. Reprinted in R. E. Shor, and M. T. Orne, *The Nature of Hypnosis* (Selected Basic Readings) (New York, 1965), vol. 6, pp. 453 ff.

83. Vol. 197, no. 1132, May 1960: W. Foster, 'The Family of Hashim', pp. 269–71.

84. Vol. CLXII, no. 4210, 9 December 1965: D. R. Martin, 'Below the Hindu Kush', p. 870.

85. Some of these articles are now reprinted in R. W. Davidson, *Documents on Contemporary Dervish Communities* (London, 1966–7).

86. *The Times*, no. 55,955, 9 March 1964. 'Elusive Guardians of Ancient Secrets', p. 12, cols. 6–8.

87. *She* (March 1963), p. 58: ('*She* Looks at religion – no.11'); and also (September 1965) 'The Hard High Life' by Mir S. Khan, pp. 68–70. (Both items illustrated.)

88. From El-Ghazali's monumental *Revival of Religious Sciences.*

89. Sentences upon Sufis and Sufism by early historical masters of the Sufis:
Dhun-Nun the Egyptian (died 860): 'A Sufi is one whose speech accords with his behaviour and whose silence indicates his state, and who discards wordly connections.'
The woman adept Rabia El-Adawia (died 717): 'The Sufi is he who neither fears hell nor covets paradise.'
Abul-Hasan Nuri (died 907): 'Sufism is the renunciation of all pleasures of the (transitory) world.'
Hujwiri (eleventh century): 'The follower of Sufism is he who seeks to reach the rank of being dead to self and alive to truth by means of struggle. He who has reached this end is called a Sufi.'
Junaid of Baghdad (died 910): 'Sufism is an attribute wherein is man's subsistence.'
Nuri: 'The Sufi has no possession, nor is he possessed by anything.'

Ibn El-Lalali (eleventh century): 'Sufism is truth without formulation.'

90. Rumi, 'AQL' = real intellect. He also said: 'The Sufi's book is not literacy and letters.' (*Mathnavi.*)

91. This is how psychological and other diagrams become 'mandalas' and 'magic figures'.

92. Various versions of the dervish teaching-stories in my *Tales of the Dervishes* (London, 1967) have been represented by Sufi masters as events which happened to them, for this reason.

93. As Professor A. J. Arberry of Cambridge puts it, the doctrine is obscure because it is 'based largely on experiences in their very nature well nigh incommunicable' (*Tales from the Masnavi*, (London, 1961, p. 19). The technical term for one form of this, the use of words written similarly which have different meanings, is *Jinas-i-Mukharif*; it is much used in poetry. Gibb (*History of Ottoman Poetry* (1900), 1, 118) shows familiarity with this system, but does not apply it in his studies.

94. Mahmud Shabistari (1317), in common with many Sufi teachers, speaks of the transient nature of formulation:

> If the Moslem knew what an idol was
> He would know that there is religion in idolatry.
> If the idolater knew what religion was
> He would know where he had gone astray.
> He sees in the idol nothing but the obvious creature:
> This is why, in Islamic Law, he is a heathen.
> (*Gulshan-i-Raz*: 'Garden of Secrets'.)

The Persian text is:

> Musulman gar bi-danist ki but chist
> Bi-danisti ki din dar butparasti'st.
> Agar mushrik zi din agah gashti
> Kuja dar din i khud gumrah gashti.
> Na did u dar but illa khalqi zahir:
> Badan illat shud an dar Shara, Kafir.

95. How little this important part of Sufi transmission is known in 'the literature of the field' is evidenced by the fact that almost the only reference to humour in Sufism at all current is made by an American student (Birge, *The Bektashi Order of Dervishes*, p. 88); and even he regards it as a 'characteristic peculiarity' of the Order which he is studying. See also Shah, *Exploits of the Incomparable Mulla Nasrudin* (London, 1966).

96. The best known case is that of Husain ibn Mansur El-Hallaj, the great Sufi martyr, dismembered alive and done to death, his corpse then being burnt, by the order of the Caliph el-Muqtadir, of the House of Haroun El-Rashid, in the year 922, for allegedly claim-

ing that he was God. Professor Louis Massignon has specialized in the Hallaj literature. See also note 101, below. The great teacher Suhrawardi, too, was executed for teaching 'ancient philosophy' in the twelfth century (see note 19, above).

97. On conditioned and indoctrined groups and movements, see R. J. Liftan, *Thought Reform* (London, 1961); J. Mann, *Changing Human Behaviour* (New York, 1965); W. J. H. Sprott, *Human Groups* (London, 1958); M. Phillips, *Small Social Groups in England* (London, 1965).

98. The story of how Uwais was visited by Companions of Mohammed after the Prophet's death is found in many books, including the well-known 'Recital of the Friends' (*Lives of the Saints*) by Fariduddin Attar, translated by A. Pavet de Courteille as *Le Memorial des saints* (Paris, 1889), pp. 11 f. See Dr B. Behari's English abridgement (*Fariduddin Attar's Tadhkiratul-Auliya*) (Lahore, 1961).

99. See the *Awarif-l-Ma'rif*, written in the thirteenth century by Sheikh Shah abudin Umar ibn Mohamed Suhrawardi (version of Mahmud ibn Ali Alkashani, translated from Persian into English by Lieut. Col. H. Wilberforce Clarke (Calcutta, 1890)).

100. The passage runs in Arabic: 'Sharibna ala dhikri alhabibi mudamatu/Shakirna bi ha min qabli an yukhlaka alkarmu.' Professor Hitti (op. cit., p. 436 calls Ibn El-Farid the only Arab mystical poet.

101. See Professor L. Massignon, *Le Diwan d'Al Hallaj* (Paris, 1955), etc.

102. See his *Turkish Nationalism and Western Civilisation* (London, 1959).

103. E.g. Ibn El-Arabi's dictum: 'People think that a Sheikh should show miracles and manifest illumination. The requirement of a teacher is, however, that he should possess all that the disciple needs.'

104. Recorded in Hujwiri, *The Revelation of the Veiled*.

105. *Munaqib*; see note 55, above.

106. He wrote *Majma el-Bahrain* ('Confluence of the Two Seas') published in translation by the Asiatic Society of Bengal.

107. In a Sufi circle even one unsuitable member will harm the

effort of the whole; this is enunciated, for instance, by Saadi in *Gulistan*, 'On the Manners of Dervishes'.

108. Omar Khayyam (d. 1123): for considerations of the Khyamic Sufi teachings, see Swami Govinda Tirtha, *The Nectar of Grace –* Omar Khayyam's Life and Works (Allahabad, 1941); and Shah, *The Sufis*, pp. 164–71. The poem quoted is quatrain 24 of the Bodleian MS, edited by E. Heron-Allen (*The Ruba'iyat of Omar Khayyam*, London 1898), p. 141. The original text is:

> Dar sauma'a wa madrasa wa deir wa kanisht –
> Tarsinda zi dozakhand wa juya-i-bihisht.
> Ankas ki zi asrar-i-khuda ba-khabar ast:
> Z'in tukhm dar andarun-i dil hich nakasht.

Khayyam's *Ruba'iyat* was retranslated and published in 1967 by Robert Graves and Omar Ali-Shah with critical commentaries.

109. See English version by Maulvi S. A. Q. Husaini, in *Ibn Al Arabi* (Lahore, 1931), VI, 1, p. 38.

110. R. Simac, 'In a Naqshbandi Circle', *Hibbert Journal* (Spring 1967), vol. 65, no. 258. See also Shah, *Exploits of the Incomparable Mulla Nasrudin* (London and New York, 1966), and *Caravan of Dreams* (London, 1968).

Part Two
CLASSICAL AUTHORS

EL-GHAZALI

THE twelfth-century philosopher and Sufi El-Ghazali quotes in his *Book of Knowledge* this line from El-Mutanabbi: 'To the sick man, sweet water tastes bitter in the mouth.'

This could very well be taken as Ghazali's motto. Eight hundred years before Pavlov, he pointed out and hammered home (often in engaging parables, sometimes in startlingly 'modern' words) the problem of conditioning.

In spite of Pavlov and the dozens of books and reports of clinical studies into human behaviour made since the Korean war, the ordinary student of things of the mind is unaware of the power of indoctrination.* Indoctrination, in totalitarian societies, is something which is desirable providing that it furthers the beliefs of such societies. In other groupings its presence is scarcely even suspected. This is what makes almost anyone vulnerable to it.

Ghazali's work not only pre-dates, but also exceeds, the contemporary knowledge of these matters. At the time of writing informed opinion is split between whether indoctrination (whether overt or covert) is desirable or otherwise, whether, too, it is inescapable or not.

Ghazali not only points out that what people call belief may be a state of obsession; he states clearly, in accordance with Sufi principles, that it is not inescapable, but insists that it is essential for people to be able to identify it.

His books were burnt by Mediterranean bigots from Spain to

* One of the most striking peculiarities of contemporary man is that, while he now has abundant scientific evidence to the contrary, he finds it intensely difficult to understand that his beliefs are by no means always linked with either his intelligence, his culture or his values. He is therefore almost unreasonably prone to indoctrination.

Syria. Nowadays they are not put into the flames, but their effect, except among Sufis, is perhaps less; they are not read very much.

He regarded the distinction between opinion and knowledge as something which can easily be lost. When this happens, it is incumbent upon those who know the difference to make it plain as far as they are able.

Ghazali's scientific, psychological discoveries, though widely appreciated by academics of all kinds, have not been given the attention they deserve because he specifically disclaims the scientific or logical method as their origin. He arrived at his knowledge through his upbringing in Sufism, among Sufis, and through a form of direct perception of the truth which has nothing to do with mechanical intellection. This, of course, at once puts him outside the pale for scientists. What is rather curious, however, is that his discoveries are so astonishing that one would have thought that investigators would have liked to find out how he made them.

'Mysticism' having been given a bad name like the dog in the proverb, if it cannot be hanged, can at least be ignored. This is a measure of scholastic psychology: accept the man's discoveries if you cannot deny them, but ignore his method if it does not follow your beliefs about method.

If Ghazali had produced no worthwhile results, he would naturally have been regarded as only a mystic, and a proof that mysticism is educationally or socially unproductive.

The influence of Ghazali on Western thought is admitted on all hands to be enormous. But this influence itself shows the working of conditioning; the philosophers of medieval Christendom who adopted many of his ideas did so selectively, completely ignoring the parts which were embarrassing to their own indoctrination activities.

Ghazali's way of thought attempted to bring to a wider audience than the comparatively small Sufi one a final distinction between belief and obsession. He stressed the role of upbringing in the inculcation of religious beliefs, and invited his readers to observe the mechanism involved. He insisted upon pointing out that those who are learned may be, and often are, stupid as well, and can be bigoted, obsessed. He affirms that, in addition to having information and being able to reproduce it, there is such a thing as knowledge, which happens to be a higher form of human thought.

The habit of confusing opinion with knowledge, a habit which is to be met with every day at the current time, Ghazali regards as an epidemic disease.

In saying all these things, with a wealth of illustration and in an atmosphere which was most unconducive to scientific attitudes, Ghazali was not merely playing the part of a diagnostician. He had acquired his own knowledge in a Sufic manner, and he realized that higher understanding – being a Sufi, in fact – was only possible to people who could see and avoid the phenomena which he was describing.

Ghazali produced numerous books and published many teachings. His contribution to human thought and the relevance of his ideas hundreds of years later are unquestioned. Let us partly repair the omission of our predecessors by seeing what he has to say about method. What was the Way of El-Ghazali? What does man have to do in order to be like him, who was admittedly one of the world's giants of philosophy and psychology?

Ghazali on the Path

A human being is not a human being while his tendencies include self-indulgence, covetousness, temper and attacking other people.

A student must reduce to the minimum the fixing of his attention upon customary things like his people and his environment, for attention-capacity is limited.

The pupil must regard his teacher like a doctor who knows the cure of the patient. He will serve his teacher. Sufis teach in unexpected ways. An experienced physician prescribes certain treatments correctly. Yet the outside observer might be quite amazed at what he is saying and doing; he will fail to see the necessity or the relevance of the procedure being followed.

This is why it is unlikely that the pupil will be able to ask the right questions at the right time. But the teacher knows what and when a person can understand.

The Difference between Social and Initiatory Activity

Ghazali insists upon the connection and also the difference between the social or diversionary contact of people, and the higher contact.

What prevents the progress of an individual and a group of people, from praiseworthy beginnings, is their stabilizing themselves upon repetition and what is a disguised social basis.

If a child, he says, asks us to explain to him the pleasures which are contained in wielding sovereignty, we may say that it is like the pleasure which he feels in sport; though, in reality, the two have nothing in common except that they both belong to the category of pleasure.

Parable of the People with a Higher Aim

Imam El-Ghazali relates to tradition from the life of Isa, ibn Maryam: Jesus, Son of Mary.

Isa one day saw some people sitting miserably on a wall, by the roadside. He asked: 'What is your affliction?' They said: 'We have become like this through our fear of Hell.'

He went on his way, and saw a number of people grouped disconsolately in various postures by the wayside. He said: 'What is your affliction?' They said: 'Desire for Paradise has made us like this.'

He went on his way, until he came to a third group of people. They looked like people who had endured much, but their faces shone with joy.

Isa asked them: 'What has made you like this?' and they

answered: 'The Spirit of Truth. We have seen Reality, and this has made us oblivious of lesser goals.'

Isa said: 'These are the people who attain. On the Day of Accounting these are they who will be in the Presence of God.'

The Three Functions of the Perfected Man

The Perfected Man of the Sufis has three forms of relationship with people. These vary with the condition of the people.

The three manners are exercised in accordance with

(1) The form of belief which surrounds the Sufi;

(2) The capacity of students, who are taught in accordance with their ability to understand;

(3) A special circle of people who will share an understanding of the knowledge which is derived from direct inner experience.

Attraction of Celebrities

A man who is being delivered from the danger of a fierce lion does not object, whether this service is performed by an unknown or an illustrious individual. Why, therefore, do people seek knowledge from celebrities?

The Nature of Divine Knowledge

The question of divine knowledge is so deep that it is really known only to those who have it.

A child has no real knowledge of the attainments of an adult. An ordinary adult cannot understand the attainments of a learned man.

In the same way, an educated man cannot yet understand the experiences of enlightened saints or Sufis.

Love and Self-Interest

If one loves someone because it gives pleasure, one should not be regarded as loving that person at all. The love is, in reality, though this is not perceived, directed towards the pleasure. The source of the pleasure is the secondary object of attention, and it is perceived only because the perception of the pleasure is not well enough developed for the real feeling to be identified and described.

You Must be Prepared

You must prepare yourself for the transition in which there will be none of the things to which you have accustomed yourself, says Ghazali. After death your identity will have to respond to stimuli of which you have a chance to get a foretaste here. If you remain attached to the few things with which you are familiar, it will only make you miserable.

Ignorance

People oppose things because they are ignorant of them.

Ceremonies of Music and Movement

Such meetings must be held in accordance with the requirements of time and place. Onlookers whose motives are not worthy shall be excluded. The participants in audition must sit silently and not look at each other. They seek what may appear from their own 'hearts'.

The Sterile Woman

A man went to a doctor and told him that his wife was not bearing children. The physician saw the woman, took her pulse, and said:

'I cannot treat you for sterility because I have discovered that you will in any case die within forty days.'

When she heard this the woman was so worried that she could eat nothing during the ensuing forty days.

But she did not die at the time predicted.

The husband took the matter up with the doctor, who said:

'Yes, I knew that. Now she will be fertile.'

The husband asked how this had come about.

The doctor told him:

'Your wife was too fat, and this was interfering with her fertility. I knew that the only thing which would put her off her food would be fear of dying. She is now, therefore, cured.'

The question of knowledge is a very dangerous one.

The Dance

A disciple had asked permission to take part in the 'dance' of the Sufis.

The Sheikh said: 'Fast completely for three days. Then have luscious dishes cooked. If you then prefer the "dance", you may take part in it.'

A Quality must have a Vehicle

Speed, which becomes a virtue when it is found in a horse, by itself has no advantages.

The Idiot Self

If you cannot find in a man an appropriate example of dedication, study the lives of the Sufis. Man should also say to himself: 'O my soul! You think yourself clever and are upset at being called idiotic. But what else are you in reality? You make clothes for winter, but no provision for another life. You are like a man in winter who says: "I shall not wear warm clothes, but place trust in God's kindness to protect me from the cold." He does not realize that, in addition to creating cold, God placed before man the means to protect himself from it.'

Man was made for Learning

A camel is stronger than a man; an elephant is larger; a lion has greater valour; cattle can eat more than man; birds are more virile. Man was made for the purpose of learning.

The Price of Knowledge

'Assuredly there is a price on this knowledge. It is to be given only to those who can keep it and not lose it.'

Book of Knowledge, quoting Ikrima

Commentary by Junubi:

This knowledge is of course the Sufi knowledge. It does not refer to book-knowledge, something which can be written down or preserved in factual form; because such material would not be diminished by exposing it to someone who might fail to benefit from it. It is the knowledge given in the time and manner which verifies and makes live the book-knowledge. 'Giving knowledge which will be lost' refers to allowing certain 'states' of recognition of truth to be engendered in an individual before that person is in a condition to preserve that state; hence he loses its advantage and it is lost.

Comment by Ahmad Minai:

Because of the difficulty of grasping this fact, and due to an understandable laziness, intellectuals have decided to 'abolish' any learning which cannot be contained in books. This is not to say that it does not exist. It makes it more difficult to find and teach, since the above-named types (intellectuals) have trained people not to look for it.

Possessions

You possess only whatever will not be lost in a shipwreck.

Gain and Loss

I should like to know what a man who has no knowledge has really gained, and what a man of knowledge has not gained.

❧ 2 ❧

OMAR KHAYYAM

OMAR Khayyam was an important philosopher, scientist and practical instructor in Sufism. His name is well known in European literature mainly because of Edward Fitzgerald, who in Victorian times published a few of Omar's quatrains in English. Fitzgerald – like, it must be noted, many Eastern scholastics – imagined that because Khayyam was at times talking about widely conflicting points of view, he himself was a victim to some sort of alternation of mind. This attitude, while characteristic of many academicians, is just about as profound as that of a man who thinks that if someone shows you something he must believe it; and that if he shows you several things, he must be subject to identification with these things.

Fitzgerald was guilty of far more, however, than poor thinking capacity. His interpolation of anti-Sufi propaganda into his rendering of Khayyam cannot be excused even by his most ardent supporters. As a result they tend to ignore this amazing dishonesty, and shout about other subjects instead.

Omar Khayyam's teaching-poems, and those of other members of his school which have become an accepted part of this material, are based upon the special terminology and allegory of Sufism. A full investigation and translation was made by Swami Govinda Tirtha in 1941, published under the title of *The Nectar of Grace*.

This book is virtually the last word on the question of the meaning (so far as it can be transposed into English) of the materials. It is interesting to note that few Western scholars have made use of this essential work in their expositions of Khayyam.

The result is that Khayyam effectively remains all but unknown.

The Secret

The secret must be kept from all non-people:
The mystery must be hidden from all idiots.
See what you do to people —
The Eye has to be hidden from all men.

Mankind

The circle of this world is like a ring:
There is no doubt at all that we are the
    Naqsh, the Design of its bezel.

Seeds like These

In cell and cloister, in monastery and synagogue:
Some fear hell and others dream of Paradise.
But no man who really knows the secrets of his God
Has planted seeds like this within his heart.

The Enemy of Faith

I drink wine, and opponents from right and left say:
'Drink no drink for it is against faith.'
Since I know that wine is against faith,
By God let me drink — the blood of the enemy is lawful to me.

Meditations

Though 'wine' is forbidden, this is according to who drinks it,
As to how much, also with whom it is drunk.

When these three requirements are fulfilled; speak truly –
Then, if the Wise may not drink 'wine', who should?

Those who try to be ostracized
And those who spend the night in prayer,
None is on dry land, all are at sea.
One is awake, and all the others are asleep.

I fell asleep, and Wisdom said to me:
'Sleeping, the rose of happiness never bloomed.
Why do you do a thing which is next to death?
Drink "wine", for you will have long to sleep.'

Friends, when you hold a meeting
You must much remember the Friend.
When you drink successfully together,
When my turn comes, 'turn the glass upside down'.

Those who have gone before us, O Cupbearer,
Are sleeping in the dust of self-pride.
Go, drink 'wine', and hear from me the Truth:
What they have only *said* is in our hands, O Cupbearer.

Under the Earth

You are not gold, ignorantly heedless one:
That, once put in the earth, anyone
Will bring you out again.

Man

Do you know what a man of earth may be, Khayyam,
A lantern of imaginings, and inside a lamp.

Omar Khayyam

Do Not Go Empty-Handed

Take some substance from Here to There —
You will make no profit if you go with empty hand.

I Am

Every clique has a theory about me —
I am mine; what I am, I am.

❧ 3 ❧
ATTAR OF NISHAPUR

Although Attar is one of the greatest of Sufi classical literary masters, and an inspirer of Rumi, his *Memorials of the Saints*, tales and teachings of Sufi sages, had to wait nearly seven and a half centuries for an English translation. In spite of the accelerating Western interest in Sufism, it was the Hindu hermit Dr Bankey Behari who published sixty-two selections from this book in 1961.

Attar wrote in all about one hundred and fourteen books, among which the most famous are the Sufic *Divine Book*, the *Parliament of the Birds*, and the *Book of Counsel*.

His teachings were carried on by means of illustrative biography, fables, maxims and apologues, which contain not only moral teaching but allegories describing specific stages in human development. In the *Parliament of the Birds*, for instance, he sketches individual phases in human consciousness, though these are represented as happening to different individuals or to a whole community.

Attar used the theme of a 'journey' or 'quest' as an analogy of the successive stages of the human soul in search of perfection.

Refusing to accept honours from the hands of the Mongol invaders of Central Asia, he is reported to have died at the hands of the soldiers of Jenghiz Khan, after having dismissed his disciples – sending them to places of safety – when he predicted the Mongol invasion of the thirteenth century.

The traditions of Sufism assert that Attar's work is important because, read as a whole, it helps to maintain the social fabric and ethical standards of Islam; while special selections from it contain initiatory material which is concealed by the heavily theological parts.

An Answer of Jesus

Some Israelites reviled Jesus one day as he was walking through their part of the town.

But he answered by repeating prayers in their name.

Someone said to him:

'You prayed for these men, did you not feel incensed against them ?'

He answered:

'I could spend only of what I had in my purse.'

The Heart

Someone went up to a madman who was weeping in the bitterest possible way.

He said:

'Why do you cry?'

The madman answered:

'I am crying to attract the pity of His heart.'

The other told him:

'Your words are nonsense, for He has no physical heart.'

The madman answered:

'It is you who are wrong, for He is the owner of all the hearts which exist. Through the heart you can make your connection with God.'

On Being Offered an Unacceptable Donation

What! Would you with a sum of money
Erase my name from the Register of Dervishes?

The Tale of Fazl-Rabbi

One day a penurious old man went to see Fazl-Rabbi to discuss some matter or other.

Because of weakness and nervousness, this ancient stuck the iron point of his walking-stick into Fazl-Rabbi's foot.

Listening courteously to what the old man had to say, Fazl-Rabbi said no word, although he went pale and then flushed, from the pain of the wound and the iron, as it stayed lodged in his foot.

Then, when the other had finished his business, he took a paper from him and put his signature to it.

When the old man had gone, delighted that he had been successful in his application, Fazl-Rabbi allowed himself to collapse.

One of the attendant nobles said:

'My lord, you sat there with blood pouring from your foot, with that old man in his dotage piercing it with his iron-tipped staff, and you said nothing, nothing at all.'

Fazl-Rabbi answered:

'I made no sign of pain because I feared that the old man's distress might cause him to withdraw in confusion, and that he might abandon his application for my help. Poor as he was, how could I add to his troubles in that manner?'

Be a real man: learn nobility of thought and action, like that of Fazl-Rabbi.

The Slave Without a Master

Wandering in a patchwork robe, his face blackened by the sun, a certain dervish arrived at Kufa, where he was seen by a merchant.

The merchant spoke to him, and decided that he must be a lost slave.

'Because of your mild manner, I will call you "Khair" [good],' he said. 'Are you not a slave?'

'That I am,' said Khair.

'I will take you home, and you can work for me until I find your master.'

'I would like that,' said Khair, 'for I have been seeking my master for such a long time.'

He worked for many years with this man, who taught him to be a weaver; hence his second name: 'Nassaj' (weaver).

After his long services, feeling guilty of his exploitation, the merchant said to him: 'I do not know who you are, but you are now free to go.'

Khair Nassaj, the great Master of the Way, travelled onward to Mecca, without regrets, for he had discovered how to continue his development in spite of having no name and being treated like a slave.

He was the teacher of Shibli, Ibrahim Khawwas and many more of the great Teachers of the Sufis. He died over a thousand years ago, at the age of one hundred and twenty.

The Magic Box

A man once wanted to sell a rough carpet, and he made a public offer of it in the street.

The first man to whom he showed it said:

'This is a coarse carpet, and very worn.'

And he bought it cheaply.

Then the buyer stood up and said to another who was walking along:

'Here is a carpet soft as silk, none is like it.'

A Sufi who was passing by had listened to the buying and the attempted selling of one and the same carpet with two different descriptions.

The Sufi said to the carpet-seller:

'Please, carpet-man, put me in your magic box, which can turn a rough carpet into a smooth one, perhaps a nothing into a jewel!'

The Moon

The Moon was asked:
'What is your strongest desire?'
It answered:
'That the Sun should vanish, and should remain veiled for ever in clouds.'

The Five Hundred Gold Pieces

One of Junaid's followers came to him with a purse containing five hundred gold pieces.
'Have you any more money than this?' asked the Sufi.
'Yes, I have.'
'Do you desire more?'
'Yes, I do.'
'Then you must keep it, for you are more in need than I; for I have nothing and desire nothing. You have a great deal and still want more.'

The Madman and the Muezzin

A muezzin in Isfahan had climbed to the top of a minaret and was giving the call to prayer.
Meanwhile, a madman was passing by, and someone asked him:
'What is he doing there, in that minaret?'
The madman said:
'That man up there is in fact shaking a nutshell which has nothing within it.'
When you speak the ninety-nine Names of God, you are, similarly, playing with a hollow nutshell. How can God be understood through names?

Since you cannot speak in words about the essence of God, best of all speak about nobody at all.

Kitab-Ilahi

The Religious Framework

One day when the Companion Omar was looking through a Jewish holy book, the Prophet Mohammed said to him:

'You are too casual with that book. If you want to gain any value from it, you will have to become a Jew. To be a perfect Jew is better than to be an incomplete Muslim; and dallying with the Jewish book is half-hearted and will give you no benefit one way or the other.

'Your mistake is that you are neither one thing nor another in behaving in this manner. You do not believe, neither do you disbelieve. What, then, is your condition, how can it be described?'

Kitab-Ilahi

A Story of Moses

Once Moses was asking God to show him one of God's friends, and a voice answered:

'Go to a certain valley and there you will find one who loves, one of the chosen, who treads the Path.'

Moses went and found this man, dressed in rags, plagued by every kind of insect and crawling thing.

He said: 'Can I do anything for you?'

The man answered: 'Emissary of God, bring me a cup of water, for I am thirsty.'

When Moses returned with the water he found the man lying dead. He went away to look for a piece of cloth for a winding-sheet. When he came back he found that the body had been all but devoured by a desert lion.

Moses was distressed beyond measure, and cried out:

'All-Powerful and All-Knowing One, you convert mud into human beings. Some are carried to paradise, others driven through tortures; one is happy, another in misery. This is the paradox which none can understand.'

Then an inner voice spoke to Moses, saying:

'This man had relied upon Us for drink and then turned back from that trust. He relied upon Moses for his sustenance, trusting in an intermediary. His was the fault in asking for help from another after having been content with Us ...'

Your heart attaches itself again and again to objects. You have to know how to keep the connection with your origins ...

Ilahi-Nama

Souls Before the Creation of the Body

Know about the time when there were souls and no bodies.

This was a time of a few years, but each of those years was one of our millennia.

The souls were all arrayed in line. The world was presented to their sight. Nine out of ten of the souls ran towards it.

Then paradise was presented to the remaining souls. Out of these, nine out of ten ran towards it.

Then hell was shown to the remaining souls. Nine out of ten of them ran away from it in horror.

Then there were only a few souls, those who were affected by nothing at all. They had not been attracted by the earth or by paradise, nor had they feared hell.

The Celestial Voice spoke to these survivors, saying:

'Idiot souls, what is it that you want?'

The souls answered in unison:

'You who know all know that it is You whom we desire, and that we do not desire to leave Your Presence.'

The voice said to them:

'Desire of Us is perilous, causes hardship and innumerable perils.'

The souls answered him:

74

'We will gladly experience anything for the sake of being with You, and lose everything in order that we may gain everything.'

Ilahi-Nama

The Test

It is related of Shaqiq of Balkh that he once said to his disciples:

'I put my confidence in God and went through the wilderness with only a small coin in my pocket. I went on the Pilgrimage and came back, and the coin is still with me.'

One of the youths stood up and said to Shaqiq:

'If you had a coin in your pocket, how could you say that you relied upon anything higher?'

Shaqiq answered:

'There is nothing for me to say, for this young man is right. When you rely upon the invisible world there is no place for anything, however small, as a provision!'

Kitab-Ilahi

About Mohammed, Son of Isa

Mohammed, son of Isa, was one of the boon-companions of the Commander of the Faithful. Because of the agility of his thought he surpassed all others.

One day he was riding through the Baghdad streets, accompanied by a multitude of attendants. The people asked one another:

'Who is this man, so dazzlingly bedecked, so well mounted, so rich?'

And one old woman who was hobbling along answered them:

'That is a poor man, not a rich one. For, had Allah not denied him his favour, he would not have such vanity as this.'

Hearing this, Mohammed, son of Isa, dismounted at once from his gorgeously caparisoned horse, and admitted that this indeed was his condition. From that moment he abandoned all desire for outward show and wealth.

The Perception of the Madman

There was a certain madman who would not take part in congregational prayers. One Friday, after much difficulty, people induced him to attend.

But as soon as the leader of the prayer started to recite, the madman started to bellow like an ox.

The people, assuming that he was only reverting to madness, but at the same time desirous of helping him, challenged him afterwards:

'Have you no idea of God, that you should make a noise like an animal in the middle of a believing congregation?'

But the madman said:

'I was only doing what the prayer-leader was doing. When he intoned, he was buying an ox, and I spoke like an ox!'

When this strange remark was reported to the leader of the prayer, he confessed:

'When I was saying GOD IS GREATEST OF ALL, I was in fact thinking about my farm. And when I got to the phrase PRAISE TO GOD, I thought that I would buy an ox. It was at that moment that I heard something bellowing.'

The Miser and the Angel of Death

A miser had accumulated, by effort, trade and lending, three hundred thousand dinars. He had lands and buildings, and all kinds of wealth.

He then decided that he would spend a year in enjoyment, living comfortably, and then decide as to what his future should be.

But, almost as soon as he had stopped amassing money, the Angel of Death appeared before him, to take his life away.

The miser tried, by every argument which he could muster, to dissuade the Angel, who seemed, however, adamant. Then the man said:

'Grant me but three more days, and I will give you one third of my possessions.'

The Angel refused, and pulled again at the miser's life, tugging to take it away.

Then the man said:

'If you will only allow me two more days on earth, I will give you two hundred thousand dinars from my store.'

But the Angel would not listen to him. And the Angel even refused to give the man a solitary extra day for all his three hundred thousand pieces.

Then the miser said:

'Please, then, give me just time enough to write one little thing down.'

This time the Angel allowed him this single concession, and the man wrote, with his own blood:

'Man, make use of your life. I could buy not one hour for three hundred thousand dinars. Make sure that you realize the value of your time.'

The Donkey's Head

An idiot saw a donkey's head on a stick in a garden.

He asked: 'What is that doing there?'

He was told: 'It has been put there to avert the evil eye!'

The fool replied:

'You are the ones with asses' brains, and that's why you have set up an ass's head! When it was alive it could not prevent the blows of the stick from hitting it. Now, when dead, how can it repel the evil eye?'

Absurdity and Ignorance

What seems to be absurdity and is not, is better than the ignorance of the man who thinks it is absurd.

Light

The true lover finds the light only if, like the candle, he is his own fuel, consuming himself.

Christians and Muslims

A Christian once became a Muslim. The very next day, however, he began to drink wine.

His mother, coming upon him in a drunken state, said:

'My son, what are you doing? In acting in this way you have spurned Jesus, and you have also failed to please Mohammed. Stay in the belief which is yours! Nobody can be a man and worship idols as well as holding to another faith.'

The Tree Unaware of its State

A man cut down a tree one day.

A Sufi who saw this taking place said:

'Look at this fresh branch which is full of sap, happy because it does not yet know that it has been cut off.

'Ignorant of the damage which it has suffered it may be – but it will know in due time.

'Meanwhile you cannot reason with it.'

This severance, this ignorance, these are the state of man.

The Arrow

When an arrow is loosed from the bow, it may go straight, or it may not, according to what the archer does.

How strange, therefore, that when the arrow speeds without deviation, it is due to the skill of the archer: but when it goes out of true, it is the arrow which receives the maledictions!

King Mahmud and the Beans

The mighty King Mahmud of Ghazna, out hunting one day, was separated from his party. He came upon the smoke of a small fire and rode to the spot, where he found an old woman with a pot.

Mahmud said:

'You have as guest today the monarch. What are you cooking on your fire?'

The crone said:

'This is a bean stew.'

The emperor asked her:

'Old lady, will you not give me some?'

'I will not,' she said, 'for this is only for me. Your kingdom is not worth what these beans are worth. You may want my beans, but I don't want anything you have. My beans are worth a hundred times more than all you have. Look at your enemies, who challenge your possessions in every particular. I am free, and I have my own beans.'

The mighty Mahmud looked at the undisputed owner of the beans, thought of his disputed domains, and wept.

Unaware

You know nothing of yourself here and in this state.

You are like the wax in the honeycomb: what does it know of fire or guttering?

When it gets to the stage of the waxen candle and when light is emitted, then it knows.

Similarly, you will know that when you were alive you were dead, and only thought yourself alive.

The Madman and the Wrestler

A tipsy madman called after the coffin-bearers of a funeral:

'Who was this man who has fallen into the claws of death?'

They answered: 'Madman, this is the body of a champion wrestler, a young man who was in the prime of his life.'

The madman said: 'He died through the power of a mighty adversary, not knowing that this would happen to him.'

The Two Rings

A man loved two women equally. They asked him to tell them which one was his favourite.

He asked them to wait for a time until his decision should be known.

Then he had two rings made, each exactly resembling the other.

To each of the women, separately, he gave one ring.

Then he called them together and said:

'The one whom I love best is she who has the ring.'

This, Too, Will Pass

A powerful king, ruler of many domains, was in a position of such magnificence that wise men were his mere employees. And yet one day he felt himself confused and called the sages to him.

He said:

'I do not know the cause, but something impels me to seek a certain ring, one that will enable me to stabilize my state.

'I must have such a ring. And this ring must be one which, when I am unhappy, will make me joyful. At the same time, if I am happy and look upon it, I must be made sad.'

The wise men consulted one another, and threw themselves into deep contemplation, and finally they came to a decision as to the character of this ring which would suit their king.

The ring which they devised was one upon which was inscribed the legend:

THIS, TOO, WILL PASS

The King Who Divined His Future

A king who was also an astrologer read in his stars that on a certain day and at a particular hour a calamity would overtake him.

He therefore built a house of solid rock and posted numerous guardians outside.

One day, when he was within, he realized that he could still see daylight. He found an opening which he filled up, to prevent misfortune entering. In blocking this door he made himself a prisoner with his own hands.

And because of this the king died.

This Space

On a wall within the *tekkia* arches of the meditation-hall of Attar, it is related, were written the words:

'Reserved for the Sage (*Hakim*) Tamtim.'

Sheikh Attar instructed his senior disciples to observe the behaviour of all newcomers towards this inscription.

He predicted that all who reacted to it in a certain fashion would develop mystical powers correctly and rapidly; and that all who said or did certain other things would leave or have to be sent away.

He never asked the disciples which postulant reacted in

which way. But they observed, over the years, that it turned out always as he predicted.

One day he was asked why he left this inscription there. He said:

'It is to show those without perceptions that apparently insignificant indications to certain experiences will betray the inner capacities or lack of them to one who knows how to make a test.'

❧ 4 ❧

IBN EL-ARABI

Mohiudin ibn El-Arabi is one of the great Sufis of the Middle Ages whose life and writings are shown nowadays to have deeply penetrated the thought of East and West alike. He was known to the Arabs as Sheikh El-Akbar, 'the Greatest Sheikh', and to the Christian West by a direct translation of this title: 'Doctor Maximus'. He died in the thirteenth century.

Whence Came the Title?

Jafar the son of Yahya of Lisbon determined to find the Sufi 'Teacher of the Age', and he travelled to Mecca as a young man to seek him. There he met a mysterious stranger, a man in a green robe, who said to him before any word had been spoken:

'You seek the Greatest Sheikh, Teacher of the Age. But you seek him in the East, when he is in the West. And there is another thing which is incorrect in your seeking.'

He sent Jafar back to Andalusia, to find the man he named – Mohiudin, son of El-Arabi, of the tribe of Hatim-Tai. 'He is the Greatest Sheikh.'

Telling nobody why he sought him, Jafar found the Tai family in Murcia and inquired for their son. He found that he had actually been in Lisbon when Jafar set off on his travels. Finally he traced him to Seville.

'There,' said a cleric, 'is Mohiudin.' He pointed to a mere schoolboy, carrying a book on the Traditions, who was at that moment hurrying from a lecture-hall.

Jafar was confused, but stopped the boy and said:

'Who is the Greatest Teacher?'

'I need time to answer that question,' said the other.

'Art thou the *only* Mohiudin, son of El-Arabi, of the Tribe of Tai?' asked Jafar.

'I am he.'

'Then I have no need of thee.'

Thirty years later in Aleppo, he found himself entering the lecture-hall of the Greatest Sheikh, Mohiudin ibn El-Arabi, of the tribe of Tai. Mohiudin saw him as he entered, and spoke:

'Now that I am ready to answer the question you put to me, there is no need to put it at all. Thirty years ago, Jafar, thou hadst no need of me. Hast thou still no need of me? The Green One spoke of something wrong in thy seeking. It was time and place.'

Jafar son of Yahya became one of the foremost disciples of El-Arabi.

The Vision at Mosul

A Seeker well versed in inducing significant inner experiences still suffered from the difficulty of interpreting them constructively. He applied to the great sheikh Ibn El-Arabi for guidance about a dream which had deeply disturbed him when he was at Mosul, in Iraq.

He had seen the sublime Master Maaruf of Karkh as if seated in the middle of the fire of hell. How could the exalted Maaruf be in hell?

What he lacked was the perception of his own state. Ibn El-Arabi, from his understanding of the Seeker's inner self and its rawness, realized that the essentials were seeing Maaruf surrounded by fire. The fire was explained by the undeveloped part of the mind as something within which the great Maaruf was trapped. Its real meaning was a barrier between the state of Maaruf and the state of the Seeker.

If the Seeker wanted to reach a state of being equivalent to that of Maaruf, the realm of attainment signified by the figure of Maaruf, he would have to pass through a realm symbolized in the vision by an encircling fire.

Through this interpretation the Seeker was able to understand his situation and to address himself to what he had still to experience.

The mistake had been in supposing that a picture of Maaruf was Maaruf, that a fire was hell-fire. It is not only the impression (*Naqsh*) but the correct picturing of the impression, the art which is called *Tasvir* (the giving of meaning to a picture), which is the function of the Rightly Guided Ones.

The Three Forms of Knowledge

Ibn El-Arabi of Spain instructed his followers in this most ancient dictum:

There are three forms of knowledge. The first is intellectual knowledge, which is in fact only information and the collecttion of facts, and the use of these to arrive at further intellectual concepts. This is intellectualism.

Second comes the knowledge of states, which includes both emotional feeling and strange states of being in which man thinks that he has perceived something supreme but cannot avail himself of it. This is emotionalism.

Third comes real knowledge, which is called the Knowledge of Reality. In this form, man can perceive what is right, what is true, beyond the boundaries of thought and sense. Scholastics and scientists concentrate upon the first form of knowledge. Emotionalists and experientalists use the second form. Others use the two combined, or either one alternatively.

But the people who attain to truth are those who know how to connect themselves with the reality which lies beyond both these forms of knowledge. These are the real Sufis, the Dervishes who have Attained.

Truth

She has confused all the learned of Islam,
Everyone who has studied the Psalms,
Every Jewish Rabbi,
Every Christian priest.

A Higher Love

The ordinary lover adores a secondary phenomenon.
I love the Real.

The Special Love

As the full moon appears from the night, so appears
her face amid the tresses.

From sorrow comes the perception of her: the eyes
crying on the cheek; like the black narcissus
shedding tears upon a rose.

Mere beauties are silenced: her fair quality is
overwhelming.

Even to think of her harms her subtlety (thought is
too coarse a thing to perceive her). If this be
so, how can she correctly be seen by such a clumsy
organ as the eye?

Her fleeting wonder eludes thought.
She is beyond the spectrum of sight.

When description tried to explain her, she overcame it.
Whenever such an attempt is made, description is
put to flight.

Because it is trying to circumscribe.

If someone seeking her lowers his aspirations (to
    feel in terms of ordinary love),
    – there are always others who will not do so.

Attainments of a Teacher

People think that a Sheikh should show miracles and manifest
illumination. The requirement in a teacher, however, is only
that he should possess all that the disciple needs.

The Face of Religion

Now I am called the shepherd of the desert gazelles,
Now a Christian monk,
Now a Zoroastrian.
The Beloved is Three, yet One:
Just as the three are in reality one.

My Heart Can Take on Any Appearance

My heart can take on any appearance. The heart varies in accordance with variations of the innermost consciousness. It may
appear in form as a gazelle meadow, a monkish cloister, an
idol-temple, a pilgrim Kaaba, the tablets of the Torah for certain sciences, the bequest of the leaves of the Koran.

  My duty is the debt of Love. I accept freely and willingly
whatever burden is placed upon me. Love is as the love of
lovers, except that instead of loving the phenomenon, I love
the Essential. That religion, that duty, is mine, and is my faith.
A purpose of human love is to demonstrate ultimate, real love.
This is the love which is conscious. The other is that which
makes man unconscious of himself.

Study by Analogy

It is related that Ibn El-Arabi refused to talk in philosophical language with anyone, however ignorant or however learned. And yet people seemed to benefit from keeping company with him. He took people on expeditions, gave them meals, entertained them with talk on a hundred topics.

Someone asked him: 'How can you teach when you never seem to speak of teaching?'

Ibn El-Arabi said: 'It is by analogy.' And he told this parable.

A man once buried some money for security under a certain tree. When he came back for it, it was gone. Someone had laid bare the roots and borne away the gold.

He went to a sage and told him his trouble, saying: 'I am sure that there is no hope of finding my treasure.' The sage told him to come back after a few days.

In the meantime the sage called upon all the physicians of the town, and asked them whether they had prescribed the root of a certain tree as a medicine for anyone. One of them had, for one of his patients.

The sage called this man, and soon found out that it was he who had the money. He took possession of it and returned it to its rightful owner.

'In a similar manner,' said Ibn El-Arabi, 'I find out what is the real intent of the disciple, and how he can learn. And I teach him.'

The Man who Knows

The Sufi who knows the Ultimate Truth acts and speaks in a manner which takes into consideration the understanding, limitations and dominant concealed prejudices of his audience.

To the Sufi, worship means knowledge. Through knowledge he attains sight.

The Sufi abandons the three 'I's. He does not say 'for me',

88

'with me', or 'my property'. He must not attribute anything to himself.

Something is hidden in an unworthy shell. We seek lesser objects, needless of the prize of unlimited value.

The capacity of interpretation means that one can easily read something said by a wise man in two totally opposite manners.

Straying from the Path

Whoever strays from the Sufi Code will in no way attain to anything worthwhile; even though he acquires a public reputation which resounds to the heavens.

SAADI OF SHIRAZ

It is hard to find words to approach a description of the achievement of the thirteenth-century classical author Saadi. Western critics are amazed that Saadi could write *The Orchard* (*Bostan*) and *The Rose Garden* (*Gulistan*), the two great classics, in the space of two or three years. These major works, known to every Persian and regarded as supreme accomplishments, contain a richness of material and beauty of poetry which are almost unparalleled. Saadi was a man of no resources, and spent most of his time as a wanderer on the face of the earth. He was instructed by the Sufi masters Gilani and Suhrawardi.

In the case of *The Rose Garden,* Saadi has accomplished the feat (still not attained in any Western language) of writing a book which is so simple in vocabulary and structure that it is used as a first textbook for students of Persian, and appears to contain only moralistic aphorisms and stories; while at the same time it is recognized by the most eminent Sufis as concealing the whole range of the deepest Sufi knowledge which can be committed to writing.

The sense of wonderment at this achievement, when one sees the different levels of material interlocked in this manner, cannot be expressed.

These two books are not only mines of quotations, proverbs and practical wisdom and texts of states of mind; they are written in such a way as to be accepted by the most blinkered of religious bigots. In this way did Saadi receive, shape and transmit the Sufi lore. His choice of the format of classical literature ensured for all time the preservation and communication of his message; for nobody could ever cut Saadi out of Persian literature, and hence Sufism is protected in this manner.

The following extracts are translated literally, to show how the texts look to the ordinary reader.

Pluck the cotton wool of heedlessness from the ear of awareness,
So that the wisdom of dead men may reach your ear.

The Door

The unfortunate one is he who averts his head from this door.
For he will not find another door.

Jewels and Dust

If a gem falls into mud it is still valuable.
If dust ascends to heaven, it remains valueless.

The Day of Battle

On the day of battle it is the slender horse – not the lumbering ox – that will be of use.

The Alchemist and the Fool

The alchemist dies in pain and frustration – while the fool finds treasure in a ruin.

The Pearl

A raindrop, dripping from a cloud,
Was ashamed when it saw the sea.
'Who am I where there is a sea?' it said.
When it saw itself with the eye of humility,
A shell nurtured it in its embrace.

Dominion

Dominion of the world from end to end
Is worth less than a drip of blood upon the earth.

The Thief and the Blanket

A thief entered the house of a Sufi, and found nothing there.
As he was leaving, the dervish perceived his disappointment
and threw him the blanket in which he was sleeping, so that
he should not go away empty-handed.

Learning

None learned the art of archery from me
Who did not make me, in the end, the target.

The Unshaped One

For one unshaped one in the community
The hearts of the Wise will suffer pain –
As if a pool had been filled with rose-water,
And a dog fell in, polluting it.

Scholars and Recluses

Give money to the scholars, so that they can study more.
Give nothing to the recluses, that they may remain recluses.

The Scorpion

A scorpion was asked:
  'Why do you not come out in winter?'
  It said:
  'What treatment do I get in summer, that I should go out in winter as well?'

      Green wood can be bent;
      When it is dry, it is only straightened by fire.

The Ark

When Noah is the captain, what is there to fear?

The Destiny of a Wolf-Cub

The destiny of a wolf-cub is to become a wolf, even if it is reared among the sons of men.

The Barren Tree

    No one throws a stone at a barren tree.

Conceit

    He who has self-conceit in his head —
    Do not imagine that he will ever hear the truth.

The Straight Path

I have never seen a man lost who was on a straight path.

Cages

When a parrot has been shut up with a crow,
He thinks it a stroke of luck to get out of the cage.

Butting

You who play at butting with a ram;
You will soon see a broken head.

A Tree Freshly Rooted

A tree, freshly rooted, may be pulled up by one man on his
own. Give it time, and it will not be moved, even with a crane.

Doing Good to the Evil

Merely doing good to the evil may be equivalent to doing evil
to the good.

Reward

Child, look for no reward from A,
If you are working in the house of B.

To Know One's Faults

In the eyes of the wise, the seeker of combat with an elephant
is not really brave.
Brave is he who says nothing unbecoming in wrath.
A lout abused a man who patiently said:
'O you of bright prospects: I am worse even than you say.
I know all my faults, while you do not know them.'

The Alternatives

The sanctuary is in front of you and the thief is behind you.
If you go on, you will win; if you sleep, you die.

The Unfed Dervish

When I see the poor dervish unfed
My own food is pain and poison to me.

That building without a firm base: do not build it high;
Or, if you do – be afraid.

Asleep and Awake

When a man's sleep is better than his waking –
It is better that he should die.

The Harvest

You will know at the harvest
That laziness is not planting.

95

Relative

A Lamp has no rays at all in the face of the sun;
And a high minaret even in the foothills of a mountain
looks low.

When you burn the woods, if you are wise
You will avoid the tigers.

Information and Knowledge

However much you study, you cannot know without action.
A donkey laden with books is neither an intellectual nor a
wise man.
Empty of essence, what learning has he –
Whether upon him is firewood or book?

The Elephant-Keeper

Make no friendship with an elephant-keeper
If you have no room to entertain an elephant.

The Dervish under a Vow of Solitude

A dervish under a vow of solitude sat in a desert as a king
passed with his retinue. Being in a special state of mind he
took no notice, not even raising his head as the procession passed.

The king, emotionally overcome by his regal pretensions,
was angry and said: 'These wearers of the patchwork robe
are as impassive as animals, possessing neither politeness nor
due humility.'

His vizier approached the dervish, saying: 'O dervish! The

Sultan of the whole of the Earth has just passed by you. Why did you not pay the required homage?'

The dervish answered: 'Let the Sultan look for homage from those who seek to benefit from his goodwill. Tell him, too, that kings are created for the protection of their subjects. Subjects are not created for the service of kings.'

Safety and Riches

Deep in the sea are riches beyond compare.
But if you seek safety, it is on the shore.

The Fox and the Camels

A fox was seen running away in terror. Someone asked what was troubling it. The fox answered: 'They are taking camels for forced labour.' 'Fool!' he was told, 'the fate of camels has nothing to do with you, who do not even look like one.' 'Silence!' said the fox, 'for if an intriguer were to state that I was a camel, *who* would work for my release?'

Gold Coins called Nobles

He who has a purse full of gold has a place like the light of men's eyes.

As the goldsmith's son so well put it:
'The noble is the man who has gold nobles.'

Talk

The learned man who only talks will never
Penetrate to the inner heart of man.

Disciples and Sages

Disciples in power are less than children;
Sages are like a firm wall.

Fools have been endowed with such a provision
That a hundred scholars would be amazed by it.

Horse and Camel

The Arab horse speeds fast. The camel plods slowly, but it goes
by day and night.

Where the Leopard May Lurk

What may appear to you a group of bushes could well be a place
wherein a leopard lurks.

The Foundation of Tyranny

The foundation of tyranny in the world was trifling at first.
Everyone added to it until it attained its present magnitude.
For the half-egg that the Sultan considers right to take by
force, his troops will put a thousand fowls on the spit.

Personal Appearance

Have the essential qualities of a dervish —
Then you can sport a Tartar shako!

If You Cannot Stand a Sting

If you cannot stand a sting, do not put your finger in a scorpion's nest.

Ambition

Ten dervishes can sleep beneath one blanket; but two kings cannot reign in one land. A devoted man will eat half his bread, and give the other half to dervishes. A ruler may have a realm, but yet plot to overcome the world.

The Danger of Ecstasy

If a dervish remained in a state of ecstasy,
He would be fragmented in both worlds.

The Dervish and the Camel Rider

When we were heading for southern Arabia, a barefooted and bareheaded dervish joined our caravan at Kufa (in the north).

I saw that he was penniless, but he strode along purposefully, reciting as he walked:

Neither do I burden a camel
Nor do I carry a camel's burden;
Neither do I rule, nor am I ruled.
Neither have I anxieties about the
Past, the Present or the Future.
Fully I breathe, fully I live life.

A certain merchant, mounted on a camel, advised him to turn back. Otherwise, he said, the dervish would certainly die of hardship and lack of nourishment.

Ignoring this advice, the dervish marched on.

When we reached Beni Hamud oasis the merchant died. The dervish, standing by the bier, exclaimed:

> I did not die of my hardships;
> But you, on your camel, have died.

Fools burn lamps during the day. At night they wonder why they have no light.

The Sick Man

> Throughout the long night a man wept
> At the bedside of a sick man.
> When day dawned the visitor was dead –
> And the patient was alive.

The Dervish in Hell

One night a king dreamt that he saw a king in paradise and a dervish in hell.

The dreamer exclaimed: 'What is the meaning of this? I should have thought that the positions would be reversed.'

A voice answered: 'The king is in heaven because he respected dervishes. The dervish is in hell because he compromised with kings.'

Heedless Man

Whoever gives advice to a heedless man is himself in need of advice.

The Poor Man's Yoghurt

If a poor man brings you a gift of yoghurt, he will have bought it at such a price that it will be two parts of water to one of real yoghurt.

The Tiger's Prey

What can the tiger catch in the dark recesses of his own lair?

The Fool and the Donkey

A foolish man was raving at a donkey. It took no notice. A wiser man who was watching said: 'Idiot! The donkey will never learn *your* language – better that you should observe silence and instead master the tongue of the donkey.'

The Road

I fear that you will not reach Mecca, O Nomad!
For the road which you are following leads to Turkestan!

❧ 6 ❧

HAKIM JAMI

Jami (1414-92) was a genius and knew it, which made ecclesiastics and literary men of his time acutely uncomfortable, since the convention was that no man was great unless he appeared intensely humble. In his *Alexandrian Book of Wisdom*, Jami shows that the Sufi esoteric transmission link of the Asian Khajagan ('Masters') was the same as that used by Western mystical writers. He cites as teachers in the Sufi transmission such names as Plato, Hippocrates, Pythagoras and Hermes Trismegistos.

Jami was a disciple of Sadedin Kashgari, the chief of the Naqshbandis, whom he succeeded in the direction of the Herat area of Afghanistan. His higher allegiance was to Khaja Obaidullah Ahrar, General of the Order.

One of Jami's succinct sayings illustrates the problem of all Sufi teachers who refuse to accept students on their own valuation of themselves:

'Seekers there are in plenty: but they are almost all seekers of personal advantage. I can find so very few Seekers after Truth.'

Nor was this his only concern. Certain religious enthusiasts in Baghdad, trying to discredit him, misquoted a passage from his *Chain of Gold*, and created a rumpus which was only stilled after a ridiculous and trivial debate in public. Most of all Jami lamented that such things could happen at all in the community called human.

Jami's writings and teachings in the end made him so celebrated that contemporary monarchs, from the Sultan of Turkey downwards, were constantly irritating him with offers of enormous amounts of gold and other presents, and appeals to adorn their courts. His acclaim by the public annoyed him, too, to the mystification of the populace, who could not understand that he wanted them not to adopt him as a hero but to do something about themselves.

He never tired of pointing out that many people who tried to overcome pride were doing so because in this way they would be able to inflate themselves with such a victory.

Luxuriant Growth

If the scissors are not used daily on the beard it will not be long before the beard is, by its luxuriant growth, pretending to be the head.

Unity

Love becomes perfect only when it transcends itself –
Becoming One with its object;
Producing Unity of Being.

The Prayer and the Nose

I saw a man prostrating himself in prayer, and exclaimed:
'You lay the burden of your nose upon the ground on the excuse that it is a requirement of prayer.'

The Teacher

The ruler is a shepherd and his flock is the people.

He has to help them and save them, not to exploit and destroy them.

Is the shepherd there for the flock, or the flock for the shepherd?

Love

Ordinary human love is capable of raising man to the experience of real love.

The Dry Cloud

The dry cloud, waterless, can have no rain-giving quality.

The Poet and the Physician

A poet went to see a doctor. He said to him: 'I have all kinds of terrible symptoms. I am unhappy and uncomfortable, my hair and my arms and legs are as if tortured.'

The doctor answered: 'Is it not true that you have not yet given out your latest poetic composition?'

'That is true,' said the poet.

'Very well,' said the physician, 'be good enough to recite.'

He did so, and, at the doctor's orders, said his lines again and again. Then the doctor said: 'Stand up, for you are now cured. What you had inside had affected your outside. Now that it is released, you are well again.'

The Beggar

A beggar went to a door, asking for something to be given to him. The owner answered, and said: 'I am sorry, but there is nobody in.'

'I don't want anybody,' said the beggar, 'I want food.'

Hypocrisy

It is recorded in the Tradition of the Masters that Jami once said, when asked about hypocrisy and honesty:

'What a wonderful thing is honesty and what a strange thing is hypocrisy!

'I wandered to Mecca and to Baghdad, and I made trial of the behaviour of men.

'When I asked them to be honest, they always treated me with respect, because they had been taught that good men always speak thus, and they had learned that they must have their eyes downcast when people speak of honesty.

'When I told them to shun hypocrisy, they all agreed with me.

'But they did not know that when I said "truth", I knew that they did not know what truth was, and that therefore both they and I were then being hypocrites.

'They did not know that when I told them not to be hypocrites they were being hypocrites in not asking me the method. They did not know that I was being a hypocrite in merely saying "Do not be hypocrites", because words do not convey the message by themselves.

'They respected me, therefore, when I was acting hypocritically. They had been taught to do this. They respected themselves while they were thinking hypocritically; for it is hypocrisy to think that one is being improved simply by thinking that it is bad to be a hypocrite.

'The Path leads beyond: to the practice and the understanding where there can be no hypocrisy, where honesty is there and not something which is man's aim.'

Pride

Do not boast that you have no pride, because it is less visible than an ant's foot on a black stone in a dark night.

And do not think that bringing it out from within is easy, for it is easier to extract a mountain from the earth with a needle.

Intellect

Stop boasting of intellect and learning; for here intellect is hampering, and learning is stupidity.

What Shall We Do

The rose has gone from the garden; what shall we do with
    the thorns?
The Shah is not in the city; what shall we do with his court?
The fair are cages, beauty and goodness the bird;
When the bird has flown, what shall we do with the cage?

The State

Justice and fairness, not religion or atheism,
Are needful for the protection of the State.

The Heaviest Wave

Before Nushirvan the Just wise sages discussed the heaviest wave in this deep of sorrow.
    One of them said that it was illness and suffering;
    Another that it was old age and poverty;
    A third that it was approaching death with lack of work.
    And in the end this one was accepted.

❧ 7 ❧

HAKIM SANAI

The Master Sanai lived during the eleventh and twelfth centuries, and is reckoned as the earliest Afghan teacher to use the love-motif in Sufism. Rumi acknowledged him as one of his inspirations.

Attempts were made by religious fanatics to brand him an apostate from Islam, but they did not succeed. Characteristically, his words have regularly been employed since then by the spiritual descendants of these narrow clerics to bolster their own pretensions. By a quite familiar process, when Sufi terminology and organization had been adopted by religious enthusiasts to the extent that the distinction between the Sufis and these superficialists had been blurred, the fanatics tried more than once to claim that Sanai was not a Sufi at all. The reason for this was that his thoughts could not be easily reconciled with narrow religiosity.

The Walled Garden of Truth, one of Sanai's most important works, is composed in such a manner as to give several readings for many passages. This effects a shift in the perceptions which is analogous to a change of focus on one and the same object. If one series of interpretation-methods is used with this book, a most interesting framework of instructional material, almost a system, is revealed.

Sanai is also known for his *Parliament of the Birds,* which is on the surface an allegory of the human quest for higher enlightenment. His *Dervish Songs* represents the lyrical presentation of Sufi experience.

Man Asleep

While mankind remains mere baggage in the world
It will be swept along, as in a boat, asleep.
What can they see in sleep?
What real merit or punishment can there be?

The Sealed Book

The human's progress is that of one who has been given a sealed book, written before he was born. He carries it inside himself until he 'dies'. While man is subject to the movement of Time, he does not know the contents of that sealed book.

Levels of Truth

What appears to be truth is a worldly distortion of objective truth.

Means and End

'Ha' and 'Ho' are sounds which are of no further use when the knowers really know.

The Infant

Man does not notice that he is like an infant in the hands of a nurse. Sometimes he is happy, sometimes sad, at what happens to him. The nurse sometimes chides the child, sometimes soothes him. At times she spanks him, at others shares his sorrow. The superficial person, the stranger passing by, may think that the nurse is unmindful of the child. How can he know that this is the way in which she must behave?

Hakim Sanai

How and Why

The essence of truth is superior to the terminology of 'How?' or 'Why?'

Follow the Path

Do not speak of your heartache – for He is speaking.
Do not seek Him – for He is seeking.

He feels even the touch of an ant's foot;
If a stone moves under water – He knows it.

If there is a worm in a rock
He knows its body, smaller than an atom.

The sound of its praise, and its hidden perception,
He knows by His divine knowledge.

He has given the worm its sustenance;
He has shown you the Path of the Teaching.

JALALUDIN RUMI

Rumi's major work, generally considered to be one of the world's greatest books, is his *Mathnavi-i-Maanavi* (*Couplets of Inner Meaning*). His table-talk (*Fihi Ma Fihi*), letters (*Maktubat*), *Diwan,* and the hagiography *Munaqib El-Arifin,* all contain important parts of his teachings.

The following selections, from all of these sources, are meditation-themes which can be taken as aphorisms and declarations of dogma, or as pieces of sage advice. Their Sufic usage, however, goes far beyond this. Rumi, like other Sufi authors, plants his teachings within a framework which as effectively screens its inner meaning as displays it. This technique fulfils the functions of preventing those who are incapable of using the material on a higher level from experimenting effectively with it; allowing those who want poetry to select poetry; giving entertainment to people who want stories; stimulating the intellect in those who prize such experiences.

One of the most revealing of his sentences is the title of his table-talk: 'In it what is in it' ('You get out of it what is in it for you').

Rumi had the uncomfortable Sufi habit of excelling in literary and poetic ability beyond all his contemporaries, while constantly affirming that such an attainment was a minor one compared with Sufihood.

How Far You Have Come!

Originally, you were clay. From being mineral, you became vegetable. From vegetable, you became animal, and from animal, man. During these periods man did not know where he was going, but he was being taken on a long journey nonetheless. And you have to go through a hundred different worlds yet.

The Way

The Way has been marked out.

If you depart from it, you will perish.

If you try to interfere with the signs on the road, you will be an evil-doer.

The Four Men and the Interpreter

Four people were given a piece of money.

The first was a Persian. He said: 'I will buy with this some *angur*.'

The second was an Arab. He said: 'No, because *I* want *inab*. '

The third was a Turk. He said: 'I do not want *inab*, I want *uzüm*.'

The fourth was a Greek. He said: '*I* want *stafil*.'

Because they did not know what lay behind the names of things, these four started to fight. They had information but no knowledge.

One man of wisdom present could have reconciled them all, saying: 'I can fulfil the needs of all of you, with one and the same piece of money. If you honestly give me your trust, your one coin will become as four; and four at odds will become as one united.'

Such a man would know that each in his own language wanted the same thing, grapes.

I am the Life of My Beloved

What can I do, Muslims? I do not know myself.
I am no Christian, no Jew, no Magian, no Musulman.
Not of the East, not of the West. Not of the land, not of the sea.
Not of the Mine of Nature, not of the circling heavens,
Not of earth, not of water, not of air, not of fire;
Not of the throne, not of the ground, of existence, of being;
Not of India, China, Bulgaria, Saqseen;
Not of the kingdom of the Iraqs, or of Khorasan;
Not of this world or the next: of heaven or hell;
Not of Adam, Eve, the gardens of Paradise or Eden;
My place placeless, my trace traceless.
Neither body nor soul: all is the life of my Beloved . . .

The Owls and the King's Hawk

A royal hawk alighted for a time on the wall of a ruin inhabited by owls. The owls feared him. He said: 'This may seem a prosperous place to you, but my place is upon the wrist of a king.'

Some of the owls shouted to the others: 'Do not believe him! He is using guile to steal our home.'

Another Dimension

The hidden world has its clouds and rain, but of a different kind.

Its sky and sunshine are of a different kind.

This is made apparent only to the refined ones – those not deceived by the seeming completeness of the ordinary world.

Profiting by Experience

Exalted Truth imposes upon us
Heat and cold, grief and pain,
Terror and weakness of wealth and body
Together, so that the coin of our innermost being
Becomes evident.

Awakening

A man may be in an ecstatic state, and another man may try to
rouse him. It is considered good to do so. Yet this state may be
bad for him, and the awakening may be good for him. Rousing
a sleeper is good or bad according to who is doing it. If the
rouser is of greater attainment, this will elevate the state of the
other person. If he is not, it will deteriorate the consciousness
of the other man.

He was in No Other Place

Cross and Christians, end to end, I examined. He was not on
the Cross. I went to the Hindu temple, to the ancient pagoda.
In none of them was there any sign. To the uplands of Herat
I went, and to Kandahar. I looked. He was not on the heights
or in the lowlands. Resolutely, I went to the summit of the
[fabulous] mountain of Kaf. There only was the dwelling of
the [legendary] Anqa bird. I went to the Kaaba of Mecca. He
was not there. I asked about him from Avicenna the philosopher. He was beyond the range of Avicenna ... I looked into my
own heart. In that, his place, I saw him. He was in no other
place.

Those Who Know, Cannot Tell

Whenever the Secrets of Perception are taught to anyone
His lips are sewn against speaking of the Consciousness.

Joha and Death

A boy was crying and shouting before his father's coffin, saying:

'Father! They are taking you to a place where nothing covers the floors. There is no light, no food; no door nor helpful neighbour ...'

Joha, alarmed since the description seemed to fit, called out to his own father:

'Respected Parent, by Allah, they are taking him to *our* house!'

Intelligence and Real Perception

Intelligence is the shadow of objective Truth.
How can the shadow vie with sunshine?

True Reality

Of this there is no academic proof in the world;
For it is hidden, and hidden, and hidden.

The Human Spirit

Go higher – Behold the Human Spirit.

Detachment Brings Perception

O Heart! Until, in this prison of deception,
    you can see the difference between This and That,
For an instant detach from this Well of Tyranny;
    stand outside.

Thou and I

Joyful the moment when we sat in the bower, Thou and I;
In two forms and with two faces – with one soul, Thou and I.
The colour of the garden and the song of the birds give the
    elixir of immortality
The instant we come into the orchard, Thou and I.
The stars of Heaven come out to look upon us –
We shall show the Moon herself to them, Thou and I.
Thou and I, with no 'Thou' or 'I', shall become one through
    our tasting;
Happy, safe from idle talking, Thou and I.
The gay parrots of heaven will envy us –
When we shall laugh in such a way, Thou and I.
This is stranger, that Thou and I, in this corner here . . .
Are both in one breath in Iraq, and in Khorasan – Thou and
    I.

Two Reeds

Two reeds drink from one stream. One is hollow, the other is
sugar-cane.

What Shall I Be

I have again and again grown like grass;
I have experienced seven hundred and seventy moulds.
I died from minerality and became vegetable;
And from vegetativeness I died and became animal.

I died from animality and became man.
Then why fear disappearance through death?
Next time I shall die
Bringing forth wings and feathers like angels:
After that soaring higher than angels —
What you cannot imagine. I shall be that.

The Man of God

The Man of God is drunken without wine:
The Man of God is sated without meat.

The Man of God is rapturous, amazed:
The Man of God has neither food nor sleep.

The Man of God is a king beneath a humble cloak:
The Man of God is a treasure in a ruin.

The Man of God is not of wind and earth:
The Man of God is not of fire and water.

The Man of God is a sea without a shore:
The Man of God rains pearls without a cloud.

The Man of God has a hundred moons and skies:
The Man of God has a hundred sunshines.

The Man of God is wise through Truth:
The Man of God is not a scholar from a book.

The Man of God is beyond faith and disbelief alike:
For the Man of God what 'sin' or 'merit' is there?

The Man of God rode away from Non-being:
The Man of God has come, sublimely riding.

The Man of God Is, Concealed, O Shamsudin!
Search for, and find – The Man of God.

Truth

The Prophet said that Truth has declared:
'I am not hidden in what is high or low
Nor in the earth nor skies nor throne.
This is certainty, O beloved:
I am hidden in the heart of the faithful.
If you seek me, seek in these hearts.'

The Science

The Science of Truth disappears in the Sufi's knowledge
When will mankind understand this saying?

Dust on the Mirror

Life/Soul is like a clear mirror; the body is dust on it.
Beauty in us is not perceived, for we are under the dust.

Action and Words

I am giving people what they want. I am reciting poetry because people desire it as an entertainment.

In my own country, people do not like poetry. I have long searched for people who want action, but all they want is words. I am ready to show you action; but none will patronize this action. So I present you with – words.

A fool's ignorance eventually harms, however much his heart is one with yours.

Work

Work is not what people think it is.
   It is not just something which, when it is operating, you can see from outside.

How long shall we, in the Earth-world, like children
Fill our laps with dust and stones and scraps?
Let us leave earth and fly to the heavens,
Let us leave babyhood and go to the assembly of Man.

The House

If ten men want to enter a house, and only nine find their way in, the tenth must not say: 'This is what God ordained.'
   He must find out what his own shortcoming was.

Owls

Only sweet-voiced birds are imprisoned.
Owls are not kept in cages.

Efforts

Tie two birds together.
They will not be able to fly, even though they now have four wings.

Seeking

Seek a pearl, brother, within a shell;
And seek skill from among the men of words.

This Task

You have a duty to perform. Do anything else, do any number of things, occupy your time fully, and yet, if you do not do this task, all your time will have been wasted.

The Community of Love

The people of Love are hidden within the populace;
Like a good man surrounded by the bad.

A Book

The aim of a book may be to instruct,
Yet you can also use it as a pillow;
Although its object is to give knowledge, direction, profit.

Epitaph of Jalaludin Rumi

When we are dead, seek not our tomb in the earth, but find it in the hearts of men.

Part Three
FOUR MAJOR ORDERS

BACKGROUND

All dervish teachers employ formulations through which to project their teachings. Taken in isolation, as in the case of people examining things with insufficient information, these procedures, materials and ideas may seem to be associated with other creeds, and with practices dating from immemorial time, or they may appear to belong to areas which are not, strictly speaking, metaphysical.

But, since the basic knowledge of the dervishes is often not known to these observers, the reasons for Sufis choosing certain methods, let alone the effectiveness of the methods themselves, remain equally unknown.

We may easily distinguish the following as outstanding methods used by dervishes in helping to engender higher states of mind in their pupils:

1. Auditory, visual and other sense-impacts.

2. Verbalized materials, including legends and parables, intended to establish in the mind not a belief but a pattern, a blueprint which helps it to operate in 'another' manner.

3. Working, worshipping, exercising, in unison, for the purpose of engendering, liberating and making flow a certain dynamic (not an emotional or indoctrination one) which furthers the 'work'.

4. The employment of places, objects, symbols and so on, which are held to supplement ordinary human cognitions, not to train them.

5. The organizing of local and other groups, composed of people chosen because of the inherent possibility of their harmonizing in an esoteric community, to encourage the development of something within the community; not a community magnetized around an idea.

6. The selection, from traditional or other formulations, of practices and procedures solely by the criterion of function. Will this work successfully, given a certain type of person in a certain culture?

7. The creation of working communities by selecting locally approved vocational and other groupings which can also be of use in the dervish 'work'. The introduction of grouping-systems which may be lacking in the local culture, because they have no psychological appeal or no economic validity.

8. The production of procedures, techniques and materials which may be used to make contact with the inner aspect of a person's being, without disrupting his habitual activities based upon local or temporal conditioning. Dervish operation is therefore a highly skilled and complex endeavour. The major characteristics of well-known dervish schools – dancing, jumping, listening to and playing music and the like – are all popularizations ignorantly imitated from an originally very sophisticated 'technology' whose expertise is the instant knowledge of the teachers as to which process applies to what circumstances.

Once these basic facts are known, two major contentions of the dervishes appear as practical and plausible ones:

1. The unity of all dervishes and of the 'work' becomes more feasible. The seeming contradiction between one 'Path' and another is removed. The practice, for instance, of the Naqshbandi sheikhs in initiating disciples into any of the Orders becomes comprehensible, even at the intellectual level. The claim as to the bankruptcy of the imitators concentrating upon a few techniques is more clearly understood.

2. The connection between the ancient practical philosophies and the present ones is seen to have been based upon the higher-level unity of knowledge, not upon appearances. This explains why the Muslim Rumi has Christian, Zoroastrian and other disciples; why the great Sufi 'invisible teacher' Khidr is said to be a Jew; why the Mogul Prince Dara Shikoh identified Sufi teachings in the Hindu Vedas, yet himself remained a member of the Qadiri Order; how Pythagoras and Solomon can be said to be Sufi teachers. It also explains why Sufis will

accept some alchemists to have been Sufis, as well as understanding the underlying developmental factors in Rumi's evolutionary philosophy, or Hallaj's 'Christianity'; why, indeed, Jesus is said to stand, in a sense, at the head of the Sufis.

The importance of this information does not, however, end here. It is essential for any would-be student of Sufism to remember that all formulations, exercises, Orders, techniques, which he studies outside a Sufi school, represent the outward cloak of a current or superseded intensive educational work which may be presented in one of very many shapes. He cannot, therefore, legitimately decide that such-and-such a Sufi principle or practice is attractive to him (and hence useful) and another not. Attractive or not, these principles and practices are working frames through which the teaching has been, or is being, projected. In dealing with historical material, especially, only imitators (however pious) think that a certain practice is to be recommended just because such-and-such a teacher employed it.

Because of the doctrine of 'time, place and people', Sufi exercises are of value:

1. To those attracted to techniques. They are people who seek a mere ordinary psychological stimulus. They are not mystics or metaphysicians, although they often think that they are.

2. For the purpose of information, to familiarize possible pupils with the variety and type of exercises used by dervishes.

3. In developing the capacities of the individual and the group only when correctly prescribed by a Sufi school which belongs to the culture from which the majority of its adherents belong. In order to benefit from recorded materials, it is absolutely necessary for the reader to examine accounts of Sufi theory and practice with a clear understanding of the foregoing points.

The surviving dervish Orders were originally set up for the purpose of regularizing and making available to selected candidates the special techniques perfected by the Founder of each Order.

Those Orders which are generally known in the East, including the Four Major Orders whose materials are studied here, have stabilized their rituals and membership nowadays exclusively on the basis of Eastern culture and the religion of Islam. Teaching in these orders is nowadays limited exclusively to Muslims.

❧ I ❧
THE CHISHTI ORDER

Khwaja ('Master') Abu-Ishak Chishti, 'the Syrian', was born early in the tenth century. He was a descendant of the Prophet Mohammed, and claimed as his 'spiritual pedigree' the inner teachings of the Family of Hashim. His followers are an off-shoot of the Line of the Masters, which later became known as the Naqshbandi ('the People of the Design').

This Chishti community, originating at Chisht in Khorasan, specialized in the use of music in their exercises. The wandering dervishes of the Order were known as Chist or Chisht. They would enter a town and play a rousing air with flute and drum to gather people round them before reciting a tale or legend of initiatory significance.

Traces of this figure occur even in Europe, where the Spanish *chistu* is found with closely similar garb and instruments – a sort of itinerant jester. It may even be that the Western dictionaries' etymological attribution of the Latin *gerere*, 'to do', for the origin of the word 'jester' is in fact a fanciful one, and that the original lies with the Afghan *chisti*.

As in the case of other Sufic Orders, the specialized methodologies of the Chishtis soon became crystallized into a simplified love for music; the emotional arousal produced by music being confused with 'spiritual experience'.

The Chishtis made their most enduring impact upon India. For the past nine hundred years their musicians have been esteemed throughout the subcontinent.

The following materials are representative of Chishti instruction and tradition.

Cause and Effect

Abu-Ishak Shami Chishti said:

My teacher, Khaja Hubaira, took me for a walk through the town one day.

A man on a donkey would not make way for us in the narrow streets, and as we were slow in getting out of his path he cursed us roundly.

'May he be punished for that behaviour,' people called out of their doorways.

The Khaja said to me:

'How simple-minded people are! Little do they realize how things really happen. They only see one kind of cause and effect, while sometimes the effect, as they would call it, appears before the cause.'

I was perplexed and asked him what he meant.

'Why,' he said, 'that man has already been punished for the behaviour which he showed us just now. Last Thursday he applied to enter the circle of Sheikh Adami, and was refused. Only when he realizes the reason will he be able to enter the circle of the elect. Until then he will continue to behave thus.'

The Garden

Once upon a time, when the science and art of gardening was not yet well established among men, there was a master-gardener. In addition to knowing all the qualities of plants, their nutritious, medicinal and aesthetic values, he had been granted a knowledge of the Herb of Longevity, and he lived for many hundreds of years.

In successive generations, he visited gardens and cultivated places throughout the world. In one place he planted a wonderful garden, and instructed the people in its upkeep and even in the theory of gardening. But, becoming accustomed to seeing some of the plants come up and flower every year, they soon forgot that others had to have their seeds collected, that some

were propagated from cuttings, that some needed extra water-
ing, and so on. The result was that the garden eventually became wild, and people started to regard this as the best garden
that there could be.

After giving these people many chances to learn, the gardener expelled them and recruited another whole band of workers.
He warned them that if they did not keep the garden in order,
and study his methods, they would suffer for it. They, in turn,
forgot – and, since they were lazy, tended only those fruits and
flowers which were easily reared and allowed the others to die.
Some of the first trainees came back to them from time to time,
saying: 'You should do this and that,' but they drove them
away, shouting: '*You* are the ones who are departing from
truth in this matter.'

But the master-gardener persisted. He made other gardens,
wherever he could, and yet none was ever perfect except the
one which he himself tended with his chief assistants. As it
became known that there were many gardens and even many
methods of gardening, people from one garden would visit
those of another, to approve, to criticize, or to argue. Books were
written, assemblies of gardeners were held, gardeners arranged
themselves in grades according to what they thought to be the
right order of precedence.

As is the way of men the difficulty of the gardeners remains
that they are too easily attracted by the superficial. They say:
'I like this flower,' and they want everyone else to like it as well.
It may, in spite of its attraction or abundance, be a weed which
is choking other plants which could provide medicines or food
which the people and the garden need for their sustenance and
permanency.

Among these gardeners are those who prefer plants of one
single colour. These they may describe as 'good'. There are
others who will only tend the plants, while refusing to care
about the paths or the gates, or even the fences.

When, at length, the ancient gardener died, he left as his
endowment the whole knowledge of gardening, distributing it
among the people who would understand in accordance with

their capacities. So the science as well as the art of gardening remained as a scattered heritage in many gardens and also in some records of them.

People who are brought up in one garden or another generally have been so powerfully instructed as to the merits or demerits of how the inhabitants see things that they are almost incapable – though they make the effort – of realizing that they have to return to the concept of 'garden'. At the best, they generally only accept, reject, suspend judgement or look for what they imagine are the common factors.

From time to time true gardeners do arise. Such is the abundance of semi-gardens that when they hear of real ones people say: 'Oh, yes. You are talking about a garden such as we already have, or we imagine.' What they have and what they imagine are both defective.

The real experts, who cannot reason with the quasi-gardeners, associate for the most part among themselves, putting into this or that garden something from the total stock which will enable it to maintain its vitality to some exent.

They are often forced to masquerade, because the people who want to learn from them seldom know about the fact of gardening as an art or science underlying everything that they have heard before. So they ask questions like: 'How can I get a more beautiful flower on these onions?'

The real gardeners may work with them because true gardens can sometimes be brought into being, for the benefit of all mankind. They do not last long, but it is only through them that the knowledge can be truly learnt and people can come to see what a garden really is.

The Group of Sufis

A group of Sufis, sent by their preceptor to a certain district, settled themselves in a house.

In order to avoid undesirable attention, only the man in charge – the Chief Deputy – taught in public. The rest of the community assumed the supposed functions of the servants of his household.

When this teacher died, the community rearranged their functions, revealing themselves as advanced mystics.

But the inhabitants of the country not only shunned them as imitators, but actually said: 'For shame! See how they have usurped and shared out the patrimony of the Great Teacher. Why, these miserable servants now even behave as if they were themselves Sufis!'

Ordinary people, only through lack of experience in reflection, are without the means to judge such situations as these. They therefore tend to accept mere imitators who step into the shoes of a teacher and reject those who are indeed carrying on his work.

When a teacher leaves a community, by dying or otherwise, it may be intended for his activity to be continued – or it may not. Such is the greed of ordinary people that they always assume that this continuity is desirable. Such is their relative stupidity that they cannot see the continuity if it takes a form other than the crudest possible one.

When Death is Not Death

A certain man was believed to have died, and was being prepared for burial, when he revived.

He sat up, but he was so shocked at the scene surrounding him that he fainted.

He was put in a coffin, and the funeral party set off for the cemetery.

Just as they arrived at the grave, he regained consciousness, lifted the coffin lid, and cried out for help.

'It is not possible that he has revived,' said the mourners, 'because he has been certified dead by competent experts.'

'But I am alive!' shouted the man.

He appealed to a well-known and impartial scientist and jurisprudent who was present.

'Just a moment,' said the expert.

He then turned to the mourners, counting them. 'Now, we have heard what the alleged deceased has had to say. You fifty witnesses tell me what you regard as the truth.'

'He is dead,' said the witnesses.

'Bury him!' said the expert.

And so he was buried.

The Spare Room

A certain man needed money, and the only way he could get it was to sell his house. He did not, however, want to part with all of it.

So he agreed, by contract with the new owners, that he would have the complete and unrestricted use of one room, in which he could keep, at any time, any of his possessions.

At first the man kept small items in his room, and used to go to see them without giving any trouble to anyone. Then, when he changed his job from time to time, he would store the tools of his trade there. Still the new owners did not object.

Finally, he started to keep dead cats in his room, until the whole house was made uninhabitable by the effect of their decomposition.

The owners applied to the courts, but the judges held that the nuisance was compatible with the contract. Eventually they sold the house back to its first owner at a great loss to themselves.

The Seven Brothers

Once upon a time there was a wise father who had seven sons. While they were growing up, he taught them as much as he could, but before he could complete their education he perceived something which made their safety more important. He realized that a catastrophe was going to overwhelm their country. The young men were foolhardy and he could not confide completely in them. He knew that if he said: 'A catastrophe threatens,' they would say: 'We will stay here with you and face it.'

So he told each son that he must undertake a mission, and that he was to leave for that mission forthwith. He sent the first to the north, the second to the south, the third to the west and the fourth to the east. The three other sons he sent to unknown destinations.

As soon as they had gone, the father, using his special knowledge, made his way to a distant country to carry on some work which had been interrupted by the need to educate his sons.

When they had completed their missions, the first four sons returned to their country. The father had so timed the duration of their tasks that they would be safely and remotely engaged upon them until it was possible to return home.

In accordance with their instructions the sons went back to the place which they had known in their youth. But now they did not know one another. Each claimed that he was the son of his father, each one refused to believe the others. Time and climate, sorrow and indulgence, had done their work, and the appearance of the men was changed.

Because they were so bitterly opposed to one another and each determined to assess the other by his stature, his beard, the colour of his skin, and his manner of speech – all of which had changed – no brother would for months allow another to open the letter from their common father which contained the answer to their problem and the remainder of their education.

The father had foreseen this, such was his wisdom. He knew that until they were able to understand that they had changed very much they would not be able to learn any more. The situation at the present is that two of the sons have recognized one another, but only tentatively. They have opened the letter. They are trying to adjust themselves to the fact that what they took to be fundamentals are really – in the form in which they use them – worthless externals; what they have for many years prized as the very roots of their importance may in reality be vain and now useless dreams.

The other two brothers, watching them, are not satisfied that they are being improved by their experience, and do not want to emulate them.

The three brothers who went in the other directions have not yet arrived at the rendezvous.

As to the four, it will be some time before they truly realize that the only means of their survival in their exiles – the superficials which they think important – are the very barriers to their understanding.

All are still far from knowledge.

Camel's-Eye View

A man once asked a camel whether he preferred going uphill or downhill.

The camel said: 'What is important to me is not the uphill or the downhill – it is the load!'

The Oath

A man who was troubled in mind once swore that if his problems were solved he would sell his house and give all the money gained from it to the poor.

The time came when he realized that he must redeem his oath. But he did not want to give away so much money. So he thought of a way out.

He put the house on sale at one silver piece. Included with the house, however, was a cat. The price asked for this animal was ten thousand pieces of silver.

Another man bought the house and cat. The first man gave the single piece of silver to the poor, and pocketed the ten thousand for himself.

Many people's minds work like this. They resolve to follow

a teaching; but they interpret their relationship with it to their own advantage.

'The Sufi is a Liar'

The Sufi is in the position of a stranger in a country, of a guest in a house. Anyone in either capacity must think of the local mentality.

The real Sufi is a 'changed' man (*abdal*), change being an essential part of Sufism. The ordinary man is not changed; hence a need for dissimulation.

A man goes into a country where nakedness is honourable, and wearing clothes is considered dishonourable. In order to exist in that country, he must shed his clothes. If he says merely: 'Wearing clothes is best, nakedness is dishonourable,' he puts himself outside the range of the people of the country which he is visiting.

Therefore he will either quit the country or – if he has functions to perform there – he will accept or temporize. If the subject of the excellence or otherwise of wearing clothes comes up in discussion, he will probably have to dissimulate. There is a clash of habits here.

There is an even greater clash between habit thought and non-habit thought. The Sufi, because he has experienced, in common with others, so many things, knows a range of existence which he cannot justify by argument, even if only because all arguments have already been tried by someone at one time or another, and certain ones have prevailed and are considered 'good sense'.

His activity, like that of an artist, is reduced to that of illustration.

On Music

They know that we listen to music, and that we perceive certain secrets therein.

So they play music and cast themselves into 'states'.

Know that every learning must have *all* its requirements, not just music, thought, concentration.

Remember:

> Useless is a wonderful milk-yield
> From a cow which kicks the pail over.

Hadrat Muinudin Chishti

How Man Raises Himself Higher

There are two things: good and that which has to become good – reality and pseudo-reality. There is God and there is man.

If a man seeks Truth, he must be eligible for the reception of truth. He does not know this. Consequently, believing in the existence of Truth, he assumes that he is therefore able to perceive it. This is not in accordance with experience, but it continues to be believed.

After my time, as an example, people will continue to use parts of what has been carefully attuned as a means to contact truth, using it as a sort of spell or talisman, to open a gate. They will play and listen to music, will contemplate written figures, will collect together, simply because they have seen all these things done.

But the art is in the right combining of the elements which help to make man worthy of his connection with real Truth, not in a pale imitation of them.

Remember always that the science (*ilm*) to effect the bridge between the external and the inner is rare and passed down only to a few. Inevitably there will be many who prefer to convince themselves of the reality of a lesser experience rather than to find the purveyor of the essence.

Hadrat Muinudin Chishti

The Mystery of the Sufis

This Urdu song is sung by followers of the nineteenth-century Chishti saint Sayed Mir Abdullah Shah, whose shrine is in Delhi. The intention is to show that Sufis are known by something which they all share, something not portrayed adequately by names, ritual or regalia; though all these things have some relevance to the mysterious interior unity of being.

I see a free man sitting on the ground.
At his lips a reed-pipe, the robe is patched, the hands work-
    worn.
Can this be one of the Great Elect?
Yes, O my Friend, it is He!

Sheikh Saadi Baba, Sultan Arif Khan, Shah Waliullah el-Amir.
Three waves from one sea. Three kings in beggar's garb.
Can they be the High Elect?
Yes, O my Friend, all is He!
All is HE, all is HE, all is HE!

Muslim, Hindu, Christian, Jew and Sikh.
Brothers in a secret sense — yet who knows it internally? . . .
O Companions of the Cave!
Why the axe, the begging-bowl?
Why the sheepskin, horn and cap?
Why the stone upon the belt?
See: when in your blood flows wine.
All is He, my Friend, is He!

Do you go to mountain-tops?
Are you sitting in a shrine?
Seek him when a Teacher comes,
Seek the jewel within the mine!
All is He, my friends, companions, ALL is HE!

2

THE QADIRI ORDER

This 'Path' was organized by the followers of Abdul-Qadir of Gilan, who was born at Nif, in Gilan district, to the south of the Caspian Sea. He died in 1166, and used terminology very similar to that which was later employed by Rosicrucians in Europe.

Hadrat ('the Presence') Abdul-Qadir specialized in the induction of spiritual states, called the Science of States. His doings have been described in such exaggerated terms by his followers that his reported personality bears little resemblance to his own definitions of the character of a Sufi master.

Ardent over-employment of ecstatogenic techniques is almost certainly the cause of the deterioration of the Qadiri organizations. This follows a common pattern in enthusiasts, when the production of an altered condition of mind becomes an end and not a means properly controlled by a specialist.

The following extracts include traditional instruction-materials from the Qadiri discipline, and also some pointed remarks by Abdul-Qadir himself.

Like Jalaludin Rumi, Abdul-Qadir was supposed to have displayed marked supernormal capacities in his early childhood, and his hagiographies are full of accounts of these.

The Rose of Baghdad

All dervishes use the rose (*ward*) as an emblem and symbol of the rhyming word *wird* ('concentration-exercises').

Abdul-Qadir, founder of the Qadiri Order, figures in an incident which gave him his title of Rose of Baghdad. It is related that Baghdad was so full of mystical teachers that when Abdul-

Qadir arrived at the city it was decided to send him a message. The mystics therefore dispatched to him, at the city's outskirts, a vessel, full to the brim with water. The meaning was clear: 'The cup of Baghdad is full to the limit.'

Although it was winter and out of season, Abdul-Qadir produced a full-blown rose, which he placed on top of the water, to indicate both his extraordinary powers and also that there was room for him.

When this sign was brought to them, the assembly of mystics cried out: 'Abdul-Qadir is our Rose,' and they hastened to usher him into the city.

The Vine

A certain man planted a vine, well known as being of a kind which produces eatable grapes only after thirty years.

It so happened that as he was planting it, the Commander of the Faithful passed by, paused and said:

'You are a remarkable optimist if you hope to live until that kind of vine bears fruit.'

'Perhaps I shall not,' said the man, 'but at least my successors will live to benefit from my work, as we all profit from the work of our predecessors.'

'In any case,' said the ruler, 'if and when any grapes are produced, bring some of them to me. That is, if both of us have escaped the sword of death which is hanging over us all the time.'

He went on his way.

Some years later the vine started to bear delicious grapes. The man filled a large basket with the choicest bunches and went to the palace.

The Commander of the Faithful received him and gave him a handsome present of gold.

The word went round: 'An insignificant peasant has been given a huge sum in exchange for a basket of grapes.'

A certain ignorant woman, hearing this, immediately filled a basket with her own grapes and presented herself to the palace guard saying: 'I demand the same recompense as the man who was rewarded this morning. Here is my fruit. If the king gives money for fruit, here is fruit.'

Word was taken to the Commander of the Faithful, whose answer was: 'Those who act by imitation and the arrogance which underlies the lack of inquiry into the circumstances which they try to imitate: let them be driven away.' The woman was sent away, but she was so annoyed that she did not trouble herself to ask the vine-grower what had really happened.

The Teacher and the Dog

A Sufi teacher, walking along a road with a student, was assailed by a ferocious dog.

The disciple was furious and cried out:

'How dare you approach my master in such a manner?'

'He is more consistent than you are,' said the Sage, 'for he barks at anyone, in accordance with his habit and proclivities; while you regard me as your master and are wholly insensitive to the merits of the many illuminates whom we have already passed on this journey, dismissing them without a second glance.'

States and Jackals

The jackal thinks that he has feasted well, when he has in fact only eaten the leavings of the lion.

I transmit the science of producing 'states'. This, used alone, causes damage. He who uses it only will become famous, even powerful. He will lead men to worship 'states', until they will almost be unable to return to the Sufi Path.

Abdul-Qadir of Gilan

The Rogue, the Sheep and the Villagers

One there was a rogue who was caught by the people of a village. They tied him to a tree to contemplate the suffering which they were going to inflict on him; and went away, having decided to throw him into the sea that evening, after they had finished their day's work.

But a shepherd, who was not very intelligent, came along and asked the clever rogue why he was tied up like that.

'Ah,' said the rogue, 'some men have put me here because I will not accept their money.'

'Why do they want to give it to you, and why will you not take it?' asked the astonished shepherd.

'Because I am a contemplative, and they want to corrupt me,' said the rogue; 'they are godless men.'

The shepherd suggested that he should take the rogue's place, and advised the rogue to run away and put himself out of reach of the godless ones.

So they changed places.

The citizens returned after nightfall, put a sack over the shepherd's head, tied him up, and threw him into the sea.

The next morning they were amazed to see the rogue coming into the village with a flock of sheep.

'Where have you been, and where did you get those animals?' they asked him.

'In the sea there are kindly spirits who reward all who jump in and "drown" in this manner,' said the rogue.

In almost less time than it takes to tell, the people rushed to the seashore and jumped in.

That was how the rogue took over the village.

The Horrid Dib-Dib

One night a thief, intending to rob an old woman, crept to the open window of her home and listened. She was lying on the bed, and the thief heard her talking, with powerful emotion, in a most strange manner. She was saying:

'Aah ... the Dib-Dib, the horrid Dib-Dib! This abominable Dib-Dib will be the end of me.'

The thief thought:

'This unfortunate woman is suffering from some terrible disease – the malignant Dib-Dib, of which I had not even heard before!'

Then, as her wails increased in volume, he began to say to himself:

'Have I, I wonder, been infected? After all, I almost took her breath as I leant in through the window ...'

The more he thought about it, the more he began to fear that he had, indeed, contracted the injurious Dib-Dib. Within a few moments he was shaking in every limb. He only just managed to totter home to his wife, moaning and groaning:

'The sinister Dib-Dib, how can there be any doubt that the accursed Dib-Dib has got me in its grip ...'

His wife put him to bed at once, greatly fearful. What dreadful thing had attacked her husband? She imagined at first that he must have been pounced upon by some wild animal called a Dib-Dib. But, as he became less and less coherent and she could still find no mark upon him, she began to fear that it was a matter of supernatural intervention.

The person whom she knew to be best qualified to deal with such a problem was, of course, the local holy man. He was something approaching a priest, learned in the Law, known as the Sage Faqih.

The woman immediately went to the house of the sage and begged him to come to see her husband. The Faqih, thinking that this might indeed be a field in which his especial sanctity could be put to use, hurried to the thief's bedside.

The thief, when he saw the man of faith beside him, thought that his end must be even closer than he had feared. Mustering all his strength, he muttered:

'The old woman at the end of the road, she has the accursed

Dib-Dib, and it has flown upon me from her. Help me, if you can, Reverend Faqih!'

'My son,' said the Faqih, although he was himself perplexed, 'bethink yourself of repentance and pray for mercy, for your remaining hours may now indeed be few.'

He left the thief and made his way to the old woman's cottage. Peering through the window, he distinctly heard her whimpering voice as she writhed and shuddered:

'Foul Dib-Dib, you are killing me ... Stop, stop, evil Dib-Dib, for you are sapping my very life's blood away ...'

And she continued for some time in this vein, occasionally sobbing and sometimes remaining silent. The Faqih himself now began to feel as if an eerie chill passed through him. He started to shake, and his hands clutching the window-frame caused it to rattle like the chattering of teeth.

At this sound the crone leapt from her bed and seized the now terrified Faqih by the hands.

'What are you, a man of respectability and learning, doing at this time of night, looking through decent people's windows?' she shrilled.

'Good but unfortunate woman,' faltered the learned one, 'I heard you speak of the awful Dib-Dib, and now I fear that it has its clutches upon my heart as well as upon your own, and that I am, physically and spiritually, lost ...'

'You incredible fool,' screeched the hag; 'to think that for all these years I have looked up to you as a man of books and wisdom! You hear someone say "Dib-Dib", and you imagine that it is going to kill *you*! Look, then, in yonder corner, and see what the appalling Dib-Dib really is!'

And she pointed to the dripping tap, which the Faqih suddenly realized was leaking with the thud of *dib-dib-dib* ...

But divines have resilience. In next to no time he felt himself marvellously restored by the relief from his troubles and hurried back to the house of the thief, for he had work to do.

'Go away,' groaned the thief, 'for you deserted me in my necessity, and the sight of so depressing a face offers little reassurance as to my future state ...'

The elder interrupted him:

'Ungrateful wretch! Do you think that a man of my piety and learning would leave a matter such as this unsolved? Attend, then, closely to my words and acts, and I shall show you how I have worked untiringly, in accordance with my celestial mandate, towards your safety and recovery.'

The word 'recovery' immediately focused the attention of both the thief and his wife upon the imposing dignity of that reputed sage.

He took some water and said certain words over it. Then he made the thief promise never to steal again. Finally, he sprinkled the prepared water over the thief with many a polysyllabic word and gesture, ending with:

'Flee, unclean and infernal Dib-Dib, whence thou camest, never returning to plague this unhappy man!'

The thief sat up, cured.

From that day to this the thief has never stolen again. Neither has he told anyone about the miraculous cure, because in spite of everything he still does not much like the sage and his ideas. And the old woman, normally a gossip, has not spread the word of the idiocy of the Faqih. She plans eventually to turn it to good account; some occasion will arise for a bartering of good turns, perhaps.

And, of course, the Faqih ... well, the Faqih is not of a mind to have the details bruited about, and he will not recite the tale either.

But, as is the way of men, each of the people involved has told his or her own version in strict confidence of course, to one other person. And that is why you have been able to know the *whole* story of the woman, the thief, the priest, and the terrible Dib-Dib.

The Thief, the Shopkeeper and the Law

A thief broke into a shop. While he was there, a sharp awl which the shopkeeper had left on a shelf entered his eye, and blinded it.

The thief went to law, saying: 'The penalty for stealing is prison, but the penalty for negligence causing injury to an eye is considerable damages.'

'He came to steal from me,' said the shopkeeper, in his own defence.

'That will be dealt with by another court,' said the judge, 'and cannot concern us here.'

'If you take all my possessions,' said the thief, 'my family will starve while I am in prison. That is clearly not fair upon them.'

'Then I shall order the shopkeeper's eye to be put out in retaliation,' said the judge.

'But if you do that,' said the shopkeeper, 'I shall lose more than the thief did, and it will not be equitable. I am a jeweller, and the loss of one eye would ruin my capacity for work.'

'Very well,' said the judge, 'since the law is impartial, and none must suffer more than he should, and since the whole community shares in the gains and losses of some of its members, bring a man who needs only one eye – an archer for instance – and put out his other eye.'

And this was done.

Help His Friends

Help His Friends, whatever their guise! One day you will hear: 'I was needy, and you did not help Me. Those who have helped My Friends, have helped Me.'

Ibn El-Arif El-Qadiri
(quoting a tradition of Mohammed the Prophet)

The Pay and the Work

A horse once met a frog. The horse said: 'Take this message to a snake for me, and you can have all the flies which surround me.'

The frog answered: 'I like the pay, but I cannot say that I can complete the work.'

The Plant

At the entrance to the house of Abdul-Qadir Gilani was one day to be seen a flower in a pot. Beside it was a notice: 'Smell this and guess what it is.'

Each person who entered was given writing materials, and was invited to write the answer, if he wished, to the conundrum.

At the end of the day, Abdul-Qadir handed a box containing the answers to a disciple. He said:

'Every one who has answered "A rose" may remain if he desires, to proceed with the teaching. Anyone who has written nothing, or anything other than "A rose", is dismissed.'

Someone asked: 'Is it necessary to resort to superficial methods to judge fitness for discipleship?'

The great teacher answered: 'I know the answers, but I wish to demonstrate for all the others that superficial manifestations signal interior character.' And he thereupon handed the company a list. This contained, although he had not seen the answers of the entrants, a list of the names of each one who had written 'A rose'.

This illustrates one meaning of the phrase: 'The obvious is the link to the True.' What Abdul-Qadir saw inwardly could be shown outwardly as well. In this way, and for this reason, is a certain kind of conduct expected of disciples.

The Transmission of *Baraka*

Abdul-Qadir called together all his adherents in Baghdad and said to them:

'I beg you never to forget what I am now going to tell you, because otherwise you will become the source of great error. I address those of you who will remain more ignorant than the others, because the Knowers and the Attainers will never make the mistake which I shall now describe.

'During the period of Duty and Repetition [certain exercises] many people acquire the capacity to affect others with a strange experience. This produces trembling, excitement and many other feelings, and signals a stage of awareness. There may be visions of great teachers, or of divine influence.

'Acting upon the unprepared "heart", such experiences must instantly be stopped, because they cannot progress to real contact with the Divine until something else has been cultivated in the disciple.

'This opening of capacity, once discovered by the ignorant or raw, spreads especially among villagers and other simple people, until they indulge it regularly, thinking it to be a true state. It is in fact merely a signal, a sign of something. When it occurs, it must be reported, and those who experience it should undergo an appropriate period of preparation.

'Persistence in this practice in the past exhausted the capacities of the followers of saints and prophets, all deludedly believing themselves to be the recipients of *Baraka* (grace). Those who Attain dare not induce this state once it has appeared. Those who indulge it may never Attain.

'Follow only the practices of the Teacher, who knows why these things occur and who has to adjust the study accordingly.'

THE SUHRAWARDI ORDER

Sheikh Ziaudin Jahib Suhrawardi, following the discipline of
the Sufi ancient Junaid, is credited with the founding of this
Order in the twelfth Christian century. As in the case of almost
all the Orders, Suhrawardi teachers are accepted by the Naqshbandis and others.

India, Persia and Africa have all been influenced in their mystical activity by the methods and personages of the Order, though
the Suhrawardis are among the most fragmented Sufic groups.

Their practices vary from the production of mystical ecstasy
to the completely quiescent exercise for 'perception of Reality'.

Instructional materials of the Order are often, to all appearance, merely legends or works of fiction. To the devotees, however, they contain materials which are essential to prepare the
ground for the experiences which the disciple must eventually
undergo. Without them, it is believed, there is a possibility
that the student may simply develop altered states of mind
which render him unfit for ordinary life.

Ben Yusuf the Carpenter

Once upon a time there was a carpenter named Nazar ben
Yusuf. He spent all his spare time for many years in studying
ancient books which contained many half-forgotten pieces of
knowledge.

He had a faithful servant, and one day he said to him:

'I have now attained the age where the ancient sciences must
be used to ensure my continued existence. I therefore want you
to help me in carrying out a process which will rejuvenate me
and make me immortal.'

When he explained the process, the servant was at first most reluctant to carry it out. The servant was to dismember Nazar and put him in a huge barrel filled with certain liquids.

'I cannot kill you,' said the servant.

'Yes, you must, for I shall die in any case, and you will be bereaved. Take this sword, and stand guard over the barrel, telling nobody what you are really doing. After twenty-eight days open the barrel and let me out. I shall be found to have regained my youth.'

So the servant agreed, and the process was started.

After a few days, however, the servant in his loneliness began to feel intensely uncomfortable, and all kinds of doubts assailed him. Then he started to become accustomed to his strange role. People came regularly to the house asking for his master, but he could only say: 'He is not here at the moment.'

Finally the representatives of the authorities arrived, suspecting that the servant had done away with his vanished master. 'Let us search the house,' they said. 'If we find nothing, we shall then take you into custody on suspicion, and it is probable that you will not be released until your master reappears.'

The servant did not know what to do, since by that time only twenty-one days had passed. But he made up his mind, and said:

'Just leave me in this room with this barrel for a few minutes, and then I shall be ready to come with you.'

He went into the room, and took the top off the barrel.

Immediately a tiny man, looking much younger but exactly like his master, though only the height of a hand, jumped out of the barrel, and ran round and round it, saying repeatedly:

'It was too soon, it was too soon . . .'

And then, as the horrified man watched, the little being vanished into thin air.

The servant went out of the room, the officers arrested him.

His master was never seen again, although there are many legends about Nazar ben Yusuf the carpenter; but these we must leave for another time.

The Girl Who Came Back from the Dead

In ancient times there was a beautiful girl, the daughter of a good man, a woman among women, rare in her loveliness and in the delicacy of her nature.

When she was of marriageable age, three young men, each apparently of the highest capacities and of great promise, sought her hand.

Having decided that they were of equal merit, the father left the final choice to her.

But months passed and the girl did not seem to be making up her mind.

And one day she suddenly fell ill. Within a few hours she was dead.

The three young men, united in grief, took her body to a cemetery and buried it in the deepest of silent agony.

The first youth made the graveyard his home, spending his nights there in sorrow and meditation, unable to understand the workings of the fate which had taken her away.

The second youth took to the roads and wandered throughout the world in search of knowledge, as a fakir.

The third young man spent his time in consoling the bereaved father.

Now the youth who had become a fakir, in his journeyings came across a certain place where a man of repute in uncanny arts resided. Continuing his search for knowledge, he presented himself at the door, and was admitted to the table of the master of the house.

When the host invited him to eat, he was about to start the meal when a small child started to cry. It was the grandson of the wise man.

The sage picked up the boy and threw him into a fire.

The fakir jumped up and started to leave the house, crying out: 'Infamous demons! I have had my share of the sorrows of the world already, but this crime surpasses those of all recorded history!'

'Think nothing of it,' said the master of the house, 'for simple things appear otherwise when there is an absence of knowledge.'

So saying, he recited a formula and waved a strange emblem, and the boy walked out of the fire, unharmed.

The fakir memorized the words and the design, and the next morning was on his way back to the cemetery where his beloved was buried.

In less time than it takes to tell, the maiden stood before him, fully restored to life.

She went back to her father, while the youths disputed as to which of them had earned her hand.

The first said: 'I have been living in the graveyard, keeping, through my vigils, contact with her, guarding her spirit's needs for earthly support.'

The second said: 'You both ignore the fact that it was *I* who actually travelled the world in search of knowledge, and who ultimately brought her back to life.'

The third said: 'I have grieved for her, and like a husband and son-in-law I have lived here, consoling the father, and helping with his upkeep.'

They appealed to the girl herself. She said:

'He who found the formula to restore me was a humanitarian; he who looked after my father acted as a son to him; he who lay beside my grave – he acted like a lover. I will marry *him*.'

The Parable of the Host and the Guests

The teacher is like a host in his own house. His guests are those who are trying to study the Way. These are people who have never been in a house before, and they only have vague ideas as to what a house may be like. It exists, nevertheless.

When the guests enter the house and see the place set aside for sitting in, they ask: 'What is this?' They are told: 'This is a place where we sit.' So they sit down on chairs, only dimly conscious of the function of the chair.

The host entertains them, but they continue to ask questions, some irrelevant. Like a good host, he does not blame them for this. They want to know, for instance, where and when they are going to eat. They do not know that nobody is alone, and that at that very moment there are other people who are cooking the food, and that there is another room in which they will sit down and have a meal. Because they cannot see the meal or its preparations, they are confused, perhaps doubtful, sometimes ill at ease.

The good host, knowing the problems of the guests, has to put them at their ease, so that they will be able to enjoy the food when it comes. At the outset they are in no state to approach the food.

Some of the guests are quicker to understand and relate one thing about the house to another. These are the ones who can communicate to their slower friends. The host, meanwhile, gives each guest an answer in accordance with his capacity to perceive the unity and function of the house.

It is not enough for a house to exist – for it to be made ready to receive guests – for the host to be present. Someone must actively exercise the function of host, in order that the strangers who are the guests, and for whom the host has responsibility, may become accustomed to the house. At the beginning, many of them are not aware that they are guests, or rather exactly what guesthood means: what they can bring to it, what it can give them.

The experienced guest, who has learned about houses and hospitality, is at length at ease in his guesthood, and he is then in a position to understand more about houses and about many facets of living in them. While he is still trying to understand what a house is, or trying to remember rules of etiquette, his attention is too much taken up by these factors to be able to observe, say, the beauty, value or function of the furniture.

Astrology

A Sufi once knew, through prescience, that a city would shortly
be attacked by an enemy. He told his neighbour, who realized
that he was a veracious but simple man, and who advised him:

'I am sure that you are right, and you should go and tell the
monarch. But, if you want to be believed, please say that you
divined it, not by wisdom, but by astrology. Then he will act,
and the town may be saved.'

The Sufi did so and the townspeople were delivered through
the correct precautions being taken.

Saying of Sheikh Ziaudin

Self-justification is worse than the original offence.

Three Candidates

Three men made their way to the circle of a Sufi, seeking ad-
mission to his teachings.

One of them almost at once detached himself, angered by
the erratic behaviour of the master.

The second was told by another disciple (on the master's
instructions) that the sage was a fraud. He withdrew very soon
afterwards.

The third was allowed to talk, but was offered no teaching
for so long that he lost interest and left the circle.

When they had all gone away, the teacher instructed his circle
thus:

'The first man was an illustration of the principle: "Do not
judge fundamental things by sight." The second was an illustration of the injunction: "Do not judge things of deep importance by hearing." The third was an example of the dictum:
"Never judge by speech, or the lack of it."'

153

Asked by a disciple why the applicants could not have been instructed in this matter, the sage retorted:

'I am here to give higher knowledge; not to teach what people pretend that they already know at their mothers' knees.'

That Makes Me Think of . . .

Suhrawardi said:

I went to see a man, and we sat talking.

There was a camel plodding past, and I said to him:

'What does that make you think of?'

He said:

'Food.'

'But you are not an Arab; since when was camel meat for food?'

'No, it is not like that,' said the man. 'You see, everything makes me think of food.'

❧ 4 ❧
THE NAQSHBANDI ORDER

The Masters

The dervish school called Khajagan ('Masters') rose in Central Asia and greatly influenced the development of the Indian and Turkish empires. The Order gave rise to many specialist schools, which adopted individual names. Many authorities regard this as the earliest of all the mystical 'chains of transmission'.

Khaja Bahaudin Naqshband (died *c.* 1389) is one of the greatest personages of this school. After his time it was known as the Naqshbandi Chain: the 'Designers', or 'Masters of the Design'.

Bahaudin spent seven years as a courtier, seven looking after animals and seven in road-building. He studied under the redoubtable Baba El-Samasi, and is credited with having returned to the original principles and practices of Sufism. The Naqshbandi sheikhs alone have the authority to initiate disciples into all the other Orders of dervishes.

Because they never publicly adopted any distinctive dress, and because their members never carried on attention-attracting activities, scholars have not been able to reconstruct the history of the order, and it has often been difficult to identify its members. Partly because it is a tradition of the 'Masters' to work entirely within the social framework of the culture in which they operate, the Naqshbandis in the Middle East and Central Asia have gained the repute of being mainly Muslim pietists.

How the Order Came Into Being

Three dervishes went on the Longest Journey.
　　When they returned, people said to them:

155

'What helped you most to complete the journey, to make your way, to endure the privations, and to accomplish the return?'

The first answered: 'Cats and mice; because observing them in the ordinary world taught me the equal importance of stillness and activity.'

The second answered: 'Food: because it enabled me to endure and to be understanding.'

The third said: 'Exercises: because they taught me to be active and unified.'

The ignorant among the hearers tried to copy this advice slavishly. They were unsuccessful, but at least they took themselves, in reality if not in appearance, out of the way of the dervishes.

The half-ignorant among the listeners said: 'We will not strictly emulate, we will try to combine these principles.'

They were unsuccessful. But at least they took themselves out of the way of the dervishes, leaving them in peace, since they thought that they now possessed all the teachings.

Then the dervishes said to those who were left:

'Now we will show you how, correctly combined, the secrets and the most ordinary of things in this life may make it possible to achieve the Longest Journey.'

This is the Teaching.

It was in this manner that the Order [of the Masters] came into being.

It is in this manner that the externalists and the inner people still behave.

Three Visits to a Sage

Bahaudin Naqshband was visited by a group of seekers.

They found him in his courtyard, surrounded by disciples, in the midst of what seemed obviously to be revels.

Some of the newcomers said:

'How obnoxious – this is no way to behave, whatever the pretext.' They tried to remonstrate with the master.

Others said:

'This seems to us excellent – we like this kind of teaching, and wish to take part in it.'

Yet others said:

'We are partly perplexed and wish to know more about this puzzle.'

The remainder said to one another:

'There may be some wisdom in this, but whether we should ask about it or not we do not know.'

The teacher sent them all away.

And all these people spread, in conversation and in writing, their opinions of the occasion. Even those who did not allude to their experience directly were affected by it, and their speech and works reflected their beliefs about it.

Some time later certain members of this party again passed that way. They called upon the teacher.

Standing at his door, they noticed that within the courtyard he and his disciples now sat, decorously, deep in contemplation.

'This is better,' said some of the visitors, 'for he has evidently learned from our protests.'

'This is excellent,' said others, 'for last time he was undoubtedly only testing us.'

'This is too sombre,' said others, 'for we could have found long faces anywhere.'

And there were other opinions, voiced and otherwise.

The sage, when the time of reflection was over, sent all these visitors away.

Much later, a small number returned and sought his interpretation of what they had experienced.

They presented themselves at the gateway, and looked into the courtyard. The teacher sat there, alone, neither revelling nor in meditation. His disciples were now nowhere to be seen.

'You may at last hear the whole story,' he said, 'for I have been able to dismiss my pupils, since the task is done.

'When you first came, that class of mine had been too serious – I was in process of applying the corrective. The second time you came, they had been too gay – I was applying the corrective.

'When a man is working, he does not always explain himself to casual visitors, however interested the visitors may think themselves to be. When an action is in progress, what counts is the correct operation of that action. Under these circumstances, external evaluation becomes a secondary concern.'

One Way of Teaching

Bahaudin was sitting with some disciples when a number of followers came into the meeting-hall.

El-Shah asked them, one by one, to say why he was there.

The first said: 'You are the greatest man on earth.'

'I gave him a potion when he was ill, and so he thinks I am the greatest man on earth,' said El-Shah.

The second said: 'My spiritual life has opened up since I have been allowed to visit you.'

'He was uncertain and ill at ease, and none would listen to him. I sat with him, and the resultant serenity is called by him his spiritual life,' said El-Shah.

The third said: 'You understand me, and all I ask is that you allow me to hear your discourses, for the good of my soul.'

'He needs attention and wishes to have notice paid to him, even if it is in criticism,' said El-Shah. This he calls the "good of his soul".'

The fourth said: 'I went from one to another, practising what they taught. It was not until you gave me a *wazifa* (exercise) that I truly felt the illumination of contact with you.'

'The exercise which I gave to this man,' said El-Shah, 'was a concocted one, not related to his "spiritual" life at all. I had to demonstrate his illusion of spirituality before I could arrive at the part of this man which is really spiritual, not sentimental.'

The Successor

Zabit ibn El-Munawwar, the mystic of high attainments, died, leaving the people of the settlement in Balkh without a real teacher. From Turkestan the venerable Elsayar, then a man of scarcely forty, was dispatched by Bahaudin to become the preceptor of this settlement.

When Elsayar (blessings upon his innermost consciousness!) arrived in Balkh and went to the Khanqah, he found the Deputy (Khalifa) sitting surrounded by his students, organizing the affairs of the community.

He was assigned a place in the kitchens. Only one pupil recognized him as the Successor, but Elsayar bade him be silent. 'Here we are both of a lowly degree,' he said.

A month later, when the Great Sheikh of Khorasan was visiting the Khanqah, he was passing the kitchens when he exclaimed:

'The Real Friend is here! And the unreal friends are everywhere else!'

Nobody understood this remark until a letter arrived from the Khajagan addressed to Elsayar as the Appointed Successor.

After that he was treated with great honour. Azimzada, the pupil who had recognized the Successor, in turn became the chief of the monastery.

The Most Ancient Masters

Bahaudin, in a reverie, cast himself back in time.

He told a group of visiting seekers:

'I have just seen, and had companionship with, the masters of the most ancient times, thought to be long dead.'

They said to him: 'Please tell us how they appeared to be.'

He said: 'Such is your attitude towards the teaching that they would have thought *you* demons.

'Matters are such that, had you seen them, you would have considered *them* quite unsuitable for companionship with you. You would not be asking questions about them.'

Why I Did That

One day a man came to the great teacher Bahaudin.

He asked for help in his problems, and guidance on the path of the Teaching.

Bahaudin told him to abandon spiritual studies, and to leave his court at once.

A kind-hearted visitor began to remonstrate with Bahaudin.

'You shall have a demonstration,' said the sage.

At that moment a bird flew into the room, darting hither and thither, not knowing where to go in order to escape.

The Sufi waited until the bird settled near the only open window of the chamber; and then suddenly clapped his hands.

Alarmed, the bird flew straight through the opening of the window, to freedom.

'To him that sound must have been something of a shock, even an affront, do you not agree?' said Bahaudin.

Indirect Teaching

A disciple attended upon El-Shah Bahaudin Naqshband of Bokhara.

After sitting in his assembly for some days, Bahaudin's chief disciple made a sign to him to approach the Sheikh and speak.

'I have come,' said the man, 'from Sheikh Ridwan. I hope that you will give me something.'

'From whom?'

'From Sheikh Ridwan.'

Bahaudin asked the man to repeat what he had said. And then he asked him again, and again, until the man was convinced that Naqshband was deaf and probably stupid.

When this interchange had gone on for an hour or more, Bahaudin said:

'I cannot hear you. I have not heard a word you have said.'

The disciple stood up and started to withdraw, muttering: 'May God forgive you!'

El-Shah, no longer deaf, immediately said: 'And you, and also Sheikh Ridwan.'

The Air of Qasr-El-Arifin

It is related that the king of Bokhara once sent for Bahaudin Naqshband to advise him on a certain matter.

His message said:

'An ambassador is coming, and I must have you with me when he is here, for consultations. Please come at once.'

Bahaudin sent this reply:

'I cannot come, since I am at the moment dependent upon the air of Qasr-El-Arifin, and have no means of bringing it with me in storage jars.'

The king was at first perplexed, and then annoyed. In spite of Bahaudin's great importance as a sage, he resolved to remonstrate with him for his lack of civility.

In the meanwhile, the ambassador's visit was cancelled, and so the king did not have to deal with him after all.

One day, months later, the king was sitting at court when an assassin leapt at him. Bahaudin Naqshband, who had entered the throne room at that moment, jumped upon the man and disarmed him.

'In spite of your discourtesy, I am indebted to you, Hadrat El-Shah,' said the king.

'The courtesy of those who know is to be available when someone needs them, not to sit waiting for ambassadors who are not going to arrive,' said Bahaudin.

Bahaudin's Answers

Many questions, one answer.
I came to a city, where people crowded around...

They said: 'Where are you from?'
They said: 'Where are you going?'
They said: 'In what company do you travel?'
They said: 'What is your pedigree?'
They said: 'What is your inheritance?'
They said: 'What is your bequest?'
They said: 'Whom do you understand?'
They said: 'Who understands you?'
They said: 'What is your doctrine?'
They said: 'Who has the whole doctrine?'
They said: 'Who has no doctrine at all?'
I said to them:
   'What seems to you to be many is one;
   What seems to you simple is not;
   What seems to you complex is easy.
   The answer to you all is: "The Sufis".'

The Sufi Who Called Himself a Dog

Maulana Dervish, chief of the Naqshbandi Order and one of
its greatest teachers, was sitting one day in his Zavia when a
furious cleric forced his way in.

'You sit there,' shouted the intruder, 'dog that you are, surrounded by disciples, obeyed by them in every particular! I, on
the other hand, call men to strive towards divine mercy
through prayer and austerities as is enjoined upon us.'

At the word 'dog', several of the Seekers rose to eject the
fanatic.

'Stay,' said the Maulana, 'for "dog" is indeed a good word.
I am a dog, who obeys his master, showing the sheep by signs
the interpretation of our Master's desires. Like a dog I infuriate
the interloper and the thief. And I wag my tail in pleasure when
my master's Friends come near.

'Just as barking and wagging and love are attributes of the
dog, we exercise them; for our Master has us, and does not do
his own barking and wagging.'

Cherished Notions

Sadik Hamzawi was asked:

'How do you come to suceed, by his own wish, the sage of Samarkand, when you were only a servant in his house?'

He said: 'He taught me what he wanted to teach me, and I learned it. He said once: "I cannot teach the others, the disciples, to the same degree, because they want to ask the questions, they demand the meetings, they impose the framework, they therefore only teach themselves what they already know."

'I said to him: "Teach me what you can and tell me how to learn." This is how I became his successor. People have cherished notions about how teaching and learning should take place. They cannot have the notions and also the learning.'

Naqshbandi Recital

But this is an old tale you tell – they say.
But surely this is a new tale you tell – some say.
Tell it once again – they say;
Or, do not tell it yet again – others say.
But I have heard all this before – say some;
Or, but this is not how it was told before – say the rest.
And these, these are our people, Dervish Baba, this is man.

Sentences of the Khajagan

RUDBARI: Heart to heart is an essential means of passing on the secrets of the Path.

MAGHRIBI: Learning is in activity. Learning through words alone is minor activity.

KHURQANI: At a certain time, more can be conveyed by distracting useless attention than by attracting it.

GURGANI: The teacher and the taught together produce the teaching.

FARMADHI: Experience of extremes is the only way towards the proper working of the mean in study.

HAMADANI: Service of humanity is not only helpful to correct living. By its means the inner knowledge can be preserved, concentrated and transmitted.

YASAVI: Local activity is the keynote of the Dervish Path.

BARQI: Aesthetics is only the lowest form of perception of the Real.

ANDAKI: Effort is not effort without *zaman, makan, ikhwan* (right time, right place, right people).

GHAJDAWANI: We work in all places and at all times. People believe that a man is important if he is famous. The converse may equally well be true.

AHMAD SADIQ: The mark of the Man who has Attained is when he does not mistake figurative for specific, or literal for symbolic.

FAGHNAVI: Our science is not of the world, it is of the worlds.

REWGARI: Stupidity is to look for something in a place where untutored imagination expects to find it. It is, in fact, everywhere that you can extract it.

RAMITANI: Information becomes fragmented, knowledge does not. What causes fragmentation in information in scholasticism.

SAMASI: Man thinks many things. He thinks he is One. He is usually several. Until he becomes One, he cannot have a fair idea of what he is at all.

SOKHARI: We send a thought to China, and it becomes Chinese, they say, because they cannot see the man who sent it. We send a man to India, and they say that he is only a Turkestani.

NAQSHBAND: When people say 'weep', they do not mean 'weep always'. When they say 'do not cry', they do not mean you to be a permanent buffoon.

ATTAR: A true document may contain seven layers of truth. A writing or speech which appears to have no significance may have as many layers of truth.

KHAMOSH: It is not a matter of whether you can learn by silence, by speech, by effort, by submission. It is a matter of how this is done, not 'that it is done'.

KASHGARI: If you still ask: 'Why did such-and-such a person teach in this or that manner, and how does it apply to me?' — you are incapable of understanding the answer deeply enough.

CHARKHI: No matter where the truth is in your case, your teacher can help you find it. If he applies only one series of method to everyone, he is not a teacher, let alone yours.

SAMARQANDI (KHWAJA AHRAR): For every trick or imagination there is a reality of which it is a counterfeit.

AL-LAHI: We do not live in the East or West; we do not study in the North, nor do we teach in the South. We are not bound in this way, but we may be compelled to talk in this way.

AL-BOKHARI: The Way may be through a drop of water. It may, equally, be through a complex prescription (ordering).

ZAHID: When you see a Sufi studying or teaching

something which seems to belong to a field other than spirituality you should know that *there* is the spirituality of the age.

DERVISH: When it is time for stillness, stillness; in the time of companionship, companionship; at the place of effort, effort. In the time and place of anything, anything.

SAMARQANDI AMIN(K)I: Pass from time and place to timelessness and placelessness, to the other worlds. There is our origin.

SIMAQI: If you take what is relative to be what is absolute, you may be lost. Take nothing, rather than risk this.

SIRHINDI: Do not talk only of the Four Ways, or of the Seventy-two Paths, or of the 'Paths as numerous as the souls of Men'. Talk instead of the Path and the attaining. All is subordinated to that.

MASUM: Essence (*Dhat*) manifests only in understanding.

ARIF: But it may *develop* independently of this. These men called daravish (dervishes) are not what you think them to be. Think, therefore, of the Real. It is something like what you think it to be.

BADAUNI: You cannot destroy us if you are against us. But you can make things difficult for us even if you think you are helping.

JAN-I-JANAN: Man can partake of the Perpetual. He does not do this by thinking he can think about it.

DEHLAVI: We spend a space in a place. Do not put up a sign to mark the place. Take rather of the material which adheres to the place, while it is still there.

QANDAHARI: You hear my words. Hear, too, that there

are words other than mine. These are not meant for hearing with the physical ear. Because you see only me, you think there is no Sufism apart from me. You are here to learn, not to collect historical information.

JAN-FISHAN: You may follow one stream. Realize that it leads to the Ocean. Do not mistake the stream for the Ocean.

Miracles and Tricks

Bahaudin once received a mendicant Qalandar who offered to perform miracles to prove that he was a representative of the greatest of all mystical masters.

El-Shah said:

'We are here in Bokhara the unique community whose faith is neither produced nor sustained, in the smallest particular, by extraordinary happenings called miracles. But it is of value for you to perform before the whole assembly of dervishes and also all those who come to see us.'

He accordingly arranged for the next festival day to be set aside for the performance of the strange Qalandar.

For a whole day the mendicant performed miracle after miracle: he brought the dead to life, he walked on water, he caused a severed head to speak, and many other wonders.

The Bokharans were in an uproar. Some of them stated that this man must be a disciple of the devil, for they did not want to adopt his way of life or to credit him with any beneficent powers. Some of the peripheral supporters of El-Shah declared themselves satisfied that a 'new Sun had arisen', and tried to make arrangements to leave for wherever his monastery might be. Some of the newer disciples of El-Shah begged him to perform similar miracles, to show that he was capable of them.

Bahaudin did nothing for three days. Then, before an immense concourse of people, he started to perform what can only be called miracles. One after another, people saw things which they could hardly believe. They saw, heard and touched such things as were not even imagined in the traditions about the wonders of the greatest saints of all time.

Then Bahaudin, one after another, showed them how the tricks were carried out, and that they were – tricks.

'Those of you who are seekers of juggling – follow the way of juggling,' he said, 'for I am at more serious work.'

Liability

One night a thief, trying to climb through the window of a house which he intended to rob, fell because the window-frame broke, hit the ground and broke his leg.

He went to court to sue the owner of the house. This man said:

'Sue the carpenter who put that window in.'

The carpenter said: 'The builder did not make the window-aperture properly.'

When the builder was called, he said: 'My fault was caused by a beautiful woman who was passing while I was working at the window.'

The woman was found, and she said: 'I was wearing a beautiful gown at the time. Normally, nobody looks at me. It is the fault of the gown, which was cunningly dyed in variegated stripes.'

'Now we have the culprit,' said the judge; 'call the man who did the dyeing, and he shall be held responsible for the harm done to the leg of the thief.'

When they found the dyer, he turned out to be the husband of the woman. It so happened that this was – the thief himself.

Falsity

One day a man went to a Sufi master and described how a certain false teacher was prescribing exercises for his followers.

'The man is obviously a fraud. He asks his disciples to "think of nothing". It is easy enough to *say* that, because it impresses some people. But it is impossible to think of nothing.'

The master asked him:

'Why have you come to see me?'

'To point out the absurdity of this man, and also to discuss mysticism.'

'Not just to gain support for your decision that this man is an impostor?'

'No, I know that already.'

'Not to show those of us who are sitting here that you know more than the ordinary, gullible man?'

'No. In fact, I want you to give me guidance.'

'Very well. The best guidance I can give you is to advise you to – think of nothing.

This man immediately withdrew from the company, convinced that the master was a fraud.

But a stranger, who had missed the beginning of these events, and had entered the assembly at the exact moment when the sage was saying 'The best guidance I can give you is to advise you to think of nothing', was profoundly impressed.

'To think of nothing: what a sublime conception!' he said to himself.

And he went away after that day's session, having heard nothing to contradict the idea of thinking of nothing.

The following day one of the students asked the master which of them had been correct.

'Neither,' he said. 'They still have to learn that their greed is a veil, a barrier. Their answer is not in one word, one visit, one easy solution. Only by continuous contact with a teaching does the pupil absorb, little by little, that which gradually accumulates into an understanding of truth. Thus does the seeker become a finder.'

'The Master Rumi said: "Two men come to you, one having dreamt of heaven, the other of hell. They ask which is reality. What is the answer?" The answer is to attend the discourses of a master until you are in harmony.'

Studies and Caravans

Sheikh Rewgari was visited by a man who pleaded long and earnestly to be accepted as a disciple.

The sheikh talked to him about his life and his problems, and then sent him away, saying: 'Your answer will be sent to you in due time.'

Then the sheikh called one of his senior adherents, and said to him: 'Go to the house of such-and-such a man (the would-be disciple) and without mentioning my name offer him a secure and profitable employment in your caravan trade.'

Soon afterwards a message came from the would-be disciple to the sheikh:

'I beg to be excused for not waiting upon you, since fortune has recently decreed that I be given an excellent position with one of the largest merchants in this town, and I must give all my time to this, in the interests of my family.'

Sheikh Rewgari on several occasions correctly divined that visitors to his presence were there only because they had suffered disappointment in their lives. This is not a rare example of his actions in this manner.

The Inner Exercises

Each Perfected Man is in a sense the same as each other one. This means that, correctly attuned through the energy of the School, a disciple can come into communication with all the Great Ones, just as they are in communication with each other, across time and place.

We have renewed the substance of the tradition of the Ancients. Many among the dedicated dervishes have not done this, and we must leave them to what they want to practise. Do not engage in disputation with them. 'You to your Way, and I to mine.'

The duties and practices of the School form one whole: the Truth, the manner of teaching and the participants form *one hand*, in which the ignorant may see only the dissimilarity of the fingers, not the combined action of the hand itself.

Bahaudin Naqshband

On Your Religion

Throughout the dervish literature you will find us saying repeatedly that we are not concerned with your religion or even with the lack of it. How can this be reconciled with the fact that believers consider themselves the elect?

Man's refinement is the goal, and the inner teaching of all the faiths aims at this. In order to accomplish it, there is always a tradition handed down by a living chain of adepts, who select candidates to whom to impart this knowledge.

Among men of all kinds this teaching has been handed down. Because of our dedication to the essence, we have, in the Dervish Path, collected those people who are less concerned about externals, and thus kept pure, in secret, our capacity to continue the succession. In the dogmatic religions of the Jews, the Christians, the Zoroastrians, the Hindus and literalist Islam this precious thing has been lost.

We return this vital principle to all these religions and this is why you will see so many Jews, Christians and others among my followers. The Jews say that we are the real Jews, the Christians, Christians.

It is only when you know the Higher Factor that you will know the true situation of the present religions and of unbelief itself. And unbelief itself is a religion with its own form of belief.

Ahmad Yasavi

The Palace of the Enlightened

Reasons for the Founding of a School

The Path (Order) of the Masters derives its substance in unbroken succession from the earliest times. It maintains its connection, in a parallel way, with both the ancients and the contemporary teachers, by direct communication of being.

Now many externalists have been confused by the fact that there are different Orders and formulations in our Path. They are the more perplexed because, although the adherents of one School esteem, revere and follow one teacher and his methods, they may well join another one at some time or other.

The reason is not far to seek, if you know how to seek it. The answer is in the ancient aphorism of ours: 'Speak to Everyone in Accordance with his Understanding.'

The task of the teacher is to teach. In order to teach he must take into account the present preoccupations and fixed ideas of his pupils. He must, for instance, use the terms of Bokhara with the Bokharan and the terms of Baghdad in Baghdad.

If he knows what he is teaching, he arranges the outer form of the means of teaching it, like building the physical shape of a school, in accordance with this. Also involved are the nature and descriptions of the disciples, and their potentiality.

Take an example in musical assemblies. We do not attend them nor do we employ music. This is because for our time and in our position there is more harm than good in it. Music, heard in the right way, improves the approach to the Consciousness. But it will harm people who are not sufficiently prepared, or of the correct type, for hearing and playing it.

Those who do not know this have adopted music as something sacred in itself. The feelings which they experience while indulging in it they mistake for sublime ones. In fact they are using it for the lower purpose of arousing sentiment, emotion which is no basis for further progress.

Dervishes join the Order most suited to their inner nature. They remain with their teacher until he has developed them as far as possible. After this they may go or be sent to another teacher, in order to participate in the special exercises which he may offer. This is because there may be a side of them which will be benefited by this specialization.

In the Path of the Masters we follow the bases of the Dervish Work. Some of our exercises are used in one way, some in another. Some are reversed, because they do not apply to this place or this time. Similarly with all other schools. It is for this reason that you will find here masters who have the Robe of Permission to enrol disciples in all the Orders, but who work with this community in accordance with its needs, based on the original science upon which all other forms are based.

Our school is founded on the verifiable and impeccable authority of our predecessors in unbroken and documented succession of spiritual pedigree. Little do you know, however, how little these externals (which satisfy you by our moral repute) count in comparison with the fundamental Truth of Experience which is our invisible, powerful inheritance.

Bahaudin Naqshband

Part Four

AMONG THE MASTERS

AMONG THE MASTERS
A Meeting with Khidr

Khidr is the 'unseen guide' of the Sufis, and it is he who is believed to be the anonymous Guide to Moses in the Koran. This 'Green One' is often referred to as 'the Jew' and he has been equated in legend with such figures as St George and Elijah. This tale – or report – is characteristic of the supernormal functions attributed to Khidr, both in folklore and among the dervish teachers.

Once, while standing on the banks of the Oxus river, I saw a man fall in. Another man, in the clothes of a dervish, came running to help him, only to be dragged into the water himself. Suddenly I saw a third man, dressed in a robe of shimmering, luminous green, hurl himself into the river. But as he struck the surface, his form seemed to change; he was no longer a man, but a log. The other two men managed to cling to this, and together they worked it towards the bank.

Hardly able to believe what I was seeing, I followed at a distance, using the bushes that grew there as cover. The men drew themselves panting on the bank; the log floated away. I watched it until, out of sight of the others, it drifted to the side, and the green-robed man, soaked and sodden, dragged himself ashore. The water began to stream from him; before I reached him he was almost dry.

I threw myself on the ground in front of him, crying: 'You must be the Presence Khidr, the Green One, Master of the Saints. Bless me, for I would attain.' I was afraid to touch his robe, because it seemed to be of green fire.

He said: 'You have seen too much. Understand that I come from another world and am, without their knowing it, protecting those who have service to perform. You may have been a disciple of Sayed Imdadullah, but you are not mature enough to know what we are doing for the sake of God.'

When I looked up, he was gone, and all I could hear was a rushing sound in the air.

After coming back from Khotan, I saw the same man. He was lying on a straw mattress in a rest-house near Peshawar. I said to myself: 'If I was too raw the last time, this time I'll be mature.'

I took hold of his robe, which was a very common one – though under it I thought I saw something glow green.

'You may be Khidr,' I said to him, 'but I have to know how an apparently ordinary man like you performs these wonders ... and why. Explain your craft to me, so that I can practise it too.'

He laughed. 'You're impetuous, my friend! The last time you were too headstrong – and now you're still too headstrong. Go on, tell everyone you meet that you've seen Khidr Elias; they'll put you in the madhouse, and the more you protest you're right the more heavily they'll chain you.'

Then he took out a small stone. I stared at it – and found myself paralysed, turned to stone, until he had picked up his saddle-bags and walked away.

When I tell this story, people either laugh or, thinking me a story-teller, give me presents.

Hasan of Basra

When he was asked: 'What is Islam, and who are the Muslims?' he answered:

'Islam is in the books, and Muslims are in the tomb.'

What Man Really Knows

Men suppose, fancifully, that they know Truth and divine perception. In fact they know nothing.

Juzjani

Sufian Thauri

A man in a dream met a Sufi who had been rewarded for his good actions. 'I was even given a reward for removing a fruit-peel from the road, when someone might have slipped upon it,' said the Sufi.

Sufian Thauri, when this was reported to him, said:

'How fortunate he was not to have been punished for each occasion upon which he gave charity and felt personal pleasure at it.'

Ghazali

Sin

Sin against God is one thing; but sinning against man is worse.

Sufian Thauri

Man Must be in the Correct State

Uwais el-Qarni said to some visitors:

'Do you seek God? If so, why have you come to me?'

The visitors only thought that they sought God. Their presence and emanations gave them away.

'If you do not,' continued Uwais, 'what truck have you with me?'

Because they were intellectuals and emotionalists, they could not understand him.

Bayazid Bistami

A fire-worshipping Magian was asked why he did not become a Muslim.

He answered:

'If you mean that I should be as good a man as Bayazid, I lack the courage. If, however, you mean that I should be as bad a man as you, I would detest it.'

Class

The lower classes of society are those who fatten themselves in life in the name of religion.

Ibn el-Mubarak

Names

You call me a Christian, to make me angry and to make yourself feel happy. Others call themselves Christians, to make themselves feel other emotions. Very well, if we are dealing in exciting words, I will call you a devil-worshipper. That should give you an agitation which will please you for some time.

Zabardast Khan

Bayazid Bistami

A devoutly religious man, who was a disciple of Bayazid, said to him one day:

'I am surprised that anyone who accepts God should not attend the mosque for worship.'

Bayazid answered:

'I, on the other hand, am surprised that anyone who knows God can worship him and not lose his senses, rendering his ritual prayer invalid.'

Service

I will not serve God like a labourer, in expectation of my wages.

Rabia el-Adawia

To be a Believer

You probably seem to yourself to be a believer, even if you are a believer in disbelief.

But you cannot really believe in anything until you are aware of the process by which you arrived at your position.

Before you do this you must be ready to postulate that all your beliefs may be wrong, that what you think to be belief may only be a variety of prejudice caused by your surroundings – including the bequest of your ancestors for whom you may have a sentiment.

True belief belongs to the realm of real knowledge.

Until you have knowledge, belief is mere coalesced opinions, however it may seem to you.

Coalesced opinions serve for ordinary living. Real belief enables higher studies to be made.

Attributed to Ali

The Blacksmith of Nishapur

Abu Hafs the blacksmith of Nishapur showed signs of strange endowments through the power of his attention, from the early days of his discipleship. He was accepted as a pupil by Sheikh Bawardi, and returned to his smithy to continue his work. While his mind was concentrated, he pulled a piece of red-hot iron from the forge with his bare hand. Although he did not feel the heat, his assistant collapsed at this unprecedented sight.

When he was Grand Sheikh of the Sufis of Khorasan, it was noted that he did not speak Arabic and used an interpreter in speaking to Arab visitors. Yet, when he visited the great Sufis of Baghdad, he spoke the language so well that the purity of his speech was unsurpassed.

When the sheikhs of Baghdad asked him to tell them the meaning of generosity, he said: 'I will hear another define it first.'

The Master Junaid then said: 'Generosity is not identifying generosity with yourself, and not considering it.'

Abu Hafs commented: 'The sheikh has spoken well. But I feel that generosity means doing justice without requiring justice.'

Junaid said to the others: 'Stand, all of you! For Abu Hafs has transcended Adam and all his race.'

Abu Hafs used to say: 'I abandoned work and then went back to it. Then it abandoned me, and I never went back to it.'

Hujwiri: *The Revelation of the Veiled*

Shibli and Junaid

Abu-Bakr, son of Dulaf, son of Jahdar ('El-Shibli'), and Abu'l Qasim el-Junaid, 'Peacock of the Learned', are two of the early classical masters of the Sufis. They both lived and taught over a thousand years ago. The story of Shibli's discipleship under Junaid, given here, comes from *The Revelation of the Veiled,* one of the most important early books on the subject. Junaid himself was spiritualized by the influence of Ibrahim, son of Adam ('Ben Adhem' in Leigh Hunt's poem), who was, like Buddha, a prince who abdicated to follow the way, and who died in the eighth century.

Shibli, a proud courtier, went to Junaid, seeking real knowledge. He said: 'I hear that you have the divine knowledge. Give it, or sell it, to me.'

Junaid said: 'I cannot sell it to you, because you do not possess its price. I cannot give it to you, because thus you would have it too cheap. You must immerse yourself in water, as I have, in order to obtain the pearl.'

'What shall I do?' asked Shibli.

'Go and become a seller of sulphur.'

When a year had passed, Junaid said to him: 'You are flourishing as a merchant. Now be a dervish, doing nothing other than begging.'

Shibli spent a year begging in the streets of Baghdad, without any success.

He went back to Junaid. The Master told him:

'To mankind you are now nothing. Let them be nothing to you. In the past you were a governor. Return now to that province and seek out every person whom you oppressed. Ask the forgiveness of each one.' He went, found them all except one, and received their pardon.

On his return, Junaid said that he still felt in some way self-important. He was to spend another year in begging. The money which he gained in this way was brought each evening to the Master, who gave it to the poor. Shibli himself got no food until the following morning.

He was accepted as a disciple. When a year was over, spent as a servant of the other students, he felt himself to be the most humble of creation.

He used to illustrate the difference between the Sufis and the unregenerate by saying things incomprehensible to the populace at large.

One day, because of his cryptic talk, he was mocked as a madman in public by detractors. He said:

> To your mind, I am mad.
> To my mind, you are all sane.
> So I pray to increase my madness
> And to increase your sanity.
>   My 'madness' is from the power of Love;
>   Your sanity is from the strength of unawareness.

Ghulam Haidar of Kashmir

Hearing a discussion among his disciples about the importance of meticulous observance of the religious law as a means to illumination, Ghulam Haidar gave orders that, on any pretext, the following were to be collected and brought before him:

One Jew, one Christian, one Zoroastrian, one Hindu priest, one Sikh, one Buddhist, one Farangi ('Frank' or Christian), one Shiah, one Sunni, one pagan, and several others. The last included traders, workmen, farmers, clerics and clerks, a baker and various women of all types.

For three years his adherents worked to collect these people in one place at one time, not telling them that their presence was required by their master. In order to do this they spread rumours of treasure in Kashmir, became merchants, sent to distant places for tutors and servants. At last all were assembled. When he was informed that they were there, Ghulam Haidar instructed that they were all to be invited to a meal at his Hall of Teaching, the Zawiya.

When all had eaten, the Pir (Ghulam Haidar) addressed the company, of whom a very large proportion were those strangers who did not adhere to his doctrine. Also present were all the disciples, who had been told to take no part in the proceedings except to watch.

The Pir spoke in several languages, explaining the need for man to dedicate himself to effort, and to master the mysteries which were his birthright, regardless of his prejudices.

Without exception the strangers were desirous of following the Pir, and their mutual enmity vanished. It is from this company that sprang the teachers known as the 'Loaves of Bread': those whose 'dough had been fashioned by the Kashmiri Pir', regardless of their basic prejudices.

After this meeting, Haidar said: 'Dough is dough,' and 'one dough is not better than another.'

Eat No Stones

A hunter, walking through some woods, came upon a notice. He read the words:

STONE-EATING IS FORBIDDEN

His curiosity was stimulated, and he followed a track which led past the sign until he came to a cave at the entrance to which a Sufi was sitting.

The Sufi said to him:

'The answer to your question is that you have never seen a notice prohibiting the eating of stones because there is no need for one. Not to eat stones may be called a common habit.

'Only when the human being is able similarly to avoid other habits, even more destructive than eating stones, will he be able to get beyond his present pitiful state.'

Why the Dog Could Not Drink

Shibli was asked:

'Who guided you in the Path?'

He said: 'A dog. One day I saw him, almost dead with thirst, standing by the water's edge.

'Every time he looked at his reflection in the water he was frightened, and withdrew, because he thought it was another dog.

'Finally, such was his necessity, he cast away fear and leapt into the water; at which the "other dog" vanished.

'The dog found that the obstacle, which was himself, the barrier between him and what he sought, melted away.

'In this same way my own obstacle vanished, when I knew that it was what I took to be my own self. And my Way was first shown to me by the behaviour of – a dog.'

Demonstration of Training

A malicious man one day invited Osman El-Hiri to eat with him.

When the sheikh arrived, the man drove him away. But when he had gone a few steps, he called him back again.

This happened more than thirty times, until the other man, overcome by the Sufi's patience and gentleness, as he took it to be, broke down and begged his forgiveness.

'You do not understand,' said El-Hiri. 'What I did was no more than a trained dog would do. When you call him, he comes; when you shoo him, he goes away. This behaviour is no mark of a Sufi, and not difficult for anyone to do.'

What the Devil Said

Once upon a time there was a dervish. As he was sitting in contemplation, he noticed that there was a sort of devil near him.

The dervish said: 'Why are you sitting there, making no mischief?'

The demon raised his head wearily. 'Since the theoreticians and would-be teachers of the Path have appeared in such numbers, there is nothing left for me to do.'

The Four Sheikhs and the Caliph

The Caliph Mansur decided to appoint one of four great Sufi sheikhs as Grand Judge of the Empire. They were called to the Palace – Abu Hanifa, Sufian Thauri, Misar and Shuraih – but on the way they made a plan.

Abu Hanifa, one of the Four Great Doctors of Law as he is now called, said: 'I shall escape from the position by an evasion. Misar will pretend that he is insane. Sufian will flee; and I predict that Shuraih will become Judge.'

Sufian accordingly took to flight and exile, to escape being executed for disobedience. The other three entered the presence of the Caliph.

First Mansur said to Abu Hanifa: 'You shall be Judge.'

Abu Hanifa replied: 'Commander of the Faithful, I cannot. I am not an Arab; I am therefore not likely to be accepted by the Arabs.'

The Caliph said: 'This has nothing to do with blood. We need learning, and you are the most esteemed sage of the time.'

Abu Hanifa insisted: 'If my words have been true, I cannot be Judge. And if they were false, I do not deserve the position, and am thus disqualified.'

Thus Abu Hanifa proved his point, and was excused.

Misar, the second reluctant candidate, now approached the Commander of the Believers and taking his hand cried:

'Are you well, you and your little ones and your cattle?'

'Take him away,' shouted the Caliph, 'for he is certainly mad.'

Only Shuraih was left, and he claimed that he was ill. But Mansur made him undergo a course of remedies, and made him Judge.

A Matter of Honour

A wandering Sufi, found in the desert, was brought to the tent of a wild Beduin chief.

'You are a scout for our enemies, and as such we shall kill you,' said the chief.

'I am innocent,' said the Sufi.

'Do you see this sword?' asked the Sufi, drawing one. 'Before you can approach me I shall kill one of your men here. When I have done so, you will have a legitimate right to avenge his death. By so doing, I shall save your honour, which is at this moment in grave danger of being sullied by the blood of a Sufi.'

Fudail the Highwayman and His Child

Fudail, son of Ayyad, was once a highwayman. After his conversion to the religious life, he felt that he was worshipping God in the right way and making amends for his crimes, for he had sought out all his victims and recompensed them.

One day, however, he had a strange experience. He had taken his little son upon his knee and kissed him. 'Do you love me?' asked the child. 'Yes, I do,' said Fudail. 'But do you not also love God, as you have often told me?' 'Yes, I believe that I do,' said his father.

'But how can you, with one heart, love two?'

It was from this moment that Fudail realized that what he

had taken for love was in fact sentimentality, and that he must find a higher form of love.

This incident was the origin of his saying:

'That which is generally considered to be the highest or noblest attainment of humankind is in reality the lowest of the high ranges possible to humankind.'

Problems of Generosity

A student, going to pay his respects to a Sufi, asked him out of curiosity: 'Why are those thirty magnificent Herat mules standing in your courtyard?'

The sage immediately said: 'They are there for you.'

The student was delighted when he heard that they were being given to him, although he said: 'I should pay some price, surely?'

'The price,' said the master, 'may be more than you can pay by yourself. But the condition is that you tell nobody that I gave the mules to you. I am not here to be known as "good" among men because of such actions. People in general think that something is "good" because of an action whose consequences and origin they cannot grasp.'

'Nothing seems smaller than your price,' said the student. He led the mules away in rapture, saying to himself: 'My teacher has indeed benefited me. This is the outer manifestation of an interior blessing.'

Soon evening fell, and within a few moments the student fell into the hands of the night patrol. Its members said to one another: 'Let us accuse this man of such-and-such a crime which we cannot in any case solve. We can suggest that he bought the mules with the profits of the theft, unless he can account for their possession otherwise. He is probably guilty of something, being ill-nurtured and poorly dressed. Some of us have seen him before, and believe in any case that he has associates of doubtful character.'

Taken before the summary court, the student at first refused to answer any questions about the origin of the mules. The examining magistrate ordered that he be put to the bastinado.

In the meantime, another body of disciples were attending the sage, who sent them, in relays, to follow the fortunes of the first man.

They reported, from time to time: 'He refuses to talk;' and: 'He is weakening – they are torturing him.'

At length the Sufi stood up and made haste to the court.

On his testimony that he had given the man the mules, the prisoner was released.

Then he addressed the court, his disciples and the public, who were perplexed at the event, thus:

'The repute of generosity has three evils: it can corrode the man who has this repute; it can harm the man who admires this generosity if he imitates it ignorantly; it can erode whoever receives generosity if he knows the giver. There should be no sense of obligation. That is why it is incumbent upon the Sufi to exercise generosity with complete secrecy.

'The highest form of generosity known to the ordinary man is equal to the lowest level of *real* generosity. It was originally instituted as a way of introducing man to liberality. It has become an idol and a curse.'

The Fortune of Man

El Mahdi Abbassi announced that it was verifiable that, whether people tried to help a man or not, something in him could frustrate this aim.

Certain people having objected to this theory, he promised a demonstration.

When everyone had forgotten the incident, El Mahdi ordered one man to lay a sack of gold in the middle of a bridge. Another man was asked to bring some unfortunate debtor to one end of the bridge and tell him to cross it.

Abbassi and his witnesses stood at the other side of the bridge.

When the man got to the other side, Abbassi asked him: 'What did you see in the middle of the bridge?'

'Nothing,' said the man.

'How was that?'

'As soon as I started to cross the bridge, the thought occurred to me that it might be amusing to cross it with my eyes shut. And I did so.'

The Flower and the Stone

When the great teacher and martyr Mansur El-Hallaj was exposed to the crowd, convicted of apostasy and heresy, he showed no evidence of pain when his hands were publicly chopped off.

When the crowd threw stones which inflicted great wounds, he made no sign.

One of his friends, a Sufi teacher, approached and struck him with – a flower.

Mansur screamed as if in torture.

He did this in order to show that he could not be hurt by anything done by those who thought that they were doing right. But the merest touch from someone who knew, like him, that he was unjustly accused and condemned was more hurtful to him than any torture.

Mansur and his Sufi companions, helpless though they were in the face of such tyranny, are remembered for that lesson, while their torturers are almost forgotten.

As he was dying, Mansur said: 'The people of the world try to do good. I recommend you to seek something of which the smallest part is worth more than all goodness: the *knowledge* of what *is* true – true science.'

Hanbal and the Conditioned Mind

Ahmad ibn Hanbal was the founder of one of the four great Schools of Law, and companion of many of the early Sufi Masters.

When he was of advanced years and very frail, a heretical party in Baghdad seized power and tried to get a ruling out of him as to the correctness of their views.

Imam Hanbal refused, so he was given a thousand lashes and put to the torture. Before he died, as he did quite soon, from this treatment, he was asked what he thought of his murderers.

He said: 'I can only say that they thrashed me because they believed that they were right and I was in the wrong. How can I claim justice against those who believe that they are right?'

Man Believes What He Thinks is True

Teaching, as was his custom, during the ordinary business of life, Sheikh Abu Tahir Harami rode his donkey one day into a market-place, a disciple following behind.

At the sight of him, a man called out: 'Look, here comes the ancient unbeliever!'

Harami's pupil, his wrath aroused, shouted at the defamer. Before long there was a fierce altercation in progress.

The Sufi calmed his disciple, saying: 'If you will only cease this tumult, I will show you how you can escape this kind of trouble.'

They went together to the old man's house. The sheikh told his follower to bring him a box of letters. 'Look at these. They are all letters addressed to me. But they are couched in different terms. Here someone calls me "Sheikh of Islam"; there, "Sublime Teacher". Another says I am the "Wise One of the Twin Sanctuaries". And there are others.

'Observe how each styles me in accordance with what he considers me to be. But I am none of these things. Each man calls another just what he thinks him to be. This is what the unfortunate one in the market-place has just done. And yet you take exception to it. Why do you do so — since it is the general rule of life?'

Which Way Round is Right?

A certain wise man was widely reputed to have become irrational in his presentation of facts and arguments.

It was decided to test him, so that the authorities of his country could pronounce as to whether he was a danger to public order or not.

On the day of the test he paraded past the court-room mounted on a donkey, facing the donkey's rear.

When the time came for him to speak for himself, he said to the judges:

'When you saw me just now, which way was I facing?'

The judges said: 'Facing the wrong way.'

'You illustrate my point,' he answered, 'for *I* was facing the right way, from one point of view. It was the donkey which was facing the wrong way.'

The Master

It is related by a Sufi master that, when he was a youth, he wanted to attach himself to a teaching master. He sought the sage, and asked to become his disciple.

The teacher said: 'You are not yet ready.'

Since the young man was insistent, the sage said: 'Very well, I will teach you something. I am going on a pilgrimage to Mecca. Come with me.'

The disciple was overjoyed.

'Since we are travelling companions,' said the teacher, 'one must lead, and the other obey. Choose your role.'

'I will follow, you lead,' said the disciple.

'If you know how to follow,' said the master.

The journey started. While they were resting one night in the desert of the Hejaz, it started to rain. The master got up and held a covering over the disciple, protecting him.

'But this is what *I* should be doing for you,' said the disciple.

'I command you to allow me to protect you thus,' said the sage.

When it was day the young man said: 'Now it is a new day. Let *me* be the leader, and you follow me.' The master agreed.

'I shall now collect brushwood, to make a fire,' said the youth.

'You may do no such thing; I shall collect it,' said the sage.

'I command you to sit there while I collect brushwood!' said the young man.

'You may do no such thing,' said the teacher, 'for it is not in accordance with the requirements of discipleship for the follower to allow himself to be served by the leader.'

And so, on every occasion, the Master showed the student what discipleship really meant, by demonstration.

They parted at the gate of the Holy City. Seeing the sage later, the young man could not meet his eyes. 'That which you have learned,' said the older man, 'is something of the nature of discipleship.'

The disciple must know *how* to obey, not merely that he must obey. The question of *whether* to become a disciple or not only comes after the person knows what discipleship really is. People spend their time wondering whether they should be disciples – or otherwise. Since their assumption (that they could be a disciple if they wished it) is incorrect, they are living in a false world, an intellectualist world. Such people have not learned the first lesson.

Hilali of Samarkand

Hilali, accompanied by five of his disciples, went on a long journey through Central Asia. From time to time Hilali made his companions act in various ways. These are some of their adventures:

When they reached Balkh and a deputation of the great people from the city came out to greet the Master, Hilali said to Yusuf Lang: 'Be thou the Master.' Yusuf was received and honoured. Reports spread of the miracles which he had accomplished merely by staying under the same roof as certain sick people. 'This is what people think Dervishhood is, and what we know it is not,' said Hilali.

In Surkhab the companions entered the town all dressed the same, none walking in front of another. 'Which is the Great Master?' asked the chief of the town. 'I am he,' said Hilali. Immediately the people fell back exclaiming: 'We knew it by the Light in his Eyes.'

'Take a lesson from this,' said Hilali to his companions.

When the company entered Qandahar they were given a feast by the Chief Sardar, all sitting in a circle. Hilali had given orders that he was to be treated as the least of the disciples, and that Jafar Akhundzada was to be treated as the Master. But the Chief Sardar said: 'Verily this least of the companions shines with the inner light, and, whatever you may say of him, I regard him as the Qutub, the Magnetic Centre of the Age.'

All saluted Hilali, who was forced to recognize that the Sardar, although a ruler, had also the capacity to perceive what other men do not perceive.

The Curse of the Beduin

One day, in the Oasis of Kufa, a rough beduin strode up to Hasan, grandson of Mohammed, and started to revile him, his father and his mother.

Hasan said: 'Beduin, are you in need? What is your trouble?'

But the beduin taking no notice at all, continued to shout and curse. Hasan had some money brought and given to the man, and spoke to him again:

'Beduin, forgiveness! This is all that there is in this house; but I say that if we had had anything else, I would have given it to you, without any reservation.'

When he heard these words, the beduin was overcome, and cried out: 'I bear witness that you are truly the grandson of the Messenger. For I had come here in order to test whether your lineage and your nature were in accord one with the other.'

Why the Dervish was at Court

One of the dicta of Hadrat Ibn El-Khafif of Shiraz was: 'A Sufi should not visit a ruler, or come out in welcome if he is visited by him.'

It was therefore a matter of surprise to two would-be Sufis who arrived at his home, when they were told that he was at the court of the king.

They changed their minds about his great sanctity and decided to walk in the city instead of paying their respects to him.

Visiting a shop, they became innocently involved in an altercation, were accused of theft, and hauled before the king for judgement.

Convinced by the shopkeeper that the two were guilty, the monarch ordered them to be killed on the spot, as an example.

Ibn El-Khafif, still at court, interceded, and their lives were spared.

'It may have been natural for you to think that I should not be at court,' said the sage to the pair; 'but learn at least that a Sufi does unexpected things for invisible but nevertheless sufficient reasons.'

The Compulsion to Teach

Bishr son of Harith was asked why he did not teach.

'I have stopped teaching because I find that I have a desire to teach. If this compulsion passes, I shall teach of my own free will.'

Time for Learning

The Sage of Ascalon would only speak to his disciples rarely. When he did, they were overcome by his ideas.

'May we have lectures at times when we can conveniently attend?' they asked, 'because when you speak some of us have family duties and cannot always be there.'

'You will have to find someone else to do that,' he said, 'because whereas I only teach when I do not feel the urge to teach, there do exist some who can teach in accordance with who is present at a fixed time. It is they who feel the urge to teach, and consequently only have the need to adapt what they say to the audience.'

If I Ask and They Refuse ...

A dervish was asked: 'Why do you not ask something from people, so that you may have food?' He said: 'If I ask them and they refuse me, there is a danger that they will suffer for it. The Prophet is reported to have said that if a sincere needy man asks, those who refuse to give him something will languish.'

How You Should Think of Me

A disciple came to Maruf Karkhi and said:

'I have been talking to people about you. Jews claim that you are a Jew; Christians revere you as one of their own saints; Muslims insist that you are the greatest of all Muslims.'

Maruf answered:

'This is what humanity says in Baghdad. When I was in Jerusalem, Jews said that I was a Christian, Muslims that I was a Jew, and Christians that I was a Muslim.'

'What must we think of you, then?' said the man.

'Some do not understand me and they revere me. Others do not either, so they revile me. That is what I have come to say. You should think of me as one who has said this.'

Saint-Worship

A Sufi sheikh was asked by a visitor:

'Is there any value in saint-worship?'

He at once said: 'It is illogical, and it is forbidden by Islam.' The inquirer went away, satisfied.

A disciple who had been present said: 'But your answer did not cover the implications of the question.'

The sheikh told him: 'The questioner was at the stage of *Shariat* (conventionalist religion). The way in which he put the question showed that there was a certain reassurance which he wanted, and he sought it from me, of whom he had heard as a reliable source of opinion. There is, however, another kind of relationship with saints, one other than worship. Visiting their tombs has a virtue. But this virtue is operative only for those who can perceive it. This man was not one of them, so this other aspect of the question was void in his case.

'A man last month asked for verification of the fact that "cures wrought by shrine-meditation were entirely due to the aspiration, not the saint". I agreed with him. He had no capacity for more complex ideas: that, in other words, this may be partly true on some occasions, wholly on others, and so on.

'It is characteristic of the blind that they can see only certain questions. Saints were men, visiting a shrine to some is bound to be "saint-worship", saint-worship is ignorant. Therefore there can be no advantage in saint-worship.

'One in a thousand, perhaps, who visits a shrine will know

inwardly why he is there and what is the nature of the virtue which he may derive from it. It is but natural that all pilgrims will imagine that they are "devout" and hence that they are all doing or experiencing exactly the same thing. Of course they are not. Have you ever tried to show a misguided man that his vision is narrow? He may listen to you in appearance. But for the sake of his own self-esteem he will reject what you *mean*, if not what you say.'

Mohammed Shah, Murshid of Turkestan

Mohammed Shah, Murshid ('Guide') of Turkestan, was a nineteenth-century teacher who took his examples from the 'juice' (real inner content) of ordinary actions and life. This is a typical account of his methods.

Mohammed Shah took a group of his Halka ('circle') to see certain sights. One was a tall minaret set beside a river. 'This was built by people who persevere,' he said.

Then he took them to see a party of Brahmin pilgrims walking to the holy Jumna river. 'These are people who persevere,' he said. On another day he took his people to watch a caravan which had come through the desert wastes of China. 'These are people who persevere,' he said. Finally he bade them go to Tibet to watch pilgrims measuring their length along the ground, making a holy journey. 'Those were people who persevere,' he told them when they returned.

After some months, he made them watch magistrates trying cases, to observe the efforts of the magistrate, the energy of the witnesses, the aspirations of the plaintiffs, the efforts of the accused. 'In all of these things you see men and women persevering,' he said.

'Men everywhere persevere. The yield of this perseverance is what is of account. This they can harvest and use. If, on the other hand, during the perseverance, they become beguiled by the thing for which they persevere, they cannot make use of the training of the struggle of perseverance. All that happens to them is that they become trained in persevering after something.'

Why the Dervish Hides Himself

Rumi's son asked him:

'How and why is the dervish hidden? Is this done by superficial disguise? Is there something within himself which he conceals?'

The Master said:

'It might be done in any way. Some write love-poems, and people think that they mean ordinary' love. The dervish may hide his true position in the Way by adopting a calling. There are writers; and some, like Baba Farid, are traders. Still others follow various different outer activities.

'This may be done for the sake of defence against the shallow. Some purposely act in a manner which society might disapprove.

'The Prophet has therefore said: "God has hidden the Men of Greatest Knowledge."

'A device may be adopted by the Followers of the Way to gain peace, when they might otherwise be hindered.'

The Master then recited:

Ever-knowing – as they hide they seek.
Appearing other than they are – to the ordinary man;
In inward light they roam – making miracles come to pass.
Yet they are *really* known – to none.

Munaqib El-Arifin

Prayers for the Dead

Sufian Thauri heard that a funeral was to take place, and he followed the coffin. He prayed at the graveside.

After the service, people began to say what a good man the deceased had been.

'I should not have prayed for that man,' said Sufian, 'for when you hear people speak well of a man, it is generally because he is a hypocrite, whether he knew it or not. If a man is not a hypocrite, there are always many who do not speak well of him.'

Thauri on Contemplation

The great Shibli went to visit the illustrious Thauri. The master was sitting so still that not a hair of him moved in any way.

Shibli asked: 'Where did you learn such stillness?'

Thauri replied: 'From a cat. He was watching a mousehole with even greater concentration than you have seen in me.'

Strange Agitation

Sahl Abdullah once went into a state of violent agitation, with physical manifestations, during a religious meeting.

Ibn Salim said: 'What is this state?'

Sahl said: 'This was not, as you imagine, power entering me. It was, on the contrary, due to my own weakness.'

Others present remarked: 'If that was weakness, what is power?'

'Power,' said Sahl, 'is when something like this enters, and the mind and body manifest nothing at all.'

The Ass

Sahl was on a journey with Ibrahim son of Adam, and fell ill.

He relates that Ibrahim sold all that he owned to spend on the sick man. One day Sahl asked for some delicacy and Ibrahim sold his donkey and bought it for him.

When he was convalescing, Sahl asked Ibrahim: 'Where is the donkey, for me to ride upon?'

'I am he,' said Ibrahim; 'ride on my shoulders.' And he carried Sahl on his back for the rest of the journey.

Ibn-Salim

A large number of people assembled in front of Ibn-Salim's house. He was asked to speak to them, in the words: 'Your disciples are here.'

He answered: 'These are not my disciples – but the disciples of my audience. My disciples are the few.'

Responsibility of the Teacher

Haji Bektash appointed Nurudin Chaqmaq as his Khalifa ('deputy') in the farthest north.

At that time Sheikh Chaqmaq already had many disciples, for he was a dervish who had attracted, through his dedication and readings of the ancient masters, several circles of pupils. Moreover, he had been in intimate contact with more than one of the teachers.

The Haji gave him teachings which on the surface were strongly at variance with the traditional customs and thoughts to which his disciples were accustomed.

Chaqmaq tried to evade his responsibility by handing over his flock to the Haji. But Haji Bektash refused, and told Chaqmaq: 'Only by acting as a channel for me to your people will you yourself become transformed.'

Chaqmaq feared that this new teaching would undermine his authority. 'If you teach only through authority, you are not teaching at all,' said Haji Bektash. Certain of Chaqmaq's disciples came to complain to Haji Bektash that their master was behaving in an eccentric manner. 'We are no longer able to have the comfort of the customary observances,' they said. 'This is exactly what I want to happen,' said the Haji.

Other disciples feared that the Haji had influenced Chaqmaq and that he would influence them similarly. This was reported to the Haji. He said: 'They see something good happening to Chaqmaq but they think it is bad. This is a fever which has to burn itself out.'

Four years passed before, entirely through the Haji's example, Chaqmaq's disciples realized that Bektash had other things to do than 'capture lame horses'. Bektash said: 'It was your own self-esteem about yourselves which made you imagine that you were something which anyone would bother himself to enslave.'

The Jewel

A young man came to Dhun-Nun and said that the Sufis were wrong, and many another thing besides.

The Egyptian removed a ring from his finger and handed it to him. 'Take this to the market stallholders over there and see whether you can get a gold piece for it,' he said.

Nobody among the market people offered more than a single silver piece for the ring.

The young man brought it back.

'Now,' said Dhun-Nun, 'take this ring to a real jeweller and see what he will pay.'

The jeweller offered a thousand gold coins for the gem.

The youth was amazed.

'Now,' said Dhun-Nun, 'your knowledge of the Sufis is as great as the knowledge of the stallholders is of jewellery. If you wish to value gems, become a jeweller.'

Whoever listens to something which is obscene is an accomplice of whoever speaks obscenely.

El-Shafai

Bayazid Bistami

Bayazid encountered a dog and started to pull his robe away from it, so that it should not defile him.

The dog, in a human voice, said:

'If I had been dry, there would have been no purpose in avoiding me. If I had been wet, you could have washed your robe. But the hate which you have towards me can never be cleansed.'

Bayazid said:

'O enlightened dog, come and stay with me for a while.'

The dog answered:

'That is impossible, because the world uses me as an epithet, and you are regarded by the world as a paragon.'

Bayazid exclaimed:

'Alas! I am not fit to live with one whom the whole world regards as inferior: how can I therefore approach the Truth which all regard as the Highest of all?'

Upon being asked: 'What is being a Sufi?' Bayazid said:

'Giving up comforts and trying to carry out efforts. That is the practice of the Sufi.'

The Idol

Someone told Uwais El-Qarni that a certain dervish sat on a tomb, dressed in a shroud and weeping.

Qarni said:

'Tell him that the method has become an idol; he must transcend the practice, for it is an obstacle.'

Money

Uwais El-Qarni was offered some money. He said:

'I do not need it as I already have a coin.'

The other said:

'How long will that last you? – it is nothing.'

Uwais answered:

'Guarantee me that I shall live longer than this sum will suffice me, and I will accept your gift.'

Do not regret the past and do not worry about the future.

Dhun-Nun

A learned man who has many friends may be a fraud, because if he were to tell them the truth, they would no longer be his friends.

Sufian Thauri

Junaid used to speak to an audience of about ten people. He always stopped talking when the number rose very much above this, and his audiences were never composed of more than twenty people.

When we speak, we are careful not to make a mistake in grammar. When, however, we act, we make mistakes and do not reach what should be our aim.

Ibrahim Ibn-Adam

The Delightful Village

They say: 'This village is delightful.'
But more delightful still is the heart of the man who can say:
'I am not delighted by delightful villages.'

Yahya Razi

The Essentials, Conduct and Occasion

Sufism is conduct. To each time its conduct. To each station its conduct. To each state its conduct.

Whoever follows the behaviour of each occasion arrives at the aim of man.

Whoever does not observe the rules of conduct is far from the mentality of Nearness.

Abu-Hafs

The Complete Man

The camel-driver has his plans; and the camel has his own plans.
   The organized mind can think well.
   The Complete Man's mind can exist well.

Rasul Shah

The candle is not there to illuminate itself.

Nawab Jan-Fishan Khan

It is a big claim, to call oneself a Sufi. Remember, anyway, that I do not call myself one.

Hadrat Abul-Hasan Khirqani

When you have not studied the Celestial Science,
While you have not put foot inside a 'Tavern',
Since you do not know your own profit and loss;
How will you attain the Friends? – on, on! On, on!

Baba Tahir Uryan

Travel – With and Without a Vehicle

If you cast yourself into the sea, without any guidance, this is full of danger, because man mistakes things which arise within himself for things arising from elsewhere.
   If, on the other hand, you travel on the sea in a ship, this is perilous, because there is the danger of attachment to the vehicle.
   In the one case, the end is not known, and there is no guidance.
   In the other case, the means becomes an end, and there is no arriving.

Niffari

A dervish master said: 'When you hear a man say: "It has been said," know that he is really saying: "Listen to what *I* am saying."'

Bishr-Al-Hafi

Observe that the things which are considered to be right today are those which were considered to be impossible yesterday. The things which are thought wrong today are those which will be esteemed right tomorrow.

Hudhaifa

Mistakes are often delightful to the minds of those who follow them.

Ibn Abbas

When asked why he did not correct the prayer of another man, Maruf Karkhi said:
'A dervish is free to instruct only after he has completed his own service.'

Assuredly, some forms of what is called knowledge are in reality ignorance, and some forms of what is thought to be eloquence are in reality incoherence.

The Prophet

Ali indicated his heart, and said:
'I have here a sufficiency of knowledge, but I cannot find anyone to whom to entrust it. There are plenty of people, but they too quickly become uncertain or sceptical. How I yearn for the really learned!'

If I am mistaken: it does not matter much to your future.
But if I am right: it is all-important to your future.

The Caliph Ali

Those Who Worship the Externals

If the Muslim knew what an idol was,
He would know that there is religion in idolatry.
If the idolater knew what religion was,
He would know where he had gone astray.
He sees in the idol nothing but the obvious creature:
This is why he is, in Islamic Law, a heathen.

Shabistari

Worship

Mankind passes through three stages.

First he worships anything: man, woman, money, children, earth and stones.

Then, when he has progressed a little further, he worships God.

Finally he does not say: 'I worship God'; nor: 'I do not worship God.'

He has passed from the first two stages into the last.

Rumi

Asceticism

First there is knowledge. Then there is asceticism. Then there is the knowledge that comes after asceticism.

The ultimate 'knower' is worth a hundred thousand ascetics.

Rumi

The Beloved

One went to the door of the Beloved and knocked. A voice asked: 'Who is there?'

He answered: 'It is I.'

207

The voice said: 'There is no room here for me and thee.'
The door was shut.

After a year of solitude and deprivation this man returned to
the door of the Beloved. He knocked.

A voice from within asked: 'Who is there?'

The man said: 'It is Thou.'

The door was opened for him.

Rumi

Emptiness

Everyone in the ordinary world is asleep. Their religion – the
religion of the familiar world – is emptiness, not religion at all.

Sanai, *Hadiqa*

Hunger

People sated with themselves are so because of their hunger for
something else. They are therefore hungry. Those who turn
back from wrongdoing, they are the ones who are at prayer; not
those who merely seem to bend in prayer. Prayer is an activity.

Sanai, *Hadiqa*

The Being of God

No human mind can attain an understanding of the form of
being which is called God.

Sanai, *Hadiqa*

Praying for Oneself

Sa'ad son of Wakas was a companion of the Prophet. In his
last years he became blind and settled in Mecca, where he was
always surrounded by people seeking his blessing. He did not
bless everyone, but those whom he did always found their way
smoothed for them.

Abdallah Ibn-Sa'ad reports:

'I went to see him, and he was good to me and gave me his blessing. As I was only a curious child, I asked him: "Your prayers for others always seem to be answered. Why, then, do you not pray for your blindness to be removed?"

'The ancient replied: "Submission to the Will of God is far better than the personal pleasure of being able to see."'

Sentimentality

Once, when Bishr was a Sufi disciple still dependent entirely upon the comfort of men, he was on the Island of Abadan. There he came across a most unfortunate man. He was suffering from leprosy, was blind, and lay on the ground with nobody near him.

Bishr went to him and raised his head on his knees, speaking some words of reassurance and humanity, feeling sorrow and compassion.

The leper then spoke out, saying: 'What stranger comes here, to stand between me and my Lord? With or without my body, I have my love for Him.'

Bishr recounts that this lesson had remained with him throughout his days.

Mashghul says: 'This story can only be understood by those who realize how the leper was preventing Bishr from indulging his own sentimentality and ruining himself, through being turned into what humanity calls a "good man". "Good" is what you do voluntarily, and not in furtherance of an appetite for indulgence taught by others in the name of humanity.'

Bishr Ibn El-Harith

The Patched Robe

There was a Jew of Damascus who was reading a holy book one day when he came across the name of the Prophet written in it.

Not liking this, he removed the name. But the next day he

found it there again. Again he took out the name; but on the third day it had appeared again.

He thought:

'Perhaps this is a sign that a true Emissary has come. I will journey southwards to Medina.'

And he forthwith started out, not tarrying until he reached the city of the Prophet.

When he arrived there, knowing nobody, he was near the Mosque of the Prophet when the Companion Anas arrived. He said to Anas:

'Friend, take me to the Prophet.'

Anas led him into the mosque, which was full of people in anguish. Abu-Bakr the Successor was sitting there at the head of the assembly. The old man went up to him, thinking he must be Mohammed, and said:

'O Chosen Envoy of God, a strayed old man has come to offer you peace.'

Hearing the title of the Prophet used, everyone present burst into a flood of tears. The stranger was uncertain as to what to do. He said:

'I am a foreigner and a Jew, and I am unaware of the rites of the Faith of Submission to the Will of Allah. Have I said something untoward? Should I have remained silent? Or is this a ritual observance? Why do you cry? If it is a ceremony, I have never heard of it.'

Omar the Companion said to him:

'We do not weep because of anything which you have done. But you must hear, unfortunate one, that it is but a week since the Prophet left the earth. When we heard his name, grief took possession of our hearts anew.'

As soon as he heard this, the ancient tore his clothes in anguish. When he had recovered a little, he said:

'Do me one favour. Let me have at least a robe of the Prophet. If I cannot see him, at least let me have this.'

Omar answered: 'Only the Lady Zohra could give us one of his robes.'

Ali said: 'But she will not allow anyone to go near her.' But they went to her door and knocked, and explained what they wanted.

The Lady Zohra answered:

'Verily, the Prophet spoke truly when he said, shortly before he died:

'"A wayfarer, who has love towards me and who is a good man, will come to the house. He will not see me. Give him, therefore, this patchwork robe as if from me, and for me treat him gently, offering salutations."'

The Jew put the robe on himself and professing Islam, asked to be taken to the Prophet's grave. It was at this tomb that he breathed his last.

Attar: *Ilahi-Nama*

Prayer of Saadi

Do to me what is worthy of Thee,
And not what is worthy of me.

Saadi: *Gulistan*

Seeing

Halls and theological colleges and learned lectures, circles and cloisters —
What use are they when there is no knowledge and there is no eye that sees?

Hafiz

The Aspect of the Dervish

The form of the objective sought by kings in prayer —
Is the appearance in the mirror of the aspect of the dervish.

Hafiz

Part Five

TEACHING–STORIES

TEACHING–STORIES

Teaching-stories are told in public and form a part of the outer activity of dervishes. They are intended to lay a basis of knowledge about Sufism and its characteristic methods of thought. They are seldom employed for didactic purposes.

The 'inner dimensions' of teaching stories, however, are held to make them capable of revealing, according to the stage of development of the student, more and more planes of significance.

It is this theory that 'one may work on different layers of the same material' which is unfamiliar to many people, who tend to prefer being told that a story has one message or one use only.

The Generous Man

There was a rich and generous man of Bokhara. Because he had a high rank in the invisible hierarchy, he was known as the President of the World. He made one condition about his bounty. Every day he gave gold to one category of people – the sick, widows, and so on. But nothing was to be given to anyone who opened his mouth.

Not all could keep silent.

One day it was the turn of lawyers to receive their share of the bounty. One of them could not restrain himself and made the most complete appeal possible.

Nothing was given to him.

This was not the end, however, of his efforts. The following day, invalids were being helped, so he pretended that his limbs had been broken.

But the President knew him, and he obtained nothing.

The very next day he posed in another guise, covering his face, with the people of another category. He was again recognized and sent away.

Again and again he tried, even disguising himself as a woman; again without result.

Finally this lawyer found an undertaker and told him to wrap him in a shroud. 'When the President passes by he will perhaps assume that this is a corpse. He may throw down some money towards my burial – and I will give you a share of it.'

This was done. A gold piece from the hand of the President fell upon the shroud. The lawyer seized it, out of fear that the undertaker would get it first. Then he spoke to the benefactor: 'You denied me your bounty. Note how I have gained it!'

'Nothing can you have from me,' replied the generous man, 'until you die. This is the meaning of the cryptic phrase: "Man must die before he dies." The gift comes after "death" and not before. And this "death", even, is not possible without help.'

Destruction of a Town

A Sufi once exclaimed, in an unguarded moment: 'I shall be the cause of the destruction of this town.'

Fortunately people thought he was mad, or just trying to frighten people. They did not harm him. But on the other hand they did not take any interest in what he was saying. He was, after all, frail and a man of no outward consequence.

One day the Sufi had climbed a tree when he fell. His body broke the wall of a reservoir below. The flood which resulted destroyed the town.

Only after the accident, when his body was found, were his words remembered.

The Magic Horse

A king had two sons. The first helped the people by working for them in a manner they understood. The second was called 'Lazy' because he was a dreamer, as far as anyone could see.

The first son gained great honours in his land. The second obtained from a humble carpenter a wooden horse and sat astride it. But the horse was a magical one. It carried the rider, if he was sincere, to his heart's desire.

Seeking his heart's desire, the young prince disappeared one day on the horse. He was absent a long time. After many adventures he returned with a beautiful princess from the Country of Light, and his father was overjoyed at his safe return and listened to the story of the magic horse.

The horse was made available to anyone who wanted it in that country. But many people preferred the obvious benefits which the actions of the first prince provided for them because to them the horse always looked like a plaything. They did not get beyond the outer appearance of the horse, which was not impressive – just like a plaything.

When the old king died, the 'prince who liked to play with toys' became, by his wish, the king. But people in general despised him. They much preferred the excitement and interest of the discoveries and activities of the practical prince.

Unless we listen to the 'lazy' prince, whether he has a princess from the Country of Light with him or not, we shall not get beyond the outer appearance of the horse. Even if we like the horse, it is not its outward shape which can help us travel to our destination.

The Cradle

A child was born, and the father went to a carpenter and asked him to make a cradle for it.

The carpenter told him to come back in a week to collect it.

When he returned it was not finished.

The man went back week after week, and still the cradle was not to be seen.

Eventually the child grew into a man. In his turn he married and his wife bore him a child.

His own father said to him: 'Go to see the carpenter and ask him whether your cradle is ready yet.'

So the young man went to the carpenter's shop and reminded him about the cradle.

'Here is an opportunity,' he said, 'for you to finish the job. I now have a small son, and the cradle will be ideal for him.'

'Be off with you!' said the carpenter: 'I refuse to be stampeded in my work just because you and your family are obsessed by what they want!'

The Three Deaf Men and the Dumb Dervish

Once upon a time there lived a poor goatherd.

Every day he took some goats to a hill overlooking the village where he lived with his family, to seek fresh grazing. He was deaf, but this did not matter to him at all. One day he found that his wife had forgotten to give him the bundle containing his midday meal; nor did she send their child with it, as in the past when it had been forgotten, even when the sun was high overhead.

'I will go home and get it,' thought the goatherd; 'I cannot stay out here all this time until sundown without a bite to eat.' Suddenly he noticed a man cutting shrubs on the hillside. He went up to him and said: 'Brother, please keep an eye on the goats and see that they do not stray, for my wife has stupidly forgotten my midday meal, and I must go back to the village for it.' Now the shrub-cutter was also deaf, and he heard not one word of what had been said, and completely misunderstood the goatherd.

He answered: 'Why should I give you any of the shrubs which I am cutting for my own animals? I have a cow and two sheep at home and I have to go far and wide for food for them.

No, leave me, I want nothing to do with the likes of you, seeking to take what little belongs to me.'

And he waved his hand in derision, laughing harshly. The goatherd did not hear what was said, and replied: 'Oh, thank you, kind friend, for agreeing; I shall be as quick as I can. Blessings be upon you, you have set my mind at ease.' He ran off to the village, and went to his own humble hut. There he found his wife sick with a fever, with the neighbour's wife in attendance. He took his food bundle and ran back to the hill. He counted the goats carefully, and they were all there.

The shrub-cutter was still busy at his task, and the goatherd said to himself: 'Why, what an excellent person this most trustworthy shrub-cutter is! He has seen that my animals have not strayed, and seeks no thanks for this service! I will give him this lame goat which I meant to kill anyway. It will make a fine meal for him and his family tonight.' So, putting the undersized lame goat upon his shoulders, he bounded down the hill, calling as he ran: 'Ho, brother, here is a present for looking after my goats while I was away. My unfortunate wife has a fever, and that explains everything. Roast this goat for your evening meal tonight; see, it has a lame leg and I meant to kill it anyway!'

But the other did not hear his words and shouted in a rage: 'Vile goatherd, I never saw what happened while you were gone, how can I be responsible for the leg of your infernal animal! I was busy cutting these shrubs, and have no idea how it happened! Be off with you, or I shall strike you.'

The goatherd was amazed at the man's enraged gestures, but he could not hear what he was saying, so he called to a passer-by who was riding a fine horse: 'Noble sir, please, I beg you, tell me what this shrub-cutter is talking about. I happen to be deaf, and do not know why he has refused my gift of a goat with such annoyance!'

Both the goatherd and the shrub-cutter began to shout at the traveller, and he got off his horse and came towards them. Now, he was a horse-thief, and as deaf as a post, and he could not hear what they were saying. He was lost, and had meant to ask them where he was. But when he saw the threatening gestures of the two other men he said: 'Yes, brothers, I stole the horse, I confess, but I did not know that it belonged to you. Forgive me, I pray, for I had a fleeting moment of temptation and acted without thinking!'

'I had nothing to do with the laming of the goat!' shouted the shrub-cutter.

'Get him to tell me why he will not accept my present,' urged the goatherd. 'I merely wanted to give it as a gesture of appreciation!'

'I certainly admit to taking the horse,' said the thief, 'but I am deaf, and I cannot hear which of you owns it.'

At that moment an aged dervish came into view, walking along the dusty road towards the village. The shrub-cutter ran to him and, pulling at his robe, said:

'Venerable dervish, I am a deaf man who cannot make head or tail of what these other two are saying. Will you please, in your wisdom, judge and explain what each of them is shouting about.'

The dervish, however, was dumb, and could not answer, but he came to them and looked searchingly into the faces of the three deaf ones, who had now stopped talking.

He looked so long and penetratingly, first at one, then at the other, that they began to feel uncomfortable.

His glittering black eyes bored into theirs, seeking the truth of the matter, trying to get a clue to the situation. But each of the others began to fear that he was going to bewitch them, or gain control over their wills in some way. And suddenly the thief sprang upon the horse, and rode it furiously away. Immediately the goatherd began to round up his animals, driving them farther up the hill. The shrub-cutter, lowering his eyes from those of the dervish, packed his shrubs into a net and hoisted it on to his shoulders, bounding down the hill towards his home.

The dervish continued his journey, thinking to himself that speech can be such a useless form of communication that man might just as well have never been given it.

My Lady Fatima and the Animals

There once was a small girl who grew up with her parents, all alone in a forest. One day she found that her father and mother were dead and she would have to fend for herself. Her parents had left behind a Mihrab, a strange carved ornament like a window-frame, which they kept hung on a wall of their hut.

'Since I am now alone,' said Fatima, 'and shall have to survive in this forest where the living things are only animals, it would be best if I could talk to them and understand their speech.'

So she spent a good part of her day addressing this aspiration to the frame on the wall: 'Mihrab, give me the power to understand animals and to speak with them.'

After a long time she suddenly had the impression that she would be able to communicate with birds, animals, even fish. So she went into the woods to try.

Soon she came to a pool. On the top of the pool was a pond-fly, which skipped about on the surface and never entered the water. Swimming in the water were several fish, and stuck to the bottom of the pond were some snails.

Fatima said, in order to start a conversation: 'Fly, why do you not enter the water?'

'Why should I, supposing that that were possible, which it is not?' asked the fly.

'Because you would be safe from the birds, which swoop down and eat you.'

'I haven't been eaten yet, have I?' said the fly.

And that was the end of the conversation.

Then Fatima spoke to the fish. 'Fish,' she said to it through the water, 'why do you not find out how to get out of the water, little by little? I have heard that some fish can do this.'

'Absolutely impossible,' said the fish; 'nobody has done that and survived. We are brought up to believe that it is both a sin and a mortal danger.' And he turned his back and dived into the shadows, unwilling to hear such nonsense.

So she called down to the snail: 'Snail, you could crawl out of the water and find nice herbs to eat. I have heard that snails can really do that.'

'A question is best answered by a question when a wise snail hears it,' said the snail. 'Perhaps you would be kind enough to tell me exactly why you have so much interest in *my* welfare? People should look after themselves.'

'Well,' said Fatima, 'I suppose it is because when a person can see more about another person, he wants to help him to attain greater heights.'

'That seems a strange idea to me,' said the snail, and crawled out of earshot under a rock.

Fatima gave up the fly, the fish and the snail, and wandered on into the forest, looking for something else to talk to. She felt that she must be able to be of use to someone. After all, she had much more knowledge than these forest-folk. A bird, she thought, for example, could be warned to store food for the winter, or to nest near the warmth of a hut, so that it would not die unnecessarily. But she did not see a bird.

Instead, she came across the hut of a charcoal-burner. He was an old man, and he sat in front of his door, burning charcoal to take to the market.

Fatima, delighted at seeing another human being, the only one other than her parents whom she had met, ran up to him. She told him her experiences of that day.

'Do not worry about that, child,' said the kindly old man; 'there are things which a human being has to learn, and those things are of vital importance to his future.'

'Things to learn?' said Fatima, 'And what should *I* want with things to learn, pray? They would only, most probably, change my way of life and thinking.' And, like the fly, the fish and the snail, she moved away out of contact with the charcoal-burner.

Fatima, daughter of Walia, spent another thirty years like the fly, the fish and the snail before she learned anything at all.

Moses and the Shepherd

This explanation of a notable passage in Rumi's *Mathnavi* was given by Khwaja Fida'i of Kars, in his *Meditations on the Couplets of Our Master Jalaludin Rumi*.

It draws attention to the different levels of human understanding, emphasizing that a man can be reached only through the ranges of association which he can conceive.

A part of the duty of every Sufi teacher, however, is to prepare his students for perception of the higher 'parallelism'. It is therefore considered to be most incorrect to emphasize the material advantages of Sufism alone in entirely conventional terms. Sufism, therefore, is not presented by teachers as a therapy or a cure for the worldly ills of man.

No man can understand more than his whole mind is capable of understanding; and for this reason it has been truly said: 'Speak to every man according to his understanding.'* As each man can perceive, so will he benefit. If a man or woman is capable only of low perceptions, he or she will seek and gain satisfaction through them.

It is related that Moses called a humble shepherd a blasphemer, because he heard the poor man offering to comb God's hair, wash His robe and kiss His hand.

God admonished Moses, indirectly teaching him, from this experience, on this occasion, that the shepherd had not the intelligence or the experience to realize that Moses was talking about an incorporeal deity. 'Thus hast thou driven away a worshipper from the nearest to Me that he could approach. There is a gradation in all men: each will perceive what he can perceive and at the stage at which he can perceive it.'

The Cap of Invisibility

In the land which is unseen to us, but in reality more real than the real, there lived a boy, and his name was Kasjan. His elder

*By tradition ascribed to Mohammed.

brother, Jankas, was hard-working and intelligent. But he, Kasjan was neither hard-working nor idle. He was neither intelligent nor stupid, but he used to apply himself to any problem he could, as well as he could.

The two brothers, neither of whom seemed to be making great progress in the Unseen Land, decided to seek their fortunes together. They walked away from their home one afternoon, and it was not long before darkness separated them, and – as for Jankas we shall hear presently. Kasjan came suddenly upon a quarrel. Three men were arguing, it seemed, about three items lying on the ground. They explained to him the trouble. Their father had died and left them a conical hat, the Kulah of Invisibility, a flying carpet, and a staff which made the carpet fly when it was beaten with it. Each one wanted all the items, or at least first choice of them. Their reasons were that they were the eldest, the middle and the youngest sons, and each on this account claimed priority.

'They are all unworthy,' thought Kasjan, but he offered to adjudicate between them. He told them all to withdraw forty paces and then turn round. Before they could finish his instructions he had placed the Kulah on his head, got on to the carpet and struck it with the stick. 'Carpet,' he commanded, 'take me to wherever my brother Jankas may be.'

Now not long before, his brother Jankas had been snatched up by a mighty Anqa bird, which had deposited him on the minaret of a mosque in Khorasan. Because Kasjan was thinking at the time, however, that Jankas must have made himself a prince at least, the carpet heard this thought and – flying with immense speed – came lightly to rest on the battlements of the king's palace of the city of Balkh in Khorasan.

The king, who had seen him alight, came out at once, saying: 'Perhaps this is the youth who it is foretold will help my daughter and yet not desire her.'

Kasjan saluted the king, and told him that he was seeking his brother Jankas. 'Before you do that,' said the king, 'I want you to help me with your special equipment and keen mind.' The princess, it transpired, used to disappear every night and return in the morning, nobody knew how. This had been fore-told and had come to pass. Kasjan agreed to help, and sugges-ted that he should watch by her bedside.

That night, through half-closed eyes, he saw the princess look to see whether he was asleep. Then she took up a needle and stuck it in his foot, but he did not move, because he was expect-ing some such thing. 'I am ready,' said the princess, and all at once a terrible spirit appeared and took her on his shoulders, and they soared together through the ceiling, without making any impression on it.

Rubbing his eyes, Kasjan immediately placed the Kulah of Invisibility on his head, sat on the magic carpet and, beating it with the stick, cried: 'Take me where the princess has gone.'

There was a rushing and a roaring, and Kasjan found him-self in the Unseen Land beyond the Unseen Land. There was the princess accompanied by the spirit. They walked through forests of trees of precious stones. Kasjan broke off a piece of jade tree with diamond fruits. Then they walked through a garden of unknown plants of unexcelled beauty. Kasjan put a few of the seeds in his pocket. Finally they stood by a lake whose reeds were shimmering swords. 'These are the swords which can kill spirits such as me,' said the spirit to the princess; 'but only a man called Kasjan can do it, so it has been fore-told.'

As soon as he heard these words, Kasjan stepped forward, seized one of the swords from the reed bed, and cut off the awful head of the spirit. He seized the princess and dragged her on to the carpet. Soon they were speeding back to the palace of the king of Balkh in Khorasan.

Kasjan took the princess at once before the king, waking him unceremoniously from his slumber. 'Your Majesty,' he said, 'here is your daughter, and I have released her from the grasp of a demon in such-and-such a manner.' And he related all that had befallen them, producing the pieces of jewel and seeds as proof. Released at last, the princess offered to marry Kasjan. But Kasjan, asking for a few moments' leave, flew on his magic carpet to find his brother Jankas.

Jankas was sleeping in a caravanserai, because he had only been able to obtain employment as a teacher in a seminary, and the pay was very low. When they returned to the court, the princess was immediately smitten by the manly features of Jankas, and she decided that she wanted to marry him instead of Kasjan.

'That is exactly what I was about to suggest,' said Kasjan and the king together. They lived happily ever after; for the kingdom was handed over to Jankas and his bride, while the king of Balkh and Kasjan together transferred themselves on the magic carpet to the Unseen Land beyond the Unseen Land, which now became their joint kingdom.

The King and the Wolf

A certain king decided to tame a wolf and make it a pet. This desire of his was based on ignorance and the need to be approved or admired by others – a common cause of much trouble in the world.

He caused a cub to be taken from its mother as soon as it was born and to be brought up among tame dogs.

When the wolf was fully grown it was brought to the king and for many days it behaved exactly like a dog. People who saw this astonishing sight marvelled and thought the king to be a wonder.

They acted in accordance with this belief, making the king their adviser in all things, and attributing great powers to him.

The king himself believed that a near-miracle had occurred.

One day, when he was out hunting, the king heard a wolf-pack coming near. As they approached, the tame wolf jumped up, bared his fangs, and ran to welcome them. Within a minute he was away, restored to his natural companions.

This is the origin of the proverb: 'A wolf-cub will always become a wolf, even if it is reared among the sons of man.'

The Water-Melon Hunter

Once upon a time there was a man who strayed, from his own country, into the world known as the Land of Fools.

He soon saw a number of people flying in terror from a field where they had been trying to reap wheat. 'There is a monster in that field,' they told him. He looked, and saw that it was a water-melon.

He offered to kill the 'monster' for them. When he had cut the melon from its stalk, he took a slice and began to eat it. The people became even more terrified of him than they had been of the melon. They drove him away with pitchforks, crying: 'He will kill us next, unless we get rid of him.'

It so happened that at another time another man also strayed into the Land of Fools, and the same thing started to happen to him. But, instead of offering to help them with the 'monster', he agreed with them that it must be dangerous, and by tiptoeing away from it with them he gained their confidence. He spent a long time with them in their houses until he could teach them, little by little, the basic facts which would enable them not only to lose their fear of melons, but even to cultivate them themselves.

His Excellency

By a series of misunderstandings and coincidences, Mulla Nasrudin found himself one day in the audience-hall of the Emperor of Persia.

The Shahinshah was surrounded by self-seeking nobles, governors of provinces, courtiers and sycophants of all kinds. Each was pressing his own claim to be appointed head of the embassy which was soon to set out for India.

The emperor's patience was at an end, and he raised his head from the importunate mass, mentally invoking the aid of Heaven in his problem as to who to choose. His eyes lighted upon Mulla Nasrudin.

'This man is to be the ambassador,' he announced; 'so now leave me in peace.'

Nasrudin was given rich clothes, and an enormous chest of rubies, diamonds, emeralds and priceless works of art was entrusted to him, the gift of the Shahinshah to the Great Mogul.

The courtiers, however, were not finished. United for once by this affront to their claims, they decided to encompass the downfall of the mulla. First they broke into his quarters and stole the jewels, which they divided among themselves, replacing them with earth to make up the weight. Then they called upon Nasrudin, determined to ruin his embassy, to get him into trouble, and in the process to discredit their master as well.

'Congratulations, great Nasrudin,' they said. 'What the Fountain of Wisdom, Peacock of the World, has ordered must be the essence of all wisdom. We therefore hail you. But there are just a couple of points upon which we may be able to advise you, accustomed as we are to the behaviour of diplomatic emissaries.'

'I should be obliged if you would tell me,' said Nasrudin.

'Very well,' said the chief of the intriguers. 'The first thing is that you must be humble. In order to prove how modest you are, therefore, you should not show any sign of self-importance. When you reach India you must enter as many mosques as you can, and make collections for yourself. The second thing is that you must observe court etiquette in the country to which you are accredited. This will mean that you will refer to the Great Mogul as "the Full Moon".'

'But is that not a title of the Persian emperor?'

'Not in India.'

So Nasrudin set out. The Persian emperor told him as they took leave : 'Be careful, Nasrudin. Adhere to etiquette, for the Mogul is a mighty emperor and we must impress him while not affronting him in any way.'

'I am well prepared, Majesty,' said Nasrudin.

As soon as he entered the territory of India, Nasrudin went into a mosque and mounted the pulpit : 'O people!' he cried, 'see in me the representative of the Shadow of Allah upon Earth! The Axis of the Globe! Bring out your money, for I am making a collection.'

This he repeated in every mosque he could find, all the way from Baluchistan to Imperial Delhi.

He collected a great deal of money. 'Do with it,' the counsellors had said, 'what you will. For it is the product of intuitive growth and bestowal, and as such its use will create its own demand.' All that they wanted to happen was for the mulla to be exposed to ridicule for collecting money in this 'shameless' manner. 'The holy must live from their holiness,' roared Nasrudin at mosque after mosque. 'I give no account nor do I expect any. To you, money is something to be hoarded, after being sought. You can exchange it for material things. To me, it is part of a mechanism. I am the representative of a natural force of intuitive growth, bestowal and disbursement.'

Now, as we all know, good often proceeds from apparent evil, and the reverse. Those who thought that Nasrudin was lining his own pockets did not contribute. For some reason, their affairs did not prosper. Those who were considered credulous and gave their money became in a mysterious way enriched. But to return to our story.

Sitting on the Peacock Throne the emperor at Delhi studied the reports which courtiers were daily bringing him, describing the progress of the Persian ambassador. At first he could make no sense out of them. Then he called his council together.

'Gentlemen,' he said, 'this Nasrudin must indeed be a saint or a divinely guided one. Who ever heard of anyone else violating the principle that one does not seek money without a plausible reason, lest a wrong interpretation be placed upon one's motives?'

'May your shadow never grow less,' they replied, 'O infinite extension of all-Wisdom; we agree. If there are men like this in Persia, we must beware, for their moral ascendancy over our materialistic outlook is plain.'

Then a runner arrived from Persia, with a secret letter in which the Mogul's spies at the imperial court reported:

'Mulla Nasrudin is a man of no consequence in Persia. He was chosen absolutely at random to be ambassador. We cannot fathom the reason for the Shahinshah's not being more select-ive.'

The Mogul called his council together. 'Incomparable Birds of Paradise!' he told them, 'a thought has manifested itself in me. The Persian emperor has chosen a man at random to represent his whole nation. This may mean that he is so confi-dent of the consistent quality of his people that, for him *anyone at all is qualified to undertake the delicate task of ambassador to the sublime court of Delhi!* This indicates the degree of perfection attained, the amazingly infallible intuitive powers cultivated among them. We must reconsider our desire to invade Persia; for such a people could easily engulf our arms. Their society is organized on a different basis from our own.'

'You are right – Superlative Warrior on the Frontiers!' cried the Indian nobles.

At length, Nasrudin arrived in Delhi. He was riding his old donkey, and was followed by his escort, weighed down by the sacks of money which he had collected in the mosques. The treasure-chest was mounted on an elephant, such was its size and weight.

Nasrudin was met by the master of ceremonies at the gate of Delhi. The emperor was seated with his nobles in an immense courtyard, the Reception Hall of the Ambassadors. This had been so arranged that the entrance was low. As a consequence, ambassadors were always obliged to dismount from their horses and enter the Supreme Presence on foot, giving the impression of supplicants. Only an equal could ride into the presence of an emperor.

No ambassador had ever arrived astride a donkey, however, and thus there was nothing to stop Nasrudin trotting straight through the door, and up to the Imperial Dais.

The Indian king and his courtiers exchanged meaningful glances at this act.

Nasrudin blithely dismounted, addressed the king as 'The Full Moon,' and called for his treasure-chest to be brought.

When it was opened, and the earth revealed, there was a moment of consternation.

'I had better say nothing,' thought Nasrudin, 'for there is nothing to say which could mitigate this.' So he remained silent.

The Mogul whispered to his vizier, 'What does this mean? Is this an insult to the Highest Eminence?'

Incapable of believing this, the vizier thought furiously. Then he provided the interpretation.

'It is a symbolic act, Presence,' he murmured. 'The ambassador means that he acknowledges *you* as the Master of the Earth. Did he not call you the Full Moon?'

The Mogul relaxed. 'We are content with the offering of the Persian Shahinshah; for we have no need of wealth; and we appreciate the metaphysical subtlety of the message.'

'I have been told to say,' said Nasrudin, remembering the 'essential gift-offering phrase' given him by the intriguers in Persia, 'that this is all we have for your Majesty.'

'That means that Persia will not yield one further ounce of her soil to us,' whispered the interpreter of omens to the king.

'Tell your master that we understand,' smiled the Mogul. 'But there is one other point: If I am the Full Moon – what is the Persian emperor?'

'He is the New Moon,' said Nasrudin, automatically.

'The Full Moon is more mature and gives more light than the New Moon, which is its junior,' whispered the court astrologer to the Mogul.

'We are content,' said the delighted Indian. 'You may return to Persia and tell the New Moon that the Full Moon salutes him.'

The Persian spies at the court of Delhi immediately sent a complete account of this interchange to the Shahinshah. They added that it was known that the Mogul emperor had been impressed, and feared to plan war against the Persians because of the activities of Nasrudin.

When he returned home, the Shahinshah received the mulla in full audience. 'I am more than pleased, friend Nasrudin,' he said, 'at the results of your unorthodox methods. Our country is saved, and this means that there will be no attempt at accounting for the jewels or the collecting in mosques. You are henceforth to be known by the special title of *Safir* – Emissary.'

'But, your Majesty,' hissed his vizier, 'this man is guilty of high treason, if not more! We have perfect evidence that he applied one of your titles to the emperor of India, thus changing his allegiance and bringing one of your magnificent attributes into disrepute.'

'Yes,' thundered the Shahinshah, 'the sages have said wisely that "to every perfection there is an imperfection." Nasrudin! Why did you call me the New Moon?'

'I don't know about protocol,' said Nasrudin; 'but I do know that the Full Moon is about to wane, and the New Moon is still growing, with its greatest glories ahead of it.'

The emperor's mood changed. 'Seize Anwar, the Grand Vizier,' he roared. 'Mulla! I offer you the position of Grand Vizier!'

'What?' said Nasrudin. 'Could I accept after seeing with my own eyes what happened to my predecessor?'

And what happened to the jewels and treasures which the evil courtiers had usurped from the treasure-chest? That is another story. As the incomparable Nasrudin said: 'Only children and the stupid seek cause-and-effect in the same story.'

Do More Than Laugh at Fools

Once upon a time there was a fool who was sent to buy flour and salt. He took a dish to carry his purchases.

'Make sure,' said the man who sent him, 'not to mix the two things – I want them separate.'

When the shopkeeper had filled the dish with flour and was measuring out the salt, the fool said: 'Do not mix it with the flour; here, I will show you where to put it.'

And he inverted the dish, to provide, from its upturned bottom, a surface upon which the salt could be laid.

The flour, of course, fell on to the floor.

But the salt was safe.

When the fool got back to the man who had sent him he said: 'Here is the salt.'

'Very well,' said the other man, 'but where is the flour?'

'It should be here,' said the fool, turning the dish over.

As soon as he did that, the salt fell to the ground, and the flour of course was seen to be gone.

So it is with human beings. Doing one thing which they think to be right, they may undo another which is equally right. When this happens with thoughts instead of actions, man himself is lost, no matter how, upon reflection, he regards his thinking to have been logical.

You have laughed at the joke of the fool. Now, will you do more, and think about your own thoughts as if they were the salt and the flour?

The Happiest Man in the World

A man who was living in comfortable enough circumstances went one day to see a certain sage, reputed to have all knowledge. He said to him:

'Great Sage, I have no material problems, and yet I am always unsettled. For years I have tried to be happy, to find an answer to my inner thoughts, to come to terms with the world. Please advise me as to how I can be cured of this malaise.'

The sage answered:

'My friend, what is hidden to some is apparent to others. Again, what is apparent to some is hidden to others. I have the answer to your ailment, though it is no ordinary medication. You must set out on your travels, seeking the happiest man in the world. As soon as you find him, you must ask him for his shirt, and put it on.'

This seeker thereupon restlessly started looking for happy men. One after another he found them and questioned them. Again and again they said: 'Yes, I am happy, but there is one happier than me.'

After travelling through one country after another for many, many days, he found the wood in which everyone said lived the happiest man in the world.

He heard the sound of laughter coming from among the trees, and quickened his step until he came upon a man sitting in a glade.

'Are you the happiest man in the world, as people say?' he asked.

'Certainly I am,' said the other man.

'My name is so-and-so, my condition is such-and-such, and my remedy, ordered by the greatest sage, is to wear your shirt. Please give it to me; I will give you anything I have in exchange.'

The happiest man looked at him closely, and he laughed. He laughed and he laughed and he laughed. When he had quietened down a little, the restless man, rather annoyed at this reaction, said:

'Are you unhinged, that you laugh at such a serious request?'

'Perhaps,' said the happiest man, 'but if you had only taken the trouble to look, you would have seen that I do not possess a shirt.'

'What, then am I to do now?'

'You will now be cured. Striving for something unattainable provides the exercise to achieve that which is needed: as when a man gathers all his strength to jump across a stream if it were far wider than it is. He gets across the stream.'

The happiest man in the world then took off the turban whose end had concealed his face. The restless man saw that he was none other than the great sage who had originally advised him.

'But why did you not tell me all this years ago, when I came to see you?' the restless man asked in puzzlement.

'Because you were not ready then to understand. You needed certain experiences, and they had to be given to you in a manner which would ensure that you went through them.'

The Sheep and the Purse

A man was walking along a road one day, followed by his sheep.

A thief went after him, cut the rope of the sheep, and took it away.

When he realized what had happened, the man ran all over the place looking for his animal. Presently he came to a well, where he saw a man apparently in despair.

Although the man did not know it, he was the very same thief.

He asked him what he was doing. The thief said:

'I have dropped a purse into this well. It contains five hundred silver coins. If you will jump in and get it back for me, I will give you a hundred silver pieces.'

The man thought: 'When one door shuts, a hundred may open. This chance is worth ten times the sheep which I have lost.'

He stripped himself and plunged into the well.

And the thief carried off his clothes.

Rumi

The Indian Bird

A merchant had a bird in a cage. He was going to India, the land from which the bird came, and asked him whether he could bring anything back for him. The bird asked for his freedom, but was refused. So he asked the merchant to visit a jungle in India and announce his captivity to the free birds who were there.

The merchant did so, and no sooner had he spoken than a wild bird, just like his own, fell senseless out of a tree on to the ground. The merchant thought that this must be a relative of his own bird, and felt sad that he should have caused this death.

When he got home, the bird asked him whether he had

brought good news from India. 'No,' said the merchant, 'I fear that my news is bad. One of your relations collapsed and fell at my feet as soon as I mentioned your captivity.'

As soon as these words were spoken the merchant's bird collapsed and fell to the bottom of the cage.

'The news of his kinsman's death has killed him too,' thought the merchant. Sorrowfully he picked up the bird and put it on the window-sill. At once the bird revived and flew to a near-by tree. 'Now you know,' he said, 'that what you thought was disaster was in fact good news for me. And how the message, the suggestion how to behave in order to free myself, was transmitted to me through you, my captor.' And he flew away, free at last.

Rumi

Part Six

THEMES FOR SOLITARY CONTEMPLATION

❧ I ❧
SOLITARY CONTEMPLATION THEMES

Solitary Contemplation Themes are chosen from great Sufis'
sayings and writings because they are held by Sufi teachers to
contain the materials which are best suited to individual study.
Their secondary use is in company, after they have been well
digested by the student.

To be a Sufi

Being a Sufi is to put away what is in your head – imagined
truth, preconceptions, conditioning – and to face what may
happen to you.

Abu Said

What Must Come

To those who seek truth in conventionalized religion:

> Until college and minaret have crumbled
> This holy work of ours will not be done.
> Until faith becomes rejection
> And rejection becomes belief
> There will be no true believer.

Abu Said

Worship

O Lord!
If I worship you from fear of hell, cast me into hell.
If I worship you from desire for paradise, deny me paradise.

Rabia

The Door

Salih of Qazwin taught his disciples:

'Whoever knocks at the door continually, it will be opened to him.'

Rabia, hearing him one day, said:

'How long will you say: "It will be opened"? The door has never been shut.'

Like Calls to Like

Hasan of Basra went to see Rabia. She was sitting in the midst of a number of animals.

As soon as Hasan approached, they ran away.

Hasan said:

'Why did they do that?'

Rabia answered:

'You have been eating meat. All I had to eat was dry bread.'

Fruit and Thistles

To an ass, a thistle is a delicious fruit.
The ass eats the thistle. It remains an ass.

Habib El-Ajami

When Avicenna Met Abu Said

When the philosopher and the Sufi met, Avicenna said:

'What I know, he sees.'

Abu Said remarked:

'What I see, he knows.'

The Sufi Call

Answer the Sufi Call, as best you are able, in this world, with a loving heart and honestly. Then you are truly safe in this world and in all the other worlds.

Salik Hamzavi

Bread

If you are entertaining a dervish, remember that dry bread is enough for him.

Harith Muhasibi

Benefit

Most of humanity do not know what it is in their interest to know. They dislike what would eventually benefit them.

Al-Nasafi

Point of View

To the sinful and vicious I am evil;
But to the good – beneficent am I.

Mirza Khan, *Ansari*

Teachers, Teachings, Taught

Teachers talk about teachings.
Real teachers study their pupils as well.
Most of all, teachers should be studied.

Musa Kazim

Service and Mastership

He who does not know about service knows even less about Mastership.

Tirmizi

Perception and Explanation

For him who has perception, a mere sign is enough.

For him who does not really heed, a thousand explanations are not enough.

Haji Bektash

To a Would-Be Dervish

My heart has become confused from the world and what is in it.
Within my heart there is nothing but the Friend.
If perfume from the rose-garden of Unity comes to me
My heart, like a rosebud, will burst its outer skin.
Speak to the recluse in his solitude and say:
Because the very edge of our prayer-niche is as the curve of the Eyebrow.
There is no real difference between the Kaaba and the idol-house
– Wherever you may look, there equally is HE.
The being of a dervish is not in what his beard and head are like:
The Path of the dervish is in qualitative exactitude.
A dervish may easily shave his head without regrets
But he is a dervish who, like Hafiz, gives up his head.

Khwaja Hafiz of Shiraz

Sufism

Sufism is truth without form.

Ibn El-Jalali

Becoming What One Can Become

To be a Sufi is to become what you can become, and not to try to pursue what is, at the wrong stage, illusion.

It is to become aware of what is possible to you, and not to think that you are aware of that of which you are heedless.

Sufism is the science of stilling what has to be stilled, and alerting what can be alerted; not thinking that you can still or alert where you cannot, or that you need to do so when you do not need it.

The following of the Dervish Path is pursuing a concealed Unity in spite of, and not by means of, the claims of diversity.

It is taking into account the means which are presented in diversity, without thinking that the externals of diversity are important in themselves.

It is approached by studying the factors of learning how to learn; not by trying to gain knowledge without correct practice in approaching it.

You come closer to being a Sufi through realizing that habit and preconception are essentials only in some studies; not by forming habits and judging by means of unsuitable preconceptions.

You must become as aware of insignificance as you think you are of significance; not seek feelings of significance alone.

The humble are so because they must be so; and worst of all men or women are those who practise humility for the purpose of pride, not as a means of travel.

The method of Sufism is as it always has been, to adopt that which is of value, when and where it is of value, and with whom it is of value; not to imitate because of awe, or to copy because of imitativeness.

The success of man in raising himself higher comes through the right effort and the right method, not merely by concentrating upon the right aspiration or upon the words of others directed to yet others.

It is as it were a trap laid for the ignoble element in you

when a man, a book, a ceremonial, an organization, a method, appears, directly or by recommendation, to have something which is applicable to all, or attracts you strongly though incorrectly.

Sayed Imam Ali Shah

Good and Evil

'Being' is absolutely good.
If it contains any evil, it is not Being.

Shabistari

Remedy

Your medicine is in you, and you do not observe it.
Your ailment is from yourself, and you do not register it.

Hazrat Ali

The World

The world has no being except as an appearance;
From end to end its state is a sport and a play.

Shabistari, *Gulshan-i-Raz*

Direction

If your teacher so directs, dye your prayer-carpet with wine.
The Seeker should not be ignorant of the techniques of the Stages.

Hafiz

Sufi Literature

There are three ways of presenting anything.
The first is to present everything.
The second is to present what people want.

244

The third is to present what will serve them best.
If you present everything, the result may be surfeit.
If you present what people want, it may choke them.

If you present what will serve them best, the worst is that, misunderstanding, they may oppose you. But if you have served them thus, whatever the appearances, you have served them and you, too, must benefit, whatever the appearances.

Ajmal of Badakhshan

Research

Only the bird understands the textbook of the rose:
For not every reader knows the inner meaning of the page.
O you who would learn the section on love from the book of knowledge –
I fear that you do not know how to fathom it by research.

Hafiz

Dumbness

He takes the tongue from those who share the secret:
So that they may not again speak the king's secret.

Nizami

The Pearl

What do ordinary people know of the value of the precious pearl?
Hafiz (protector), give the unique essence only to the elect.

Hafiz

Happiness and Sadness

Whoever gets some knowledge, however little, is happy. Whoever has it taken from him is sad.

Ibn-Idris El-Shafai

Real Goodness

Better than being what you imagine to be good is to be with those who really are good.

Worse than doing something evil is to be with those who are evil.

Bayazid

Death

Sleep with the remembrance of death, and rise with the thought that you will not live long.

Uwais El-Qarni

Commenting on a Recluse

He has established himself upon a mountain
So he has no Work to do.
A man should be in the market-place
While still working with true Reality.

Sahl

Eight Qualities of the Sufi

In Sufism, eight qualities must be exercised. The Sufi has:
Liberality such as that of Abraham;
Acceptance of his lot, as Ishmael accepted;
Patience, as possessed by Job;
Capacity to communicate by symbolism, as in the case of Zacharias;
Estrangement from his own people, which was the case with John;
Woollen garb like the shepherd's mantle of Moses;
Journeying, like the travelling of Jesus;
Humility, as Mohammed had humility of spirit.

Junaid of Baghdad

Where it Went

I saw a child carrying a light.
I asked him where he had brought it from.
He put it out, and said:
'Now you tell me where it is gone.'

Hasan of Basra

Affinities

People who are alike feel an affinity. The attraction of opposites
is a different case. But people who are alike are often mistaken
by superficialists for people who are unalike. As an example,
one is greedy for love, another is greedy to love. The uninfor-
med or outward thinker will immediately imagine and pro-
claim that these are opposites. The converse, of course, is the
truth. The common factor is greed. They are both greedy people.

The famous man and his follower are sometimes the same.
One wants to give his attention, the other to attract attention.
Both being chained by an obsession with attention, they fly
together, 'pigeon with pigeon, hawk with hawk'.

Simabi

Riches

Aim for knowledge. If you become poor it will be wealth for
you: if you become rich it will adorn you.

El-Zubeir son of Abu-Bakr

Discipleship

With a Guide you may become truly Human.
Without a Guide you will remain mainly Animal.
If you can still say: 'I could not submit to any man'
— You are still worthless for the road.

247

But if you say: 'I wish to submit', in the wrong way
– The road will never find you, and you are lost.

Zulfikar son of Jangi

'I'

Knowledge proceeds from:
  'What am I?'
  To: 'I do not know what I am.'
  To between 'Perhaps I am not' and 'I will find myself'; to between 'I will find myself' and 'I am', to 'I am what I know myself to be', to 'I am'.

Abu-Hasan El-Shadhili

Small Change

When a man is a beggar, he thinks that small change is a fortune. It is not. In order to rise above beggarhood, he must rise above small change, even though he uses it as a means. Used as an end, it will become an end.

Ibn Ikbal

What Looks After You

Knowledge is better than wealth. You have to look after wealth; knowledge looks after you.

Ali

Destructive

Three things in this life are destructive:
Anger, Greed, Self-esteem.

The Prophet

❦ 2 ❦
A SUFI NOTEBOOK

On Service

Service is the performing of duty without either reluctance or delight. The dutiful is neither an exploited slave nor one who seeks reward. People will get out of the performing of duty what they can get out of it. If they put aside immediate enjoyment of duty and also immediate reluctance to duty, they are in a position to benefit from the other content in service. This it is which refines their perceptions.

On Seeking

Seeking truth is the first stage towards finding it. After the seeking comes the realization that Truth is also seeking the Seeker himself. The third stage, which is the one in which the Sufi is learning from the Way, is when learning reaches a special stage: when the Seeker realizes that he is acquiring knowledge in a range beyond 'seeking' and 'finding', or 'being sought'.

On Effort

Effort and work have many different forms. One reason for the institution of a Guide is that he knows when to direct the disciple's effort and work, and when not to direct it. He also knows the kind of effort and work which each individual should do. Only the ignorant mistake any work for useful work, or extra effort at any time they wish for even little effort at a right time.

On Idolatry

'Idolatry' is when attention is fixed upon some intermediary person or thing at a time and by a person when this should not take place. It is mistaking the vehicle for the content. Most institutions are, knowingly or otherwise, encouragers of idolatry. It is for this reason that potential Sufis require the constant attention of a mentor to direct their attention according to possibilities.

On Discipleship

In the Dervish Way discipleship is an essential requirement. But the distinction must be made between the people who only imagine that they should be disciples – those whose greed has been aroused in disguise – and those who actually can become disciples, and where and when this stage can take place profitably.

On Mastership

The way in which a Master teaches is often incomprehensible to the students. This is generally because they are trying to understand the workings of something when in reality they are in urgent need of its benefits. Without its benefits they will never be able to understand its working.

On Companionship

There is the companionship of humanity and the companionship of transmission. Those who lack family or other forms of companionship will seek them even at times and places where associating together with others is useful for transmission. Few people know about this, partly because the one word (companionship) is generally used to denote two states, each of them quite different.

On Literature

Remarks of local application are often taken as being of general or universal application. When a Teacher says: 'Shun literature', he is speaking about a certain audience and a certain time. It is the failures among his students who misunderstand and preserve literature as a key to understanding, or else do the reverse, saying: 'The Master denied literature, therefore we will all, and always, deny it.'

On Exercises

Greed is the dominant, though well concealed, characteristic of those who imagine that exercises are the entry to knowledge. They are as important, and as independently irrelevant, as the use of a hand without one or two of the fingers.

On Appearances

The ordinary man judges a person not by his inner attainments but by his apparent actions and what he looks like superficially, and by what people say about him. This method is suitable, however, only for some kinds of judgement, not for others. What a person seems to be like will depend upon what one knows of him. As an example, a man carrying a spiked stick is not necessarily a murderer, he may be an elephant-driver. The elect often violate the superficial canons of appearance in order not to be affected by the behaviour of the mass with its artificial criteria, and also at times in order to demonstrate, to those who can see it, that conduct alone does not demonstrate interior worth.

On Faith and Religion

Those who are regarded as believers or religious people, and who are incapable because of habit from behaving in any other manner, may be called religious but cannot be regarded as having faith. If, on the other hand, this is faith, then some other word should be used to convey the kind of faith which is not produced by the parents or surroundings of a person.

On Love

What is generally called love can be harmful to the lover and the object of the love. If this is the result, the cause cannot be called love by a Sufi, but must be called 'attachment' in which the attached is incapable of any other conduct. Love not only has different intensities, but it also has different levels. If man thinks that love only signifies what he has so far felt, he will veil himself thereby from any experience of real love. If, however, he has actually felt real love, he will not make the mistake of generalizing about it so as to identify it only with physical love or the love of attraction.

On Study in the World

Sufism is a study which is not scholastic. Its materials are taken from almost every form of human experience. Its books and pens are in the environment and resemble nothing that the scholastic or enthusiast even dreams about. It is because recitations, effort and books are included in this kind of study, and because Sufi teachers are called 'Teacher', that the fact of a specialized communication has become confused with academic or imitative study. There is, therefore, 'Sufi Study' and 'ordinary study', and the two are different. The position is as if 'mouse' and 'elephant' had both been given the same name. Up to a point (being quadrupeds, being grey, having tails) this inexactitude is of no moment. After that, it becomes necessary to distinguish between the two. This distinguishing takes place in a Sufi circle.

On Dervish Assemblies

Superficial students imagine that when dervishes meet they are all of similar rank, or that any dervish can attend the meetings of any other, the difference being only in degree. In fact, it is the composition of the circle which is as important as the circle itself. Similarly, rank in the Way may hold good in one assembly and not in another. This is why teachers in one circle become pupils in another. Collections of interested parties, religious enthusiasts and would-be learners grouped together are often mistakenly called 'dervish circles'. These may or may not be preliminary to such circles, but they are not circles.

On Differences between Schools

Many things are said and written about differences in opinion, teaching and writings between Sufis. Externally there may be differences, dictated by the environment, but essentially there is no difference. To wrangle about Sufi differences is as stupid as to wrangle as to whether a coat should be spun from the bud of this or that cotton-plant. That is the extent of its significance.

Parable, Idiom and Metaphor

If your teacher is speaking to you in your native tongue, you will have to regard the idioms which he uses as idiomatic, and not intended to be analysed literally. When he gives you a parable, you will have to know it before you can apply it. When a thing is said metaphorically, it is meant metaphorically. Literal things are not to be taken as metaphorical.

On Higher Levels of Understanding

If you use ordinary intellect to try to unravel something which you do not understand in Sufism, you will go astray, because the intellect is too ingenious for the task. Understanding comes only by keeping the elusive within your mental grip. Many a test has been failed because it was too subtle. Be aware of subtleties.

On Annoyance and Unconcernedness

Nobody is annoyed unless there is a reason. If you annoy others it may be because they imagine you to be annoying, or it may be that you annoy them because of your speech or conduct. If you are, or anyone else is, unconcerned by a source of annoyance, this may be either laudable or deprecable. You cannot judge by annoyance.

On 'States'

'States' are basically three: counterfeit or imagined, genuine and irrelevant. Like the physician, it is the sheikh who knows which is which, knows the ailment or state of health by the symptom. He also knows the desirability of the induction or otherwise of states. The height of folly is to assume that the presence or absence of a 'state' is in itself indicative of something good or bad.

On Reading, Hearing, Being Present

The materials of study may constitute only the action of being present, without intense reactions, at an assembly of the Wise. It may at one time mean reading, at another, audition. Sometimes the reader or instrumentalist may be one of the initiated. At other times he should on no account be such. This science has been verified and only blunderers experiment with it.

On Repentance

Repentance means turning back or giving up completely something that was of powerful attraction. Pleasure gained through repentance is in most cases as bad as the original offence, and no permanent improvement can be expected by those who pride themselves in reformation. The repentance of the ignorant is when people feel strong reactions to giving something up, or seek forgiveness for something. There is a higher form, the repentance of the Wise, which leads to greater knowledge and love.

On Hope and Fear

Being moved between hope and fear (the fear of God and the hope of His forgiveness) is the earliest state of Sufihood. Those who stay in this state are like the ball played from one part of the field to the other. After a time this experience has its benefit and after that it has its disadvantages. Following the Path without the lower qualities of hope and fear is the objective. A higher objective is when there is neither bribe nor stick. Some need hope and fear; they are those who have had it prescribed for them.

Pahlawan-i-Zaif

Part Seven
GROUP RECITALS

GROUP RECITALS

Group recitals are selected from available material on the basis that their greatest value is extracted when they are studied in company. They are also studied in solitude. When this is done, the student is instructed to read the recitals in any order different from the sequence in which they appear here. His choice of sequence is believed to form a part of the study itself. The present sequence is the group-recital sequence.

The Price

One day two dervishes were arguing.

Ibrahim ben Adam said to one of them:

'The life of renunciation has been wasted upon you. You got it cheaply, and so you do not value it.'

The dervish sneered and said:

'And what price, pray, did you pay for being a dervish?'

Ibrahim said:

'I exchanged it for the kingdom of Balkh, and even then I regard that as a cheap price, brother.'

The Gardener

One day Ibrahim was working as a gardener when his master asked him to give him some pomegranates.

He brought several, but they were all sour.

His employer said:

'You have been in my employment for such a long time, and yet you do not know which of the pomegranates is sweet?'

Ibrahim answered:

'I was employed to tend them, not to taste them; how can I know which ones are sweet?'

It was then that the owner of the orchard realized that this must be Ibrahim ben Adam.

The Caravanserai

Once Khidr went to the king's palace and made his way right up to the throne.

Such was the strangeness of his appearance that none dared to stop him.

The king, who was Ibrahim ben Adam, asked him what he was looking for.

The visitor said:

'I am looking for a sleeping-place in this caravanserai.'

Ibrahim answered:

'This is no caravanserai, this is my palace.'

The stranger said:

'Whose was it before you?'

'My father's,' said Ibrahim.

'And before that?'

'My grandfather's.'

'And this place, where people come and go, staying and moving on, you call other than a caravanserai?'

The Book

Ibrahim dreamt once that he saw the angel Gabriel.

The angel had a book in his hand, and Ibrahim asked what it contained.

Gabriel said:

'In this book I am writing the names of the friends of God.'

Ibrahim asked:

'Is my name to be there?'

The angel replied:
'Ibrahim, you are not a friend of God.'
Ibrahim answered:
'That is so, but I am a friend of the friends of God.'
For a time Gabriel said nothing. Then he addressed Ibrahim:
'I have received instructions to record your name at the head
of this list; for hope is born of lack of hope.'

Religion

All religion, as theologians – and their opponents – understand the word, is something other than what it is assumed to
be.

Religion is a vehicle. Its expressions, rituals, moral and other
teachings are designed to cause certain elevating effects, at a
certain time, upon certain communities.

Because of the difficulty of maintaining the science of man,
religion was instituted as a means of approaching truth. The
means always became, for the shallow, the end, and the vehicle
became the idol.

Only the man of wisdom, not the man of faith or intellect,
can cause the vehicle to move again.

Alauddin Attar

Prayer

The great sheikh Simak taught this as the prayer-secret:

Man can pray only to the extent of his capacity. If he is alone,
or taught to pray through books or in seminaries, he cannot
understand or take part in the reality of prayer.

One who has learned to pray, and who carries with him the
illumination, can pass a portion of it to another man: so that
he too can learn and develop prayer in himself.

Written prayer is meaningless.

The Meaning of Culture

The Sufic understanding of culture is not that which is understood by the ordinary man, who limits the meaning.

Sheikh Abu Nasr Sarraj speaks of these three forms of culture:

Worldly culture, which is merely acquiring information, opinions and learning of a conventionalized kind;

Religious culture, which is repetitious, following rules and discipline, behaving in a ethically acceptable way;

Sufi culture, which is a self-development, realizing what is relevant, concentration and contemplation, cultivation of inner experience, following the path of Search and Nearness.

What Sufism Teaches

Sufism teaches how to purify one's self, improve one's morals and build up one's inner and outer life in order to attain perpetual bliss. Its subject matter is the purification of the soul and its end or aim is the attainment of eternal felicity and blessedness.

Sheikh El-Islam Zakaria Ansari

Choosing

'Choosing' (*istifa*) is the emptying of the heart of all things other than the search for completion. This resembles a visualization that the body is empty, and that all thoughts have left it for a moment, during which time the true thoughts flood in.

Hujwiri

The Way in Which They Bring Their Teaching

Do not expect the way in which they bring their teaching to be wholly within your ordinary way of understanding. A pearl may be carried in a leather purse. The ignorant cry out: 'This square object with a flap does not look like the necklace which has been described to me.'

Arif Yahya

Asked why a certain Sufi sheikh did not appear to the outward eye to follow a religiously devout life, Nizamuddin Awliya said: 'Kings bury their treasures in one of two places. The first, and obvious one, is in the strong-room, which can be burgled, emptied or usurped. The other, and more enduring one, is in the earth, in a ruin where nobody would think of looking for it.'

Formula of Osman of the West

O Mustafa, O Mustafa,
  Rais-i-Karawan-i-ma!
    (Perfected One, Perfected One, Leader of our Caravan!)
    In the Name of the Friend!
    Hoo, Friend!
We say *Hoo* for the Chain of Transmission, for the leaders of the Orders, for the strugglers for Truth, for the dervishes present and absent.
    Hoo!
We invoke the power of the Baraka of the Community and the Great Ones upon our assembly.
    Hoo!
We dedicate our activity this day to the Deepest Consciousness in all its forms of being!
    Hoo!
The Invocation may commence.

Eternal Sufism

Continuously, in commemoration of the Friend — we drank wine before the creation of the vine.

Ibn El-Farid

The Seed of Sufi Knowledge

The true seed was made in Adam's time. The miracle of life, existence.

It germinated in the period of Noah. The miracle of growth, rescue.

By the time of Abraham it had sent forth branches. The miracle of spreading, maintenance.

The epoch of Moses saw the making of the grapes. The miracle of fruit.

The time of Jesus was that of the ripening of the yield. The miracle of tasting, joy.

Mohammed's time saw the pressing of clear wine. The miracle of attainment, transformation.

Bayazid Bistami

In the Presence of a Wise One

Even if you have only been present, in silence, at the assembly of a Wise One, you have gained more potentiality than you could, by ordinary thinking, ever imagine.

Mirza Asim

The Aim

The hidden meaning in existence is like a tree subsisting.

And the deeply hidden fruit of it is man, O Master.

The aim of the bough — O One without a Teacher — is ripened fruit, not just another tree alone.

Ablahi Mutlaqtar

To the Prince

O Fortune, you have ennobled my mind;
By this book you have elevated me.
The idea was not mine that you should be
    the companion of my state.
You opened the door of my domain.
You showed me the treasure of guidance.
We came together in this message which
    you sent the King
When you constrained me from fanciful thoughts,
I spoke words of this sublimity.
When the King's gaze fell upon it,
He accepted it a hundredfold . . .

                                        The *Halnama* of Arifi

The Assemblies of Wisdom

A man will fill himself with book-studies and facts. He, or an-other man, will fill himself with exercises and practices.

In both of these there is the sensation of accomplishment, and of significance.

But, just as in order to fill a pot we must have a pot, something with which to fill it, and a sense of measure – only by the correct application of these factors can man really succeed in his task of true fulfilment.

Only in this way can he find himself. In many other ways he can think that he has found himself, or that he is finding himself, or that someone can find him for himself. We cannot be concerned about such people except to be solicitous for their peace of mind and bodily health.

In order to reach and apply the measure of which I speak, a man must find an Assembly of Wisdom. It is here, and no-where else, that the measure is to be acquired.

There! You have had your warning. Now go and find the

assembly of wisdom. You will find one whose true usefulness corresponds exactly with your inner sincerity. If you are a hypocrite, you will fall among hypocrites, no matter what they seem to you to be like, or what you seem to them to be like, or what they seem to each other to be like.

The Qalandar Bahadur Shah

How the Search for Knowledge is Frustrated

It is frustrated by pretence.

There is that which man knows within himself. He does not recognize it for what it is. He pretends that he can, or cannot, understand it. He does not know that he needs a certain preparation.

There is what man thinks that he knows, but does not. He only knows about a part of the things which he knows. This partial knowledge is in some ways worse than no knowledge at all.

There is also what man does not know, and cannot know at any given stage. This, however, he believes that he must know. He seeks it, or something that will seem to him to be this thing. Since he has no real measuring-stick, he starts to pretend.

Study-theme of the Azamia Dervishes

The Prelude to Realization

O Sufi! Wine becomes clear only after forty days.

And a man must be Solomon before his magic ring will work.

Hafiz

Symptoms

One man has a headache, another blurred vision.

Both are caused by the wrong food.

Say: 'Your digestion is upset', and both will reply: 'Away, fool! We seek relief to head and eye, not absurdity.'

Hamami

Remembering

Everything is dependent upon remembering. One does not begin by learning, one starts by remembrance. The distance of eternal existence and the difficulties of life cause one to forget.

It is for this reason God has commanded us:

'Remember!'

Sheikh Ismail Hakki

The Problem of Music

Be sure that you do not train yourself to music, in case this holds you back from even higher perceptions.

Ibn Hamdan

Wild Utterances

We give out strange phrases to ordinary people because our experiences cannot be put in their ordinary phrases. I have known that which cannot be described, through and through, and that which is in it overwhelms all ordinary definition.

Ibn Ata

The Atom

Crack the heart of any atom: from its midst you will see a sun shining. If you give all you have to Love, I'll be called a Pagan if you suffer a molecule of loss. The soul passed through the fire of Love will let you see the soul transmuted. If you escape the narrowness of dimensions, and will see the 'time of what is placeless', you will hear what has never been heard, and you will see what has never been seen; until they deliver you to a place where you will see 'a world' and 'worlds' as one. You shall love Unity with heart and soul; until, with the true eye, you will see Unity ...

Sayed Ahmad Hatif

Thou Art There

The flitting of a light in desert dusk – thou art there.

The weary duty of the Magian's forced ritual – thou art there.

The movement in response to another movement – thou art there.

Not in the book of the scribe, but in the smile at it – thou art there.

The Grace of the graceful, not the mind of the graceful – thou art there.

The question and answer: between them, not in them – thou art there.

Between the lumbering paces of the elephant – thou art there.

In harmony, in love, in being itself, in truth, in absoluteness – thou art there.

The pearl rejected by the oyster-fancier – thou art there.

The inexplicability of non-rhythm, of seeming change – thou art there.

The interchange, pulsation, sweetness, silence, rest:

In congruity and in incongruity – thou art there.

In the glow, the spark, the leaping flame, the warmth and the burning; in the relaxation and the agitation: Thou art there!

Haykali

To Reach the Degree of Truth ...

None attains to the Degree of Truth until a thousand honest people have testified that he is a heretic.

Junaid of Baghdad

Death does not visit more than once. Be prepared, therefore, for its coming.

Abu-Shafiq of Balkh

Obedience

The lowest form of obedience is performing actions for someone else. The high form of obedience is when one desists from behaviour which one desires to carry out. The highest form of obedience is to be able to carry out no action at all. When this is possible, the other forms of obedience are also possible. Together they make up what people, ignorantly, imagine to be one single thing, 'obedience'.

The first thing to learn is that what you have been accustomed to calling obedience is always either habit or servitude, whether it gives you pleasure or not.

Anisa Imtihani

That Which You Admire in the Sufis . . .

Whatever you admire in the achievements of the ocean of Sufis is as a droplet compared with their real attainments; which are hidden from you while you look at their external face alone.

Musa Kazim

The Path and the Gate

A path and a gateway have no meaning or use once the objective is in sight.

Hujwiri

What to Do and What to Have Done

All wisdom can be stated in two lines:

What is done for you – allow it to be done.
What you must do yourself – make sure you do it.

Khawwas

Saving Oneself

Have you heard the tale told by the incomparable Master of our Path, Maulana Rumi? It is this one to which I refer:

There was once a man who owned some livestock, and when he heard that Moses knew the language of animals, he prevailed upon him to teach him.

Armed with this knowledge, he listened to what his animals said. The cock told the dog that the horse was going to die soon, and the man understood. So he sold the horse before he incurred any loss.

Some time later, again using his knowledge, he overheard the cock telling the dog that the mule would die before long, and so he was able to sell him, too, so as to avoid any loss.

The cock next said that the man's slave was about to die. The man gleefully sold the slave, in order to save himself money. He was very pleased with himself, and imagined that this was the value of knowledge, to help man in his day-to-day affairs.

Now, however, the man heard the cock telling the dog that he, the man, was about to die. He ran in panic to see Moses, seeking his advice as to what to do.

Moses said: 'You can go and sell yourself now!'

Take heed of this teaching: that the knowledge of how to see the characteristics of others avails man nothing in respect of his greatest need – himself.

Anis Ahmad ibn El-Alawi

The Tattooed Lion

Once there was a man who wanted to have a lion tattooed on his back.

He went to a tattoo artist and told him what he wanted.

But as soon as he felt the first few pricks, this man began to moan and groan: 'You are killing me. What part of the lion are you marking?'

'I am just doing the tail now,' said the artist.

'Then let us leave out the tail,' howled the other.

So the artist started again. And again the client could not stand the pricks. 'What part of the lion is it this time?' he cried, 'for I cannot stand the pain.'

'This time,' said the tattooist, 'it is the lion's ear.'

'Let us have a lion without an ear,' gasped the patient.

So the tattooist tried again. No sooner had the needle entered his skin than the victim squirmed again: 'Which part of the lion is it this time?'

'This is the lion's stomach,' wearily answered the artist.

'I don't want a lion with a stomach,' said the other man.

Exasperated and distraught, the tattoo artist stood awhile. Then he threw his needle down and cried: 'A lion without a head, with no tail, without a stomach? Who could draw such a thing? Even God did not!'

Rumi

The Saint and Essence

The saint is subordinated to his Essence:
A devotee, but in the Way of Essence.
His work arrives at its end
When its beginning arrives again at its end.

Shabistari

Evolution

First of all he came into the inert world. From minerality he developed, into the realm of vegetation. For years he lived thus. Then he passed into an animal state, yet bereft of any memory of his being vegetable – except for his attraction to Spring and to blossoms.

This was something like the innate desire of an infant for its mother's breast. Or like the affinity of disciples for an illustrious guide. When the shadow is no more, they know the *cause* of their attachment to the teacher ...

From realm to realm man went, reaching his present reasoning, knowledgeable, robust state; forgetting earlier forms of intelligence.

So too shall he pass beyond the current form of perception. There are a thousand other forms of Mind ...

But he has fallen asleep. He will say: 'I had forgotten my fulfilment, ignorant that sleep and fancy were the cause of my sufferings.'

He says: 'My sleeping experiences do not matter.'

Come, leave such asses to their meadow.

Because of necessity, man acquires organs. So, necessitous one, increase your need.

Rumi

Dark and Light

Evening precedes morning, and night becomes dawn.

Hafiz

Immortality

The honour of man is his learning. Wise people are torches lighting the path of truth. In knowledge lies man's opportunity for immortality. While man may die, wisdom lives eternally.

Ali

Fools and Wickedness

More harm is done by fools through foolishness than is done
by evildoers through wickedness.

                                        The Prophet

Men and Knowledge

There are many trees: not all of them bear fruit.
  There are many fruits: not all of them may be eaten.
  Many, too, are the kinds of knowledge: yet not all of them
are of value to men.

                            Jesus, son of Mary,
                    according to the Book of Amu-Darya

Men and Kings

  Kings rule men, wise men rule kings.

                            Abu El-Aswad

If You Like Asceticism

Asceticism can be a weakness, the fulfilment of a desire, and
due to lack of real fortitude.

                                      Hasan of Basra

Think

  All men, except for the learned, are dead.

                                      Sahl of Tustar

What is Identity?

When someone knocked on the door, Bayazid called out:
'Whom do you seek?'
The caller answered:
'Bayazid.'
Bayazid replied:
'I, too, have been seeking "Bayazid" for three decades, and
I have not yet found him.'

What the Wise Do

The wise man is he who does today what fools will do three
days later.

Abdullah ibn Mubarak

The Answer

We wrote a hundred letters, and you did not write an answer.
This, too, is a reply.

Zauqi

Sleeping

O you who fear the difficulties of the road to annihilation – do
not fear.
It is so easy, this road, that it may be travelled sleeping.

Mir Yahya Kashi

Man

With a hundred thousand perceptors the sphere revolves round
the earth, seeking Man.
  But where is Man?

Astrabadi

The Dog and the Blows

I saw a guard hitting a dog with a stick.
  The dog was howling as it suffered the strokes.
  I said: 'O dog, why has he struck you?'
  He said: 'He cannot bear to see one better than himself.'

Shibli

The Price

O you who say 'Why buy wine with your life?' – ask this
question of our Cup Bearer, who has made the price so cheap.

Fighani

We are Alive

  We are waves whose stillness is non-being.
  We are alive because of this, that we have no rest.

Abu-Talib Kalim

What is Virtue?

Look around you at people who have virtues. You will find that
many people have not been ennobled by their practices, though
they have that repute. The practice of virtues is in itself next to
nothing.
  A thread is not made into a jewel because it passes through
the holes in a series of pearls.

I was unable to learn, let alone teach, until I had realized that a desolate place is not made fertile merely by the presence of a treasure beneath the ground.

Hamid Qalindoz

Knowing

He who knows and does not know that he knows: he is asleep. Let him become one, whole. Let him be awakened.

He who has known but does not know: let him see once more the beginning of all.

He who does not wish to know, and yet says that he needs to know: let him be guided to safety and to light.

He who does not know, and knows that he does not know: let him, through this knowledge, know.

He who does not know, but thinks that he knows: set him free from the confusion of that ignorance.

He who knows, and knows that *he is*: he is wise. Let him be followed. By his presence alone man may be transformed.

I who know, and do not know that I know: let me become one, whole. Let me be awakened.

I who have known, but do not know: let me see once more the beginning of all.

I who do not wish to know, and yet say that I need to know: let me be guided to safety and to light.

I who do not know, and know that I do not know: let me, through this knowledge, know.

I who do not know, but think that I know: set me free from the confusion of that ignorance.

He who knows, and knows that *he is*: he is wise. Let him be followed. By his presence alone man may be transformed.

We who know, and do not know that we know: let us become one, whole. Let us be transformed.

We who have known, but do not know: let us once more see the beginning of all.

We who do not wish to know, and yet say that we need to know: let us be guided to safety and to light.

We who do not know, and know that we do not know: let us, through this knowledge, know.

We who do not know, but think that we know: set us free from the confusion of that ignorance.

He who knows, and knows that *he is*: he is wise. Let him be followed. By his presence alone man may be transformed.

As with our forebears
So with our successors.
So with us.
We affirm this undertaking.
So let it be.

Sarmoun Recital

The Swimmer

Man in ordinary life finds difficulties and seeks happiness.

He cannot attain satisfaction or permanently overcome difficulties when he is in a state of ignorance and incapacity.

He can, however, arrive at a state in which he believes that his difficulties are gone, or even that he knows things which he does not know.

This is the state of those who manipulate their minds, or who allow themselves, because of the tension of their state, to adopt the assurances and techniques of the ignorant.

Man is like a swimmer who is fully dressed and hampered every moment by his clinging clothes. He must know why he cannot swim before steps can be taken to make it possible.

It is no solution for him to have the impression that he is swimming properly; for this may make him feel better and prevent him from arriving at the farther bank of the river.

Such men and women drown.

Latif Ahmad

The Teacher

Seek the appearance of a Teacher who does not seem to be the kind of teacher expected by the thinker or the pious. This is because among the thinkers and the pious there are some who will recognize him in any case. But those who have merit and ability for the *way* and are not accustomed to the behaviour of the thinking and the pious will reject the Teacher if he wears the appearance of those whom they do not understand.

Najmuddin Kubra

Touching the Patchwork Robe

Simply touch the patchwork robe of a Complete Man, and you incur the greatest benefit possible to an unregenerate individual. You owe such a man a very great debt. Similarly, attendance at the meeting of a pretended Sufi will drain from you a part of your very life.

Halima Hanim

The Celestial Apple

Ibn-Nasir was ill and, although apples were out of season, he craved one.

Hallaj suddenly produced one.

Someone said: 'This apple has a maggot in it. How could a fruit of celestial origin be so infested?'

Hallaj explained:

'It is just because it is of celestial origin that this fruit has become affected. It was originally not so, but when it entered this abode of imperfection it naturally partook of the disease which is characteristic here.'

Part Eight

LETTERS AND LECTURES

LETTERS AND LECTURES

Sufi teachers distinguish sharply between letters and lectures given for a specific audience and those which are of literary, emotional or cultural value alone. All Sufi teachings are held, basically, to belong to their own time. The Sufi message in written form is regarded as being of limited effectiveness, both in depth and in durability. This is because 'that which is introduced into the domain of Time will fall victim to the ravages of Time'. Consequently, as in the waves-of-the-sea metaphor which Sufis so often use, Sufism is constantly renewed by successive exemplar-teachers.

These teachers do not only reinterpret past Sufi materials; they select, adapt, introduce, and in so doing enable the literary materials to continue a dynamic function.

Sufi students may or may not be encouraged to familiarize themselves with the traditional Classics of Sufism. It is the Sufi Guide, however, who indicates to each circle or pupil the curriculum: the pieces from the Classics from letters and lectures, from traditional observances which apply to a particular phase of society, to a particular grouping, to a certain individual.

This usage of materials sharply divides Sufi ideology from any other on record. It is this attitude which has prevented Sufism from crystallizing into priestcraft and traditionalism. In the originally Sufic groupings where this fossilization has indeed taken place, their fixation upon a repetitious usage of Sufi materials provides a warning for the would-be Sufi that such an organization has 'joined the world'.

The following section consists of materials taken from current usage and regarded by contemporary Sufis of the school of 'supercession of ephemeral materials' as applicable to the present situation of man.

The materials themselves range back and forth between the works and sayings of the most ancient Sufis on record and currently projected teachings based on Sufic principles.

It is interesting to note, from the point of view of contemporary psychology, how study-groups – in Sufism as elsewhere – always face a challenge. This challenge is as to whether the group will stabilize itself early on comforting props (like certain drills, exercises, readings, authority-figures) or whether the group has in itself sufficient stability to reach for a reality beyond exterior, social factors.

It is the composition of the group which will decide this. If its members already have a sound social equilibrium, they will not need to convert their study atmosphere into the source of stability and reassurance. If the members have already acquired physical and intellectual satisfactions, they will not need to attempt to extract these from their Sufic group.

It is the seekers of social, intellectual and emotional stabilization who are the unsuccessful candidates for Sufi teaching in genuine schools. Imitation schools (knowingly or otherwise) use Sufi externals – including such letters and lectures as these – and operate as disguised social-psychological groups. This very valuable though Sufically sterile activity is not the quest for 'higher knowledge about man'.

This is not to say that the automimetic groupings which many people take for Sufi ones are instantly recognizable by a candidate as mere social groupings. On the contrary, if the intending student is himself in need of reassurance, adventure, catharsis, social and psychological equilibrium, he will only too gratefully and unquestioningly be attracted to the lower level of activity.

This is because he will be responding to what the group is offering in practice, not what Sufism can offer.

Traditionally, again, groups of Seekers have collected together in order to commemorate the practices and theories of Sufism, in the hope that their desires will be consummated by the appearance of a genuine teacher. This basis for study is more hazardous than is commonly supposed, for when the membership of a group is largely composed of people who use it for lower psychological purposes, the group as a whole will tend to lose the capacity and desire for recognizing higher levels of materials.

In such cases, the natural development of a social sense in the grouping stunts aspiration. Only the introduction of different types of people into the group, in order at least to restore it to a normal cross-section of people, would be likely to revive this group's possibilities. But a social group of this kind is almost by definition hostile to such introductions; people who seem to think in a different manner are regarded as hostile or ineligible.

What is Sufism?

The question is not 'What is Sufism?', but 'What can be said and taught about Sufism?'

The reason for putting it in this way is that it is more important to know the state of the questioner and tell him what will be useful to him than anything else. Hence the Prophet (Peace and Blessings upon him!) has said:

'Speak to each in accordance with his understanding.'

You can harm an inquirer by giving him even factual information about Sufism, if his capacity of understanding is faulty or wrongly trained.

This is an example. The question just recorded is asked. You reply: 'Sufism is self-improvement.' The questioner will assume that self-improvement means what he takes it to mean.

If you said, again truly: 'Sufism is untold wealth', the greedy or ignorant would covet it because of the meaning which they put upon wealth.

But do not be deceived into thinking that if you put it in a religious or philosophical form, the religious or philosophical man will not make a similar covetous mistake in taking, as he thinks, your meaning.

Idris ibn-Ashraf

Remembering

When we say: 'You are a drop of water from an illimitable Sea', we refer both to your present individuality, as a drop, to all your past individualities, as successive drops and waves, and also to the greater bond which unites all these phases with all other drops as well as with the greater Whole. When viewing this Whole, if we do it from the point of view of the grandeur of a Whole Sea, we shall briefly glimpse something of the greatness of the drop in its possible function as a conscious part of that Sea.

In order to know the relationship between the drop and the Sea, we have to cease thinking of what we take to be the interests of the drop.

We can only do this by forgetting what we take ourselves to be, and remembering what we have been in the past, and also remembering what we are at the moment, what we really are; for the relationship with the Sea is only in suspension, it is not severed. It is the suspension which causes us to make strange makeshift assumptions about ourselves, and also to blind us to true reality.

Exercises of remembering present and recent experiences are designed to provide us with the capacity for remembering farther back; remembering that which is in suspension or abeyance, and that for which we long, though we do not know it.

If this primary exercise in remembering does not lead to bridging the gap to remembering our ancient, perennial commitment, the Pact, one of three things is wrong: the teacher, the student, or the circumstances. This is why we must have a live teacher, an awakening student and the correct circumstances.

Even these present remarks will reach only those whom they can reach. Their physical preservation is but a tiny part of their reality. Unlock them with a teacher, not alone.

Haji Bahaudin, Dervish of Bokhara

Knowledge – Action – Love

Love is a Way to Truth, to Knowledge, to Action.

But only those who know of real love can approach these things by means of love. The others have misunderstood certain other feelings for those of real love.

Weakest of all are those who idealize love and seek to approach it before they can give it anything or take anything of it.

Truth is a Way to Love, to Knowledge, to Action. But only those who can find real Truth can follow its Path as a Way. Others (not in the right because they are in the majority) imagine that they may find Truth, even though they do not know where to seek it, since what they call truth is something less.

Knowledge is a Way to Action, to Love, to Truth. But since it is not the kind of knowledge that people hold it to be, they do not benefit from it. It is everywhere, but they cannot see it, and call out for it while it is beside them all the time.

Action, too, is a Way. It is a Way to Love, to Truth, to Knowledge. But what action when and where? Action with whom, and towards what end? What is the kind of action which we mean when we say it is a Way? Such a different action as to mean that man may carry it out without knowing it. Again he will generally be so immersed in action of another kind that he will not be able to perform the right action which he needs.

So, although we may be misjudged for saying this, we affirm as a real fact that: Exalted Truth has blessed the Teachers with the understanding of the knowledge of the Ways. Let us prattle no more of 'I seek Love'; 'I desire Knowledge'; 'I wish for Truth'; 'my object is Action'; unless we want men to know that we are empty, and in reality seek nothing.

Love is Action; Action is Knowledge; Knowledge is Truth; Truth is Love.

Rauf Mazari, *Niazi*

Symbols

Man is a symbol. So is an object, or a drawing. Penetrate beneath the outward message of the symbol, or you will put yourself to sleep. Within the symbol there is a design which moves. Get to know this design. In order to do this, you need a Guide. But before he can help you, you must be prepared by exercising honesty towards the object of your search. If you seek truth and knowledge, you will gain it. If you seek something for yourself alone, you may gain it, and lose all higher possibilities for yourself.

Khwaja Pulad of Erivan

This Alone is True

When the Sufi says: 'This alone is true', he is saying: 'For this time and this person and this purpose, we must concentrate our attention as if this alone is true.'

In doing this, the Sufi is helping to teach you just as surely as if he were a schoolmaster saying: 'This is A and this is B, this alone is true for the period during which we are studying it.'

In this way man learns literacy. In this way man learns metaphysics.

Sensitive yet unperceptive people often attack Sufis for behaving like this, because of their own lack of patience and cooperativeness. If you do not give a workman a chance to do his job, you can hardly accuse him of over-dedication to it.

Remember, if a dog barks and this annoys you, he may be signalling danger – while you think that he is barking at you. You have misunderstood him.

Hakim Tahirjan of Kafkaz

The Unity of Knowledge

What I have learned as a Sufi is something that man cannot credit because of what he has already been taught. The easiest thing to grasp in Sufism is one of the most difficult for the ordinary thinker. It is this:

All religious presentations are varieties of one truth, more or less distorted. This truth manifests itself in various peoples, who become jealous of it, not realizing that its manifestation accords with their needs. It cannot be passed on in the same form because of the difference in the minds of different communities. It cannot be reinterpreted, because it must grow afresh.

It is presented afresh only by those who can actually experience it in every form, religious and otherwise, of man.

This experience is quite different from what people take it to be. The person who simply thinks that this must be true as a matter of logic is not the same as the person who experiences that it is true.

Khwaja Salahudin of Bokhara

Now That I am Dead

Now that I am dead, you may read something of the truth of the Sufi. Had this information been given to you, directly or indirectly, when I was perceptibly among you, you would all, except for a few, have fed your acquisitiveness and love of wonder alone from it.

Know, then, that what the Sufi master is doing for the world and for its people, great and small, is often not seen by the observer.

A Sufi teacher uses his powers to teach, to heal, to make man happy and so on according to the best reasons for using the powers. If he shows you no miracles, this does not mean that he is not doing them. If he declines to benefit you in the way you wish, it is not because he cannot. He benefits you in accordance with your merit, not in response to a demand by you. He has a higher duty; this is what he is fulfilling.

Many among you have had your lives transformed, have been rescued from perils, have been given chances – none of which you have recognized as benefits. But you have had these benefits just the same.

Many of you, though you are looking for a fuller life, would have no life at all were it not for the efforts of the Community of the Friends. Many of you who are poor, would be cursed if you were rich. Many of you are still rich because of the presence of a Man of Wisdom. Many of you who have been at my school think that you have been taught by me. In actuality, you have been physically present in our assemblies, while you were being taught in another assembly.

All these things are so foreign to your customary thoughts that you are not yet in a position to recognize them.

My task has been to benefit you. The task of making that benefit perceptible to you is that of others.

Your tragedy is that, while waiting for me to vouchsafe miracles and make perceptible changes in you, you have invented miracles which I did not perform, and have developed a loyalty to me which is of no value at all. And you have imagined 'changes' and 'help' and 'lessons' which have not taken place. The 'changes', the 'help', the 'lessons', however, are there. Now find out what they really are. If you go on thinking and doing what I told you to do and think, you are working with yesterday's materials which have already been used.

Mirza Abdul-Hadi Khan of Bokhara

Baraka*

You who talk about Baraka may be the enemies of Baraka. And that a man or woman should be an enemy of what he wants to love is inherent in being a man – but only a certain kind of man.

*Often rendered in English as 'blessing', 'special virtue'.

In common parlance, Baraka is something which, through a divine influence, renders man safe. This is true; but safe only for a purpose. Again, in ordinary speech, people try to make use of Baraka to give them something. This is sheer greed. The superstitious ask for Baraka from the tomb of a saint. It is there but what they get is not Baraka, unless the intention was right.

Baraka adheres to things as well as people, but it will give itself only to the worthy. For practical purposes Baraka is not there at all.

When there is no real Baraka, such is the thirst of man for it that his emotionality will ascribe to his hopes and fears the virtue of Baraka. Thus he will feel pride, sadness, strong emotion, and call it Baraka. Especially prone to being wrongly called Baraka is: a feeling which man gets from something safe, familiar, arousing.

But only the Sufis have real Baraka. They are its channel, just as the rose is the channel for its perfume. They can give you Baraka, but only if you are faithful to them, which is being faithful to what they represent.

If you seek Baraka, my friend, seek the Sufi. If he seems brutal, he is straightforward, and this is his divine Baraka. If you want imagination you will frequent for companionship those who seem to you to give reassurance and the lifting of depression alone. Take this if it is your need. But call it not Baraka. To gain Baraka, you must give unstintingly of what you have before you can receive. Receiving before you give is illusion and a sinful thought. If you have already given – give again, and in this spirit.

Sheikh Shamsudin Siwasi

The People of the House

The Sufi Way was handed down through the People of the House [the descendants of Mohammed the Prophet]. And yet it did not come down simply by the blood-line. Here is a paradox.

Therefore some will say: 'So it was conveyed as a secret passed only to a few, cherished by the House?' Yet it did not come down merely in this manner. Therefore, says the logician, it must have come down through the People of the House rediscovering it from another source? But this is not the method of its being transmitted. No, it was passed down, and it is still communicated, through a Fourth Manner. A way of 'being' outside all these things. When you understand this, you understand the Secret. I tell you this because it is useful, not for mystification.

The 'Servant of the People of the House', in *That Which is Most Hidden*.

Knowledge

Knowledge is generally confused with information. Because people are looking for information or experience, not knowledge, they do not find knowledge.

You cannot avoid giving knowledge to one fitted for it. You cannot give knowledge to the unfit; that is impossible. You can, if you have it, and if he is capable, fit a man for receiving knowledge.

Sayed Najmuddin

On Entering, Living in – and Leaving – the World

Man, you enter the world reluctantly, crying, as a forlorn babe;
Man, you leave this life deprived again crying again, with regret.
Therefore live this life in such a way that none of it is really wasted.
You have to become accustomed to it after not having been accustomed to it.
When you have become accustomed to it, you will have to become used to being without it.

Meditate upon this contention.

Die, therefore, 'before you die', in the words of the Purified
  One. Complete the circle before it is completed for you.

Until you do, unless you have – then expect bitterness at the
  end as there was in the beginning; in the middle as there
  will be at the end.

You did not see the pattern as you entered; and when you
  entered – you saw another pattern.

When you saw this apparent pattern, you were prevented from
  seeing the threads of the coming pattern.

Until you see both, you will be without contentment – *Whom*
  do you blame? And *why* do you blame?

Hashim the Sidqi, on Rumi

Studying with the Famous

People tend to want to study under famous teachers. Yet there
are always people not considered distinguished by the public
who could teach them as effectively.

Ghazali

A teacher with a small following, or no apparent following
at all, may be the right man for you. In nature, small ants do
not swarm to see elephants, in hope of gain. An illustrious
master may be of use only to advanced scholars.

Badakhshani

If a teacher of great repute tells you to go to study under
someone who is apparently not outstanding, he knows what
you need. Many students feel slighted by advice like this, which
is in fact to their advantage.

Abdurahman of Bengal

I have learned what I have learned only after my teachers had
freed me of the habit of attaching myself to what *I* regarded as
teachers and teachings. Sometimes I had to do nothing at all

for long periods. Sometimes I had to study things which I could not link in my mind, no matter how I tried, with higher aspirations.

Zikiria ibn El-Yusufi

Those who are attracted by externals, who look for the outward signs of teachership, who rely on emotion in studies or reading any book they might choose – those are the pond-flies of the Tradition; they skip and skim upon the surface. Because they have words for 'profound' and 'significant', they think, incorrectly, that they know these experiences. This is why we say that, for practical purposes, they know nothing.

Talib Shamsi Ardabili

Take care you do not mistake indigestion for something else. You may visit a great man or read his book and you may feel attraction or hostility. Often this is only indigestion in the student.

Mustafa Qalibi of Antioch

If I were embarking upon the Way anew, my plea would be: 'Teach me how to learn and what to study.' And, even before that: 'Let me really wish to learn how to learn, as a true aspiration, not simply in self-pretence.'

Khwaja Ali Ramitani
addressing a Yemeni delegation

'Differences' in Sufi Teaching

When a Sufic form arises, many people will fail to recognize it. These are Sufi formalists, who copy techniques and believe that this is the same as the Way. Since the form belongs to time, like an old cloak, those who simply emulate old forms will be unable to recognize the forms of the actual time in which they live.

Thus, for instance, Hallaj was stoned by some who thought

that they themselves were Sufis, before they understood his meaning. Hence, when the Sufi way was first preached in mosques some said: 'This is heresy'; others: 'This is a secret not to be put publicly.' The former were narrow clerics, the latter narrow conformists to Sufi externals.

Sufi schools are like waves which break upon rocks: from the same sea, in different forms, for the same purpose.

Ahmed El-Badawi

Which Do You Seek – Appearance or Reality?

Uwais El-Qarni stood alone in the desert, supported on a staff. He met the Prophet in no corporeal form; yet he knew the secrets of the Companions. And none denies that he was a Sufi saint: may God sanctify his mysteries!

Dhun-Nun the Egyptian spoke in riddles, and taught with the Egyptian hieroglyphs. None denies that he was our teacher.

El-Hallaj and Suhrawardi, murdered by authority for saying things unpopular in our time: both were our teachers.

Our Master Bahaudin of Bokhara used no words in his communications to the heart. Yet he spoke as truly as man ever spoke.

Ahmed el-Rifai incurred, for himself and his successors, the name of mountebank and exhibitionist. In the secret he was unified with us.

Men thought that Jalaludin and Faridudin Attar were mere poets. Hafiz spoke of Wine, Ibn El-Arabi of Woman, Ghazali seemed to say that all is allegory.

None denies that they are one.

All engaged in this holy work of ours.

Shabistari spoke of idolatry; Maulana Chisht heard music; Khaja Ansar was a religious chief. Khayyam, Abi-Khair and Rumi denied religious form.

But none denies among the People of the Way that all were one.

Yusuf Qalander wandered the earth's face.

Sheikh Shattar transformed men at a glance.

Ali el-Hujwiri passed for a mere explainer.

All, as one, engaged upon our holy task.

Abdul-Qadir of Gilan from Persia, and Salman and Saadi; Abu-Bakr of Arabia, and Nuri and Jafari; Baba Farid, Ben-Adam from the Afghans; Jami of Khorasan, Bektash of the Turks, Nizamudin of India, Yusuf of Andalusia.

All, as one, engaged upon our holy work.

What, asks the shallow mind, is the behaviour of the Sufis which marks them out for us as Masters? What are the forms of the Exercises of which we may boast? What Path will make a suitable Path for me? What are the places which give birth to Teachers? What are the habits and assurances which bring man to Truth?

Desist you fools! Before it is too late – decide: do you want to study appearance, or Reality?

Nawab Jan-Fishan Khan

The Sufi Path

Sufism is the teaching as well as the fraternity of the Sufis, who are mystics sharing the belief that inner experience is not a department of life, but life itself. Sufi means 'love'.

In the lower reaches the members are organized into circles and lodges. In the higher – *sakina* (stillness) – form, they are bound together by *baraka* (blessing, power, sanctity) and their interaction with this force influences their lives in every way.

Sufism is a way of life, believed by the members to be the essence and reality of all religious and philosophical teachings. It leads to the completion of mankind and womankind, through the institutions of discipleship, meditation and practice. The latter is the 'living of reality'.

Wisdom or completion, according to the Sufis, is to be distinguished from intellectualism, scholasticism and the like, which are merely tools. The Path teaches to what extent these tools can be used; and also how to amalgamate action with destiny.

'Sufism', says a teacher, 'is the Path taken by Sufis in their actual living and working according to a form which is not like other forms: which leads them to the full development of their mental, physical and metaphysical powers. They are organized initially in groups under the guidance of a Guide (teacher) until the relationship which is self-perpetuating is established.

'The Fraternity is called the Brotherhood, the Order, and the Way, or Path. It may be called the Building, on the analogy that something is being built by the association of the members. The Teacher is called a Master, Sheikh, Sage, Knower, Guide, Leader, Ancient, or Director. The Disciple is called a Directed One, Devotee, Lover, or Postulant.

'The Lodge is called a monastery, temple, hermitage, and so on. It may or may not have a physical form.'

In addition to being a metaphysical system intermeshed with ordinary life, Sufism holds that its members will excel in their chosen vocations.

Sufism is taught, not by tedious methods of 'A to Z' textbooks or teachings, but by the interplay of the minds of the teacher and the taught. Eventually, when the relationship is well enough established, the Sufi continues on his own, and becomes a 'Perfected Person'.

Insan-i-Kamil

Sufism is not preached, and it is even taught in some cases by example and guidance which may be unknown to the learner's ordinary faculties.

Zalim Abdurrahman

The Sufi

He may be like Khidr, the Green One, who travels the earth in a variety of guises, and by means unknown to you. If it be his 'station' he will be found herding the sheep one day, sipping from a golden goblet with a king the next.

If he is your teacher, he will make you benefit from his luminescence, whether you know it at the time or not.

When you meet him, he will act upon you, whether you know it or not.

What he says or does may seem inconsistent or even incomprehensible to you. But it has its meaning. He does not live entirely in your world.

His intuition is that of the rightly guided, and he always works in accordance with the Right Way.

He may discomfit you. That will be intended and necessary.

He may seem to return good for evil, or evil for good. But what he is really doing is known only to the Few.

You may hear that some men oppose him. You will find that few men really do so.

He is modest and allows you to find out what you have to find out slowly.

When you first meet him, he may seem to be very different from you. He is not. He may seem to be very much like you. He is not.

Salik

The Martyrs

Mansur el-Hallaj was dismembered while still alive, and is the greatest Sufi martyr. But can you name the person who cut him up? Suhrawardi was murdered by the law, but what was the name of his executioner? Ghazali's books were thrown into the flames, but by the hand of whom? Nobody remembers these people's names, for the Sufis decline to reiterate the names of the infamous. Everyone knows the names of Ghazali, of Mansur and of Suhrawardi.

But take it in another way. We remember, and we honour, the names of our great teachers. But do we remember what it was that they taught? How many people, not being Sufis, who revere the very mention of any of these three, as paying the highest penalties for their work, trouble themselves to inquire what these men should have been doing which was so important?

We may not know the names of the miscreants, but their successors have avenged themselves upon us; because they have shrugged aside Hallaj, adopted their opponent Ghazali as one of their own, and pretended that Suhrawardi was merely obsessed.

They have avenged themselves on humanity for forgetting them. Are we going to allow them to win, once and for all?

Who among us is going to follow the path, and in so doing say to the scholastics and clerics: 'Enough, brother, Ghazali, Suhrawardi and Mansur still live!'?

Itibari

Teachings of the Sufis

Many people practise virtues or associate with wise and great people, believing that this is the pursuit of self-improvement. They are deluded. In the name of religion, some of the worst barbarities have been committed. Trying to do good, man has done some of his worst actions.

The flaw comes from the absurd assumption that mere connection with something of value will convey a corresponding advantage to an unaltered individual.

Much more is necessary. Man must not only be in contact with good: he must be in contact with a form of it which is capable of transforming his function and making him good. A donkey stabled in a library does not become literate.

This argument is one of the differences between Sufi teaching and the attempted practice of ethic or self-improvement in other endeavours.

The point is generally neglected by the reader or student. Talib Kamal said: 'The thread does not become ennobled because it goes through the jewels.' And: 'My virtues have not improved me, any more than a desolate place is made fertile by the presence of a treasure.'

A treasure is a treasure. But if it is to be put to work to re-create a ruin, the treasure must be used in a certain way.

Moralizing may be a part of the process. The means of transforming the man is still needed. It is this means which is the Sufi secret. Other schools, very often, are not at the point where they can see beyond the first stage; they are intoxicated with the discovery of ethic and virtue, which they therefore conclude constitute a panacea.

Abdal Ali Haidar

How Strange a Thing is Man

Just try to conceive for a moment that you are a being unlike a human being. Unperceived by man, you enter one of his abodes. As an observer, what would you make of the cause or the objective of his actions? Assume that you have no experience of humanity.

The man whom you are observing lies down and falls asleep. You do not sleep, because you are not of his nature. How could you understand what he has done or why? You would be forced to say: 'He is dead'; or perhaps: 'he is mad'; or again: 'this must be a religious observance.' You would be forced, because of your lack of material to which to refer this man's actions, to attribute them to the nearest action known to you, in your own world.

Now, while we still watch this man, we find that he wakes up. What has happened? We may think: 'He has miraculously revived', or something of that sort. He goes to the fountain and washes himself. We say: 'How odd!'

Now the man is cooking something in a pot, and sweat stands on his brow. 'A religious observance ... or perhaps he is the slave of this strange leaping, luminous thing called fire, and has to serve it in this way ...'

In short, everything which he does seems insane, incomplete or motivated by causes which arise in our own imagination — if we are that visitor who uses his own scale, or none at all, to measure the human activity.

So it is with the dervish. He laughs, he cries. He is kind, he is cruel. He repents, talks of wine, shuns people and then goes to visit them. He serves mankind and says that he is serving God. You talk of God and he may protest and say that you are ignorant. What are you to make of such a man?

He is a man of another world. You attribute his actions to the kind of actions you know about; his knowledge to the kind of thing which you call knowledge; his feelings you compare with what you take them to be. His origins, his Path, his destiny: you look at them all from only one point of view.

How strange a thing is man!

But there is a way to understand him. Leave off all preconceptions as to what our dervish may be. Follow his explanations or his symbols of the Sufi Path. Be humble, for you are a learner lower than all learners; for you have to know the things which will alone enable you to learn. No, I cannot teach you the Qalandar Path. I have but warned you. Go, seek a Sufi and plead first for forgiveness for your heedlessness, for you have been too long asleep.

Oration of Qalandar Puri

Congregations

Imam Ghazali has noted, in his *Revivification of the Sciences of Religion,* that of the Baghdad masters, although there were dozens, only two or three commanded audiences of more than a few. These great masters, however, are some of those whose teachings have had the greatest effect.

Moreover, there are many adepts who teach without being known and many known ones whose disciples are and remain unknown.

The collection of assemblies, it has been rightly observed by a master, always tends towards what we call the forming of a tribe. Man likes to congregate. To encourage congregating is dangerous unless explicit is the knowledge of the prevention of mere associations and not the creation of a correct collection of people in whom can move the spirit.

Abd-El-Majid Tanti

Imitations and Honesty

Mountebanks, charlatans, pretenders and the deluded comprise, from time to time, the majority of those who are reputed to be spiritual teachers.

Because the pretenders are so common and numerous, people judge each and every sage according to whether he behaves like them.

They have adopted the wrong principle. You look at hundreds of oysters and this tells you how to recognize an oyster again when you see one. You cannot tell by the same method which oysters contain pearls.

The low level of human thought is in fact the accomplice of the imitation Sufi.

'How shall I know a real Sufi?' you say.

I say: 'Become honest, for like calls to like.' If you really were honest, you would not need to ask the question. Since you are dishonest, you do not deserve much more than you get.

Haidar-i-Sirdan

Man and Teacher

A builder was commissioned by a good man to construct and prepare a house which was to be given to the needy.

The builder started work; but soon he found himself surrounded by people. Some of them wanted to learn how to build houses. Of these, only a few had the necessary ability. Some of the people remonstrated with the builder, saying:

'You select only the people whom you like.' Others reviled him, saying: 'You are building this house for yourself.'

The builder said to them: 'I cannot teach everyone. And I am building this house for some needy person.'

They replied: 'You have produced the excuse after the accusation, and merely in order to answer it.'

He said: 'But what if it is the truth? Is it still to be called a lie?'

They told him: 'This is sheer sophistry; we will not listen.'

The builder carried on with his work. Some of his assistants became so attached to the house that, for their own good, he sent them away. The detractors cried:

'Now he begins to show his true colours. See what he has done to his only real friends: cast them out!'

One of the builder's friends explained: 'He has done this for a sufficient reason. It is for the good of the others.'

'Then why does he not speak for himself, explaining it in detail to us all?' they cried.

The builder, sacrificing time which was needed in the making of the building, went to them himself, and said:

'I am here to tell you what I have done and why.'

They immediately shouted: 'See, having found that his hireling cannot convince us, he has come in person, trying to deceive us! Do not listen to him.'

The builder went back to his work, while the others called after him: 'See how he slinks away ... he cannot confuse us, for we are clear-thinking people.'

One of the people, who was more fair-minded than the rest, said to them:

'Could we not come to some accommodation in this matter; perhaps the builder is really trying to do something good. On the other hand if he is not, we can perhaps determine the situation on the basis of facts, not opinions.'

A few of the people agreed, though the majority dissented. This majority were divided among those who thought that the fair-minded man was in the builder's pay and those who thought that he was weak of intellect.

The few now approached the builder saying:

'Show us an authorization from your charitable employer, so that we may be convinced.'

But when the authorization was presented to them, it was found that none of them could read.

'Bring me a man who can read, and I shall be delighted, so that we can have an end to this,' said the builder.

Some of these few went away in disgust, saying:

'We asked for proof, and all he does is mutter about reading and writing . . .'

Others searched and returned with sharp-witted and crafty illiterates who claimed that they could read. All of these, assuming that nobody in the world could read, asked the builder for large sums of money in exchange for attesting the truth of his authorization. He refused to conspire with them.

Literate people, you see, are very scarce in that country. Those who can read and write are not trusted by the populace, or else have other things to do.

The facts of the situation are these. People interpret them as they desire.

Mudir Ali Sabri

Obedience

If you cannot be obedient, you cannot learn anything. Obedience is a part of attention.

You must be obedient to your teacher. From the exercise of this obedience, you will be able to learn how dishonest your mind is.

To lament and supposedly repent of disobedience may be considered a worthy thing to do. It is worthy only for the unworthy: those who cannot aim any higher.

If you are given a time, and you arrive at the place of your teacher early, you are being greedy. If you arrive late, you are being disobedient.

If your teacher indicates that for a time you shall not study, and even if he seems to neglect you, it is for a reason. This has often been done when study has become a vice with a person. To try to make him act otherwise towards you is an act of disobedience.

Sholavi relates:

I first met my Guide when I was sixteen years of age. He agreed to teach me, and gave me three lessons. I did not see him, or even hear of him, again until I was forty-one years old. His first words to me on that occasion were: 'You can now begin your work.'

Umm El-Hasan

Growth, Deterioration and Renewal

Real teaching starts with the Guardians, Lords of Knowledge and Understanding. It does not start with Love, Effort or Action, because real love, effort and action are made possible only through real knowledge.

But when too many even slightly covetous people appear or remain in a community, they turn methods into beliefs, and believe what they should practise.

There are two conditions which can lead to the perishing of a group. In the first, there is too much insincerity in the people in charge. In the other a little insincerity spread among all the members constitutes the equivalent of one or more wholly selfish people.

The insincerity-flaw retards the progress of the leaders and of the others alike. Only searching self-examination can reveal it to them. If it were not for this flaw, they and the community would have arrived at their destination. It is well known, of course, that the worse the degree of self-esteem, the less able is the victim to detect it, or even contemplate it.

To revert to the behaviour of the infected group:

These individuals and their followers choose thoughts and actions which themselves smother most of the hope of success in human fulfilment. They may try to form a permanent organization to aim for enlightenment. They probably subject everyone to the same exercises and observances. Forgetting the original intention, they turn practices and illustrative tales into a sort of history, which they try to teach. If they possess literature and contemporary memories of teachers ('masters'), they use them to bolster a belief in their own rightness and the correctness of their procedures. They frequently use but a single method of interpretation of literature and tradition, training people and not enabling them to become illuminated.

The Centre has by this stage effectively disappeared. The work has instead become a kind of kingdom, intent upon conserving but not knowing what to conserve. The leaders and their adherents remain frozenly attached to its body, making it a place of imitation which conserves minor or irrelevant outward forms. They generally esteem, under other names, raw emotionality.

Concurrently, there comes into being over-veneration of men, of groups and legend, and hostility towards others, and sometimes impatience. What was originally a unity splits into groups of varying interpretation or concentration, generally useless, and observations which are inaccurate. By this point almost all reality and potentiality have departed. The community has been effectively invaded and possessed without this development having been registered by its members. The truth may be obscured by the continued use, by the 'lame' community, of words and outward aspects, biographical reminiscences, and other facets of the original knowledge. Certainly its members will believe that by these tokens they are continuing on the right path.

Their only hope of retrieval is in the exercise of concentrated efforts towards sincerity.

This pattern is one reason why from time to time the Guardians must emerge and announce to the possessors of ears the renewal of the high tradition by means of apposite working. By now, naturally, to the strayed ones, these words will sound strange or inimical, like the speech of reason seems to the demented – absurd.

One result of the condition is that without intending it the Guardians incur, variously, both over-enthusiastic support and also opposition to themselves in different sections of their audience. Both reactions are unpromising, if expected, signs, just as objectionable as apathy.

Working together the parties must overcome these tendencies if success in reviving the teaching is to be achieved.

This is the story of every age upon earth. The only real variant is the time-span during which this behaviour takes place.

Those who have only little knowledge, and think that they have more than that of ordinary folk, are no less open to reason and to teaching than those who have no knowledge at all of the Tradition. This irony is a further complication.

And yet they are better able to make progress in the Way once the outer husk of ageing has been softened. They sometimes retain potentialities whose presence involves us in a chance to offer rescue. It is in the furtherance of this duty, based upon our knowledge of the Tradition, the teaching and the conditions of parties (groups), that we can exercise skill, action, love and effort.

When the husk of people or groupings is too hardened, such individuals and communities will remain like hard nuts which are being rapidly carried down a river, heedlessly.

The water of compassion and understanding will not be able to soften them enough to help them sprout into seedlings before they reach a dam where they will pile up, abandoned and, unfortunately, uncomprehending.

Nawab Mohammed Ali Shah, *Nishan-i-Ghaib*

Readings in Sufi Philosophy

Reading anything and everything in Sufism is like reading all kinds of books on different subjects without the necessary basis. It is a calamity, and, like indiscriminate medication, may make a man worse than before he started.

Sufi writings are always addressed to a special audience. This audience is not the same in Bokhara as in Basra, in Spain as in Africa.

Yet the values of studying special collections of Sufi readings made by a Sufi cannot be exaggerated.

These values include:

The selection of passages which will help a given community to find its way.

The preparation of the student for the enlightenment which is supplied by the master in person when the time is ready;

A corrective against the monotony of ordinary repetition of doctrine and practice, which dulls without our knowing it.

A corrective against the excitement which is our daily lot, and which manipulates us without our knowing it.

Read, therefore, what has been prepared for you, so that you may earn the blessing of eternal felicity.

Hadrat Bahaudin Naqshband

Part Nine

QUESTIONS AND ANSWERS
ON SUFISM

1. Sufism and Islam (Mohammed Ali El-Misri)

2. Deep Understanding (Rais Tchaqmaqzade)

*Answers to questionnaires submitted to
a Cairene and a Bokharan Sufi*

I

SUFISM AND ISLAM

Question 1: What are the bases of Sufism?
Answer: The chief basis of Sufism is faith. Islamic faith (*Iman*) has six pillars. These are: God Exists; God is One; There are Angels; There are Prophets; There is a Day of Restoration; There is Fate.

Question 2: How are these things to be understood, since none of them is subject to ordinary verification by most people?
Answer: They are recorded in the mind and experienced in the 'heart'.

Question 3: What is the completion of Sufism?
Answer: The perception of the above statements in the 'heart'.

Question 4: What is the difference between the Transformed and other people?
Answer: The understanding of the Transformed is something other than what the ordinary people call knowledge.

Question 5: What is the knowledge of ordinary people?
Answer: It is imitative; learned through the training of instructors; thought to be real, though it is not.

Question 6: How is real faith developed?
Answer: By arriving, through certain practices, at the Path which is only one out of the seventy-two possible Paths open to man. It is possible, after following an imitative Path, to rise to the real one, but it is difficult.

Question 7: What outward religious forms do the Transformed follow?
Answer: The majority follow the observances of Islam and the People of the Tradition, and the directorship of rites established

by Sheikh Mataridi of Samarkand. Those who follow the exercises of Islam in the Four Major Schools are generally termed the People of Salvation.

Question 8: When he was asked his sect, Bayazid Bistami said: 'I am of the Sect of God.' What does this mean?

Answer: All the confessional divisions mentioned above are regarded as of the Sect of God.

Question 9: Sufis refer to themselves as phenomena, ideas, animals and vegetables. Why?

Answer: The Prophet has said that man on the Day of Restoration is raised up in the form of one or other animal, corresponding to his leading characteristic. His form appears to change to that of the animal or other form which he internally resembled, rather than to his human shape. In his sleep, man sees himself as human; he may, however, see himself, according to his dominant tendency as a sheep, a monkey, or a hog. It is a misunderstanding of this that has produced the belief that human life passes into that of animals (transmigration), interpreted literally by ignorant people without perceptive insight.

Question 10: Sufis use symbols and advocate ideas which are opposed to the established social requirements, and alien to the phraseology normally employed for higher things. They talk of beloveds, wine-glasses and so on. How can this be understood?

Answer: To the Sufi, religion as understood by ordinary man is a coarse, external thing. Their symbols are indicative of certain states. They are as legitimate as using the symbol 'God' for something which one does not know at all, apart from the illusion of it which is caused by emotion.

Question 11: How can the Koran be the eyebrow of a mistress?

Answer: How can it be marks made by carbon and gum on pieces of paper with wood from a swamp?

Question 12: Dervishes say that they see God. How can this be possible?

Answer: It is not literally true; it is emblematic of certain states.

Question 13: Can an individual not be seen by means of his externals or manifestations?
Answer: Not an individual; only his externals or manifestations are seen. When you see someone coming towards you, you may say: 'I have seen Zaid'; but you have merely seen what you can see of the externals and superficiality of Zaid.

Question 14: According to Muslim belief, it is blasphemous for the dervishes to say: 'We do not fear Hell, or covet Heaven.'
Answer: They do not mean this. They mean that fear and coveting are not the ways in which a man should be trained.

Question 15: You state that there is no contradiction between external behaviour or belief and the inner perceptions of the Sufis. This being so, why do Sufis persist in hiding certain things from others?
Answer: That which is concealed is not against good conduct, but against ordinary understanding. The most elevated scholar cannot understand that which he has not experienced, and it is therefore in concealment from him.

Question 16: If a person knew only religious faith and not the special science of the Sufis, would his religious faith be less than that of a Sufi?
Answer: No, his belief would be the most perfect of religious beliefs, it could not be inferior to the religious belief of a Sufi.

Question 17: What is the difference between the prophets, the saints, those who have high knowledge and great initiates?
Answer: If they have religious faith, their faiths are all equal. Their difference lies in their knowledge not their feelings. A king is the same as his subjects in having two eyes, a nose and a mouth. He is different in character and in functions.

Mohammed Ali El-Misri

❧ 2 ❧
DEEP UNDERSTANDING

Question 1: For how long has Sufism existed?
Answer: Sufism has always existed. It has been practised in a very wide variety of ways; the outer shells of these being different, the less-informed have been misled into thinking that they are essentially different.

Question 2: Is Sufism the interior meaning of Islam, or does it have wider application?
Answer: Sufism is the knowledge whereby man can realize himself and attain permanency. Sufis can teach in any vehicle, whatever its name. Religious vehicles have throughout history taken various names.

Question 3: Why should a person study Sufism?
Answer: Because he was created to study it; it is his next step.

Question 4: Yet many people believe that teachings which are not called Sufism are their next step.
Answer: This is due to the human peculiarity of having two forms of understanding: the Greater Understanding and the Lesser Understanding. The Greater Understanding is when a person wants to understand but instead develops only a conviction that a certain path is true. The Lesser Understanding is the shadow of the Greater Understanding. Like a shadow, it is a distortion of reality, preserving only a part of the original.

Question 5: Does the fact that Sufis have been such famous and respected figures not attract people to the study?
Answer: The Sufis who have been publicly known are only a minority of the total of the Sufis: those who could not keep out of prominence. The attraction to a greatly esteemed figure

by a potential student is a part of the Lesser Understanding. Later he may know better.

Question 6: Is there a conflict between Sufism and other methods of thought?
Answer: There cannot be, because Sufism embodies all methods of thought; each has its usefulness.

Question 7: Is Sufism restricted to a certain language, a certain community, a certain historical period?
Answer: The obvious face of Sufism at any given time, place or community may often vary because Sufism must present itself in a form which will be perceptible to any people.

Question 8: Is this why there have been Sufi teachers with so many different systems and who have flourished in so many different countries?
Answer: No other reason.

Question 9: Yet people like to make journeys to visit teachers in other countries, whose languages they may not even understand.
Answer: Such actions, unless undertaken under special instructions for a certain purpose, can be of use only in the Lesser Understanding.

Question 10: Is there a difference between what a man or woman wants to find, and what he needs to find, for his inner life?
Answer: Yes, almost invariably. It is the function of the teacher to arrange the right operation of the answer to needs, not wants. Wants belong to the sphere of Lesser Understanding.

Question 11: Is your division of Understanding into Greater and Lesser common to all Sufis?
Answer: Nothing which is put into words is common to all Sufis.

Question 12: What is common to all forms of Sufism?
Answer: The being of the teacher, the capacity of the disciples, the peculiarities of individuals, the interaction between the members of the community, the Reality behind forms.

Question 13: Why do some Sufi teachers initiate disciples into several different Orders?

Answer: Because these Orders represent teaching entities which are constructed to deal with people in accordance with their personal individuality. People are different from one another.

Question 14: But collecting information about Sufis and their teachings cannot but be a good enterprise leading to knowledge?

Answer: This is a question of Lesser Understanding. Information about the activities of one body of Sufis may be harmful to the potential of another.

Question 15: Why are there so few indications of the schools of Ahmad Yasavi of Turkestan and Ibn El-Arabi of Andalusia?

Answer: Because, in the realm of Greater Understanding, the workshop is dismantled after the work is finished.

Rais Tchaqmaqzade

FOR THE BEST IN PAPERBACKS, LOOK FOR THE

In every corner of the world, on every subject under the sun, Penguin represents quality and variety – the very best in publishing today.

For complete information about books available from Penguin – including Pelicans, Puffins, Peregrines and Penguin Classics – and how to order them, write to us at the appropriate address below. Please note that for copyright reasons the selection of books varies from country to country.

In the United Kingdom: For a complete list of books available from Penguin in the U.K., please write to *Dept E.P., Penguin Books Ltd, Harmondsworth, Middlesex, UB7 0DA*

In the United States: For a complete list of books available from Penguin in the U.S., please write to *Dept BA, Penguin, 299 Murray Hill Parkway, East Rutherford, New Jersey 07073*

In Canada: For a complete list of books available from Penguin in Canada, please write to *Penguin Books Canada Ltd, 2801 John Street, Markham, Ontario L3R 1B4*

In Australia: For a complete list of books available from Penguin in Australia, please write to the *Marketing Department, Penguin Books Australia Ltd, P.O. Box 257, Ringwood, Victoria 3134*

In New Zealand: For a complete list of books available from Penguin in New Zealand, please write to the *Marketing Department, Penguin Books (NZ) Ltd, Private Bag, Takapuna, Auckland 9*

In India: For a complete list of books available from Penguin, please write to *Penguin Overseas Ltd, 706 Eros Apartments, 56 Nehru Place, New Delhi, 110019*

In Holland: For a complete list of books available from Penguin in Holland, please write to *Penguin Books Nederland B.V., Postbus 195, NL–1380AD Weesp, Netherlands*

In Germany: For a complete list of books available from Penguin, please write to *Penguin Books Ltd, Friedrichstrasse 10 – 12, D–6000 Frankfurt Main 1, Federal Republic of Germany*

In Spain: For a complete list of books available from Penguin in Spain, please write to *Longman Penguin España, Calle San Nicolas 15, E–28013 Madrid, Spain*

Idries Shah

THINKERS OF THE EAST

Idries Shah, author of *The Way of the Sufi*, has long been 'recognized as the leading interpreter of Sufi methods and practice to the Western world' – *The Times Literary Supplement*.

This anthology of 'Studies in Experientialism' is a collection of entertaining anecdotes and 'parables in action' illustrating the eminently practical approach of Eastern dervish thinkers. Distilled from the teachings of more than a hundred sages in three continents, these extracts provide an entertaining but lucid introduction to Sufic thought.

'The language is beautifully clear and concise' – *Church Times*.

'Racily translated and very readable' – *The Times Literary Supplement*.

and

LEARNING HOW TO LEARN

Learning How to Learn is the definitive introduction to a way of thinking that has inspired men and women all over the world.

Drawing on his many successful books, lectures and radio and television programmes, Idries Shah takes the questions of housewives and businessmen, philosophers and assembly-line workers to show how the traditional Sufi concepts can resolve our social, psychological and spiritual problems. The classic Sufi writings, Eastern parables of Jesus, encounters with contemporary teachers and students and Western mass-circulation journals are only some of the examples used to offer us the means of looking at ourselves and our institutions in a new way.

'*Learning How to Learn* pioneers where we, in our time, face the biggest challenges: human nature itself, how to understand our organizations and cultures ... It is as if a veil has been stripped off ordinary life, and we become freer in our actions, our choices' – from the introduction by Doris Lessing.

THE TEACHINGS OF DON JUAN:
A YAQUI WAY OF KNOWLEDGE
Carlos Castaneda

'A uniquely important contribution to our burgeoning psychedelic literature; indeed perhaps one that deserves to replace the comparatively amateurish efforts of Huxley, Watts, Burroughs and Leary ... don Juan projects a quality of experience beside which scientific exactitude stands in peril of paling into insignificance' – Theodore Roszak in the *Nation*.

In 1960 Carlos Castaneda first met don Juan, a Yaqui Indian feared and shunned by the ordinary folk of the American South West because of his unnatural powers. During the next five years don Juan's arcane knowledge led him into a world of beauty and terror, ruled by concepts far beyond those of western civilization. Using psychedelic drugs – peyote, jimson weed and a mushroom called 'humito' – Castaneda lived through encounters with disembodied spirits, shamans in the form of huge wolves, and death in the shape of silver crows. Three times he met Mescalito, the god of the peyote. Finally, after a night of utter terror in which he knew that his life was threatened by forces which he still cannot fully explain, he gave up his struggle to become a Man of Knowledge. After several months of indecision, he wrote this extraordinary book.

Also published

A SEPARATE REALITY
JOURNEY TO IXTLAN
TALES OF POWER
THE SECOND RING OF POWER
THE EAGLE'S GIFT

Penguin Classics

THE BHAGAVAD GITA

Translated by Juan Mascaró

Sanskrit literature can boast some of the most beautiful and profoundly moving works of all times – the songs of the *Vedas*, the *Upanishads*, the *Bhagavad Gita* and many others. It is essentially a romantic literature, interwoven with idealism and practical wisdom, expressing a passionate longing for spiritual vision.

The eighteen chapters of the *Bhagavad Gita* (c. 500 B.C.) encompass the whole great struggle of a human soul. The three central themes of this immortal poem – Love, Light, and Life – arise from the symphonic vision of God in all things and all things in God.

THE UPANISHADS

Translated and selected by Juan Mascaró

The Upanishads represent for the Hindu approximately what the New Testament represents for the Christian.

The earliest of these spiritual treatises, which vary greatly in length, were put down in Sanskrit between 800 and 400 B.C. This selection from twelve Upanishads, with its illuminating introduction by Juan Mascaró, reveals the paradoxical variety and unity, the great questions and simple answers, the spiritual wisdom and romantic imagination of these 'Himalayas of the Soul'.

'Your translation ... has caught from those great words the inner voice that goes beyond the boundaries of words' – Rabindranath Tagore in a letter to the translator.

BUDDHISM

Christmas Humphreys

The religion-philosophy known to the West as Buddhism is in number of adherents and range of teaching one of the largest in the world. Born in India in the sixth century B.C., it became the religion of Ceylon, Siam, Burma, and Cambodia, which adhere to the older or Southern School, while the developed Mahayana School is found in various forms in Tibet, Mongolia, China, Korea, and Japan. Its range of thought is equally vast. It includes the most exalted philosophy yet achieved by man, a psychology from which the West is slowly beginning to learn, a religion which has satisfied untold millions for 2,500 years, a Middle Way of self-development to self-enlightenment and a range and depth of spiritual science, mysticism, and religious art which cannot be found elsewhere.

To compress such a wealth of human thought into a single volume is difficult, but here is not only the history and development of Buddhism and the teaching of the various Schools, but also its condition in the world today.

A Pelican Book